GOERING—AIR LEADER

Hermann Goering, 1938

Goering
AIR LEADER

Asher Lee

DUCKWORTH

First published in 1972 by
Gerald Duckworth & Company Limited
43 Gloucester Crescent, London W.C.2

© 1972 Asher Lee

ISBN 0 7156 0622 0

Printed in Great Britain by
Bristol Typesetting Co., Ltd.

Contents

List of Illustrations

The frontispiece and plates III and V are from *Hermann Goering: Werk & Mensch* (Munich, 1938); plate IV from the Radio Times Hulton Picture Library; and the rest by courtesy of the Imperial War Museum, London.

Introduction

IN PREPARATION for writing this book I have had great help in three major ways. From 1939 to 1945, my British and American intelligence colleagues continually sharpened and reformed my views on Hermann Goering and his Air Force. The list of these professional helpers is long. I apologise for many omissions. To begin with may I mention just four of many Americans—Telford Taylor, Henry Berliner, Al Macormack and Bill Finan : thank you for not accepting anything I said or wrote about Goering without critical comment of a high order. I must also mention my American friend William Wister Haines, whose sardonic humour helped me over the humps many a time. The British colleagues who tempered my views on Hermann Goering were many and varied. If I begin with three professional Royal Air Force officers, S/Ldr Taffy Williams, S/Ldr Knights-Whittome and Wing Commander Coope, it is because they gave me a valuable grounding in aircraft and aviation in my first groping year of RAF service. It was from them that I first learnt some basics about radar, fuel octanes, runways, wing-loading and many other military aircraft matters, which a civilian needed to grasp to understand Goering and German Air Force affairs.

Others who contributed to the slow build-up of my views on Goering and his Air Force included many British civilians in uniform from many spheres of life. Joe Hurst and Drew Bovill, both schoolmasters as I was, had to become air strategists—at least that was the 1939-1945 billing. Then there was Wedgwood Benn, father of our present Parliamentarian; M. C. Allom, man of business and Surrey County fast bowler and now a cricket legislator; Gilbert Frankau, novelist; Harry Hylton-Foster, lawyer and later Speaker of the House of Commons. More important there were lawyers Ron Horne, Tom Burgess and

Ellice Hearn, whose legal training enabled them to weigh evidence with an even hand. And I am especially grateful to Professor Geoffrey Barraclough, a gifted historian who applied his penetrating mind to the problems of assessing Goering's planning potential. We benefited particularly from his splendid summary despatches to Churchill and Stalin. I have mentioned one woman who gave us fundamental help, Ellice Hearn. She was, in a word, brilliant; but Pat Murray, Dorothea Ralli, Patsy Lindsell and others convinced me that there is a role for women in senior staff work in the world of modern defence. I owe thanks also to Jim Rose, the quiet-humoured liberal journalist, and to many university dons who toiled on our behalf.

I am grateful also to the senior ranks of the RAF and the USAAF for taking our views on Goering and his Air Force with critical kindliness. I remember Lord Tedder's justified statement on our estimate of Goering's modest potential reaction to the June 1944 invasion of Normandy. He wrote, 'Read this with a jaundiced eye.'

Lord Portal, Royal Air Force Commander-in-Chief, could skilfully reduce even the longest piece on Goering and his Air Force to a sentence or two, and leave no surplus or bias. United States Army Air Force Generals Carl Spaatz, Fred Anderson, Ira Eaker, James Dolittle and others were highly democratic and gave us a fair hearing without pulling rank.

So much for phase one of my Goering apprenticeship. It was the more difficult part, for our theories were tested daily in the reality of Luftwaffe bomber, fighter, reconnaissance and air transport operations. The second and third stages were a more leisurely business.

In the period 1948 to 1970, I made about a dozen trips to Germany to talk to German Air Force officers at both the command decision and the pick and shovel levels. I spoke to about a hundred in all. They ranged from General Kammhuber, who in the 1950s followed Hermann Goering as Commander-in-Chief of the Luftwaffe, and General Adolf Galland, Chief of German fighter units and fighter operations, to Leutnants Loechner and Pyritz who were junior officers, but highly intelligent and fair-minded. The first was in Luftwaffe signals and the second a very nice sensitive reconnaissance and later air transport pilot. I must thank them all for giving me their time.

I. Loerzer, Fokker and Goering during World War One

II. Military Aircraft Trials, 1918

III. Goering's First Solo

IV. Goering in the Cockpit of a Fighter, 1916

Then came the growing piles of post-war papers. First there were the documents, which one has, in part, had to skip spasmodically because they carried too much weight. But I have ploughed through them as best I could in the last two and a half decades. For the texts of the interviews with Goering carried out by USAAF intelligence personnel I have to thank US General Scare for putting me on the right track, also Derek Wood, Editor of *Interavia* in London.

In tracing Luftwaffe documents, I was given great help by the Director of the Imperial War Museum, Dr Noble Frankland, and by his staff. Mr L. A. Jacketts of the Air Historical Branch of the Defence Ministry in London and the personnel of the Air Historical Branch of the Bundeswehr both gave valuable assistance.

Finally, I wish to thank the publishers who have kindly given permission to quote other writers' views on Hermann Goering. They are Methuen for the quotations from Adolf Galland's memoirs *The First and the Last;* Weidenfeld and Nicolson for the right to quote the views of Albert Speer in his *Inside the Third Reich* and also those of Telford Taylor in *The Breaking Wave.* Thanks are also due to Macdonald for permission to quote from William Green's *War Planes of the Third Reich;* to Hutchinson for the right to print views on Hermann Goering taken from *The Narrow Margin* by Derek Wood and Derek Dempster; and to Heinemann for permission to quote from Ciano's diary and from the fine biography of Hermann Goering by Roger Manvell and Heinrich Fraenkel.

I have named only some of the people who have helped to sharpen my wits on Hermann Goering since the autumn of 1939. They are in no way responsible for the picture of the Nazi air leader offered here. In the last resort the most crucial source is oneself. For that source selects and moulds the data presented.

ASHER LEE

London
July 1971

CHAPTER ONE

Youth and First Combats

HERMANN WILHELM GOERING was conceived in Haiti and born in Bavaria, at the Marienbad Sanatorium at Rosenheim on 12 January 1893. He died at about ten minutes to eleven on the late evening of 15 October 1946 at the age of 53.

At the time of Goering's birth, his father, Heinrich Goering, was the German Consul General in Haiti having previously served Germany in a consular capacity in London and South West Africa. It was in London that Heinrich married Hermann Goering's mother on 28 May 1885. He was then a widower of 45 and had already sired five children. Relatives had taken them off Heinrich Goering's hands and left him free to roam. He met and married Franziska (Fanny) Tiefenbrunn, a lively buxom Bavarian girl of Austrian origin who was durable and energetic. Hermann Goering's mother was emotional and temperamental. She handed on some of this uneven histrionic strain to her son. Hermann's father on the other hand was orderly, rigid and honest with a capacity for hard work. The future Commander in Chief of the German Air Force derived more of his temperament from his mother than his father. But from the latter he may have acquired the will to work hard.

In those days Haiti was not a suitable place in which to bring a child into the world. And so, in October 1892, Fanny Goering journeyed back to Bavaria and three months later gave birth to a son who was to make the world's news headlines much more often than either of his modestly placed parents could have foreseen.

Six weeks after Hermann Goering's birth he was parted from his mother and the rupture continued for the next three years. Franziska Goering went back to Haiti to look after her husband and her other three children, Karl, Olga and Paula. The infant

Hermann was left in the care of a friend of the family, Frau Graf, who lived in Fuerth in Southern Germany.

The Freudian psychologist might well ponder the effect on Hermann Goering of spending the first three years of his life without the close affection of either father or mother. In the absence of clinical evidence one can only speculate. Was Goering, in both his marriages, subconsciously looking for women to replace the motherly love he had missed in the vital period of his early infancy? Even Hermann Goering himself could not be sure. But both his wives Karin and Emmy gave him much of the maternal protective love of which he seemed to be in need at times of worry and crisis.

Hermann Goering's links with professional soldiers can be traced back to an early age. When he was three his father gave up his work as consul in Haiti and returned in 1896 to Berlin. There he worked for a few months at the German Foreign Office and then retired on a small pension. For the next five years the Goering family lived modestly in a small suburban house in the Friedenau district of Berlin. On Sundays Heinrich Goering would take young Hermann to see the military parades at Potsdam. During the week the retired civil servant would have some friends in to drink or for a meal. They included a number of officers of the Prussian Army who would talk of the great victorious days of 1866 and 1870. The young son listened eagerly. When Hermann was five Heinrich Goering bought him a Hussar uniform. This is said to have inspired in the lad the desire to become an officer in the German Army. Certainly the atmosphere in his father's home was conducive to such an ambition. And the fact that young Hermann Goering never seemed to be on very friendly terms with his school books no doubt also helped to pave the way to a military career.

A Jewish doctor, Hermann (von) Eppenstein, emerged at this stage to change the rather straitened circumstances of the Goering family. He had attended Goering's mother at the birth of her first child Karl in Africa. He was a wealthy bachelor and a bon viveur who became Hermann Goering's godfather and also Fanny Goering's lover. He owned two castles, one at Mauterndorf near Salzburg in Austria and the other at Veldenstein near Nuremberg. He gave the Veldenstein Castle to the Goering family as a home and also contributed to the cost of the education of his young godson Hermann. Veldenstein Castle helped to give Goering his taste for grand houses.

His early education was fitful but varied. It gave no indication that young Hermann was destined for all but the very highest role in Germany's future. He went to his first school at the age of seven in 1900, at Fuerth in South Germany. But by most accounts he was wild, difficult to control, spoiled by his father and very keen to play at soldiers and avoid books. His father seems to have exercised little influence on his young son except to encourage his interest in military matters. When the lad was at the school in Fuerth he bought young Hermann a Boer uniform complete with broad-brimmed hat and khaki shorts. The Boer uniform, the lead soldiers with which he liked to play and the fisticuff fighting at school were all indications pointing to his first military career in the German Army.

Hermann Goering's next port of learning was a boarding school at Ansbach. Here the discipline was much stricter than at Fuerth. Young Hermann was now eleven. He is credited by one of his German biographers, Gritzbach, with organising a strike among the boys against the poor food. It would be tempting to suggest that here were the incipient signs of the subsequent leader and gourmand who loved good food. But the pattern of the links between the young adolescent Goering and the full grown man are as tenuous to trace as in other lives. Certainly, the disciplinary influences in his youth were not very firm. And later on his air leadership was undisciplined in some respects. Indulgence and lack of control marked both his early adolescence and to some extent the rest of his life.

The young lad gave plenty of promise of physical bravery. In his early youth he turned, during his holidays, to the arduous risks of mountaineering and became a skilled climber for one of such tender years. By the time he was fifteen he had scaled the 12,000 foot peak of the Grossglockner. There are stories told, some no doubt apocryphal, of his utter fearlessness and general disregard for danger. But they square with one's firm knowledge of the way he acted later as a man in time of war.

It was the early signs of pugnacity, physical courage and lack of interest in academic studies which no doubt encouraged his father and godfather, von Eppenstein, to send him at the early age of twelve to the military cadet school at Karlsruhe in the

province of Baden. They probably both felt that he would there
have to face the discipline he seems to have avoided at his two
previous schools. His home life had been much too indulgent
for a lad who probably needed a tight rein. He spent some four
years at this junior military academy where he studied infantry
matters and German history and learnt the etiquette of clicking
heels and kissing ladies' hands. His progress confirmed the view
that the military life was to be the one for him.

When he was sixteen Hermann Goering transferred to a
Military Training College at Lichterfelde near Berlin. For the
next three years he was a happy teenager enjoying the wearing
of uniforms, the social life of a military academy and the group
discipline of a Kadettenkorps. In March 1912 at the age
of nineteen, after achieving high marks at the Lichterfelde
Academy, he was commissioned in the Prinz Wilhelm No. 112
Infantry Regiment. Its headquarters were at Muelhausen near
the borders of France.

Before he could adjust to his new life as an officer in the
German Army, two key events occurred in his family life, both
in 1913. His father died shortly after leaving Veldenstein and
moving the family to Munich, which was later to be the headquarters of Hitler's Nazi Party. At the funeral, Hermann Goering
is said to have wept openly despite his officer's uniform. This
was a foretaste of the many gusts of public emotion which were
to follow later. A short while before his father's death, his mother
Franziska had broken off her relationship with von Eppenstein
after a series of tedious quarrels. But perhaps the most important
event of 1913 for Hermann Goering was his meeting with
Lieutenant Bruno Loerzer, who was to introduce Goering to
military aviation and so reset the course of his entire life. Loerzer
was then a fellow infantry officer at Muelhausen. He struck up a
friendship with Hermann Goering which helped to sweeten the
dullish routine of German garrison life. In the regimental mess
the prospect of the coming war was, of course, the recurrent
theme of major interest. Lieutenant Hermann Goering was a
popular member of the regiment who is said to have held his
liquor well. His subsequent capacity for drinking wine and spirits
would tend to confirm this. He was also popular with the ladies
of Muelhausen as a dancer and a cheerful conversationalist. One
can find no record of him as a lady-killer. In the more serious

business of the Prinz Wilhelm Infantry Regiment No. 112 he put his young healthy vigour into the drill and manoeuvres, which assumed a more serious nature as the months of 1914 went by. Like many young men his attitude to war was double-edged. In the mess he revelled in the prospect. In a letter to his mother he expressed his deep foreboding.

When war broke out in August 1914 Goering's regiment was immediately withdrawn from Muelhausen and stationed behind the Rhine as a precautionary measure. This kind of move did not suit the young Hermann Goering. Nor was he pleased when his friend Bruno Loerzer was seconded to a flying school at Freiburg. Goering was put in charge of an infantry platoon but it was some weeks before he went into action. His first military mission was intended to be purely a local exploratory reconnaissance. But true to his character, even at this early stage, Goering overstepped the line of duty allocated to him by his superiors. His mission was simply to reconnoitre the French position at Muelhausen and to report on their strength and disposition. An armoured train ferried Goering and his platoon across the River Rhine. But when they reached the suburbs of Muelhausen Goering became ambitious far beyond the call of duty. He captured some French bicycles and horses to give himself and his men greater mobility, proceeded to the Town Hall, exchanged fire with the French and then returned to base. The next day at dawn he set off again with a section of his platoon on bicycles, with the declared intention of capturing the French general Paul Pau who commanded the advanced enemy troops in the Muelhausen area. The plan misfired. One of Goering's N.C.O.'s nervously fired his rifle prematurely and so gave the alarm. Goering and his platoon section swung back hastily towards the German lines riding their bicycles at top speed. And so Goering's first military operation collapsed in retreat and confusion. But he had shown bravery, initiative and imagination. These qualities were fairly typical of him; but the flights of imagination often required the brake of discipline and more attention to mundane detail.

On his return to the Prinz Wilhelm Regiment headquarters, Goering was naturally reproved by his senior officers. The plot that failed had put a valuable German armoured train in jeopardy but had contributed nothing to the general success of the reconnaissance operation. But Goering's military masters were not displeased with him. In the fighting near Muelhausen, Saarburg and Baccarat in the closing months of 1914 he developed into a courageous, experienced and conscientious officer with a penchant for reconnaissance and intelligence operations. He became adjutant of the 2nd Battalion of his regiment. His unit captured French prisoners who yielded valuable information, directed German artillery fire from forward positions close to the French front line trenches and made their own direct valuable visual observations. Hermann Goering was now winning his infantry spurs in war in an atmosphere of local optimism which expected that the German army would be in Paris within a few months.

Then came one of those sharp reverses of fortune which, in Hermann Goering's life, were often followed by a blazing streak of good luck. The dampness of trench warfare got into his bones and he was removed to the military hospital at Freiburg crippled by rheumatic pains. He chafed at the dreary inactivity of the hospital ward. When he discovered that his friend Bruno Loerzer had been seconded to the local air training school in Freiburg he sent him an urgent letter. Loerzer went to visit Goering and regaled him with aviation short stories that fired Goering with enthusiasm and envy. He went to visit the Freiburg air training school and immediately filed an application for transfer to it. On the day Goering's application was turned down, Bruno Loerzer qualified as a pilot and was posted to an operational unit of the German Air Force.

At the Nuremberg trials in 1946, Goering was to hold much discourse about the rights and duties of an officer. He emphasised the importance of discipline and obedience and stressed how impossible war would be if officers were allowed to do as they pleased, to move according to their inclination and to attack or retreat as they thought best.

Early in 1915, he showed his disregard of military discipline once again. The German army authorities had ruled that Goering was to stay in the infantry arm. But he followed Bruno Loerzer to the Darmstadt base of the young German Air Force and got his friend to agree to use him as an observer. For a few indeterminate weeks Hermann Goering was a kind of unofficial, unpaid air gunner-observer in No. 25 Field Air Detachment of the

Fifth German Army, under the command of the German Crown Prince Friederich Wilhelm. A military court had sentenced Goering to three weeks confinement to barracks for leaving his infantry unit. But the punishment never caught up with him. He spent the spring of 1915 in the skies of the Western Front in the observer's seat of Bruno Loerzer's plane. The Loerzer-Goering team was a success. They carried out a succession of reconnaissance flights in which Goering both photographed and sketched enemy troop concentrations and gun positions. In accordance with the custom of the day Goering used a hand camera and leant dangerously over the side to take his pictures. The armament of his plane consisted of one ordinary Mauser revolver.

The main target of these reconnaissance flights in the spring of 1915 was the fortifications of Verdun against which the German armed forces were concentrating. The photographic plates would be rushed back to the air base at Stenay, some twenty miles north-east of Rheims, for rapid developing. Then the two airmen, both now twenty-two years old, would be called into conference with senior officers to interpret and elucidate the details on the photographs and to give an account of their visual observations. They were thus involved to some extent in the strategy of the German Fifth Army. Their reports were often made, so the story goes, in the unorthodox vigorous language of enthusiastic young airmen. Very soon Hermann Goering was to make the acquaintance of his Commander-in-Chief, the Crown Prince Wilhelm. He also met a number of other wealthy and influential members of the German aristocracy.

The French Air Force planned an air attack on the army headquarters of Prince Wilhelm. Goering and Loerzer took off with other German planes and successfully intercepted the raid. The Crown Prince narrowly escaped a direct hit from the French bombing which damaged the German Army headquarters buildings. Both Loerzer and Goering were personally decorated by Prince Wilhelm with the Iron Cross First Class for their action against the French bombers.

Two other important things happened in 1915 to the now ambitious young Goering. First he was admitted to the close social and professional circle of his Commander-in-Chief and received a number of dinner invitations from the Crown Prince

B

and his friends. And in the early autumn of 1915 he was sent
to the Freiburg Training School to embark on a spectacular
career as a fighter pilot. He passed his flying tests easily enough.
In those days training courses were short and intensive. By late
October 1915 he had returned to the front to rejoin his friend
Bruno Loerzer. Both pilots were transferred to the Fifth Fighter
Squadron (*Jagdstaffel*).

Hermann Goering's first combat experience as a fighter pilot
was far from glamorous. On a misty November morning in 1915,
his Albatross D.V. fighter took off with the rest of the squadron
against a raiding force of British Handley-Page bombers pro-
tected by Sopwith fighters. Visibility was not good. Anxious for
his first kill he dived to attack the British bombers, fired his
single machine-gun, put an enemy gunner out of action and set
an engine of one of the Handley-Page bombers on fire. But he
was unaware of the imminent presence of about a dozen hostile
British Sopwith fighters. After a short air battle the petrol tank
of Goering's aircraft was pierced, his engine was hit and he
himself badly wounded in the leg and hip. He was lucky
to escape his pursuers and to crash land in the cemetery of a
church behind the German lines. He was operated on at once
and, but for immediate medical care, might have bled to
death.

Goering was to be out of action for more than six months.
And so he had plenty of time to ponder his life past, present and
future. As sometimes happens to convalescent warriors he fell in
love during this period of suffering. She was Marianne Mauser,
the daughter of a rich agriculturalist. Goering became unofficially
engaged to her. But the romance was never very profound. The
attachment lasted until the end of the war and was broken off
by Goering a few weeks after the Armistice was signed.

Goering left hospital in the summer of 1916 and joined the
German Air Force fighter unit of which his friend Bruno Loerzer
was then Commandant. During the next year or so, Goering
established a growing reputation as a fighter pilot and in May
1917 was put in command of Squadron No. 27 operating on
the Flanders front. There is no reason to doubt the many reports
that he was a brave and inspiring leader. Like most fighter pilots
he lived dangerously and had his share of luck. On one occasion
he was set upon by French fighters and but for the intervention

of his friend Bruno would almost certainly have been shot down. He force-landed with a heavily damaged undercarriage and his fuselage punctured by bullets. On another combat occasion Goering rescued Loerzer from a similar plight. For some time Loerzer and Goering commanded respectively the German Air Force 26th and 27th Fighter Squadrons (*Staffeln*) which operated on the Flanders front and struggled for air survival against the mounting allied air offensive of 1917. To combat the growing French and British air strength the German Air Force created stronger fighter formations of several grouped squadrons, known as a *Jagdgeschwader* (Fighter formations), with a normal combat strength of about 50 planes. The first of them was commanded by Manfred von Richthofen. Both Goering and Loerzer belonged initially not to the famous Richthofen Circus but to No. 3 Fighter Geschwader based at Iseghem near Ypres in Belgium. The ebb and flow of the 1917-1918 air battles brought Hermann Goering new responsibilities culminating in the leadership of the Richthofen Geschwader.

On 21 April 1918 Baron von Richthofen failed to return from combat against a British formation of fighters. Von Richthofen was credited with shooting down 80 British and French aircraft. He was probably Germany's best known war hero and had set new standards in leadership of fighter squadrons in the German Air Force. Before his death he had nominated Lieutenant Reinhard as his successor. But within three months, Reinhard was killed when test-flying an improved version of the Albatross plane. On that very day, 3 July 1918, and at the same airfield, the Adlerhorst near Berlin, Hermann Goering test-flew the same type of Albatross machine an hour or so after Captain Reinhard had crashed to his death. Within a week Goering was appointed Commander of the Richthofen Geschwader and so reached the peak of a German fighter pilot's war career.

There is little doubt that Goering's combat record and skill as an air leader justified this appointment, although some might say with reason that Ernst Udet, who claimed to have shot down 60 enemy planes, should have been appointed. Goering had, by May 1918, achieved his twentieth claimed air victory and with it the award of 'Pour le Mérite', the German equivalent of the Victoria Cross. In addition to the Iron Cross, he had also been awarded the Airmen's Gold Medal, the Zaehring Lion (with swords), the Hohenzollern Medal (also with swords) and the Order of Karl Friederich. He had shown energy, organising ability and courage as Commander of 27th Fighter Squadron and he could perhaps hope to maintain the fine combat record of the Richthofen Circus.

But his period as Commander of the Richthofen Geschwader, from July to November 1918, was one of disaster and retreat for which Goering was, of course, in no sense to blame. The French twin-engined Caudron bombers were proving difficult to shoot down because German fighter aircraft ammunition did not easily penetrate their armour plating. The new British Sopwith Camel and SE5 fighters and the French Spad 140 and 200 machines were technically superior to the Albatross plane with which the Richthofen Geschwader was now being fitted. The growing preponderance of Anglo-French air power ruled the skies on the Western Front and made great holes in the ranks of Goering's fighter squadrons.

It is perhaps surprising to find that, less than a month after he was appointed to command the Richthofen Circus, Goering went off on four weeks leave despite the state of German air crisis. Was this a habit of his? He certainly pursued it when he became Commander in Chief of the German Air Force in the late 1930s and in the early 1940s. When on leave he took the opportunity of developing his contacts with the Fokker Aircraft Industry and the German B.M.W. Aero-Engine Works. Goering was genuinely interested in the technical problems of engines and equipment; he also had a keen business sense which was later to extend from aeronautics to economics and the world of art. Fokker was to help provide him with a fresh career when the crash of Germany's defeat came.

And it was not long delayed. When Goering returned to the Richthofen Geschwader towards the end of August 1918, there was nothing but gloomy news from the unit's adjutant Karl Bodenschatz, who was to become an important person very close to Goering for most of his subsequent aeronautical career. It was he who had handed Goering the famous Richthofen walking-stick, the emblem of command, when he was appointed leader a month or so before. And both before and during the Second World War, it was Karl Bodenschatz who attended many of Hitler's conferences, sometimes to attempt to bridge the growing gap between the Fuehrer and the Commander in Chief of the Luftwaffe.

During the few months in which Goering commanded the Richthofen Fighter Geschwader operating in Flanders skies, it gained few fresh laurels in air combat. Pilot casualties were heavy. Because of the heavy losses there was a merger in the late summer of 1918 with Fighter Geschwader No. 3 commanded by von Greim who was to be a prominent Luftwaffe commander in the Second World War. In fact at the end of the Second World War he replaced Goering for a few weeks.

The war diary of the Richthofen Geschwader for the period of Goering's command makes gloomy reading; but no fault of leadership or courage can be reasonably ascribed to him personally. He remained in active air combat right to the end. But on the ground the German armies were in full retreat, and in the air the Anglo-French allies, aided by American pilots, had at last won air superiority. November 1918 was a month of chaos and disorder during which Goering felt the full bitterness of defeat and said a provisional goodbye to the German Air Force. The rumours grew about the abdication of the Kaiser, the riots in Berlin, and the mutiny in the German Navy and also among Army elements. In the meantime Goering retreated with his aircraft and men in good order to an airfield west of Tellancour. Then, on Armistice Day, the Richthofen Geschwader elements that remained were flown back to Germany, some landing at Mannheim and some at Darmstadt. It was at Darmstadt that Lieutenant Hermann Goering signed his last order as Commander of the unit which was then disbanded. He was granted the honorary rank of Captain on demobilisation.

During the last ten days or so, spent with his fellow pilots, Goering encountered for the first time something of the harsh realities of mob politics. When some of the Richthofen Geschwader aircraft landed at Mannheim a Workers' Council had taken charge of the airfield. Its members disarmed Goering's pilots and sent them on to Darmstadt by road. Goering burst into a typical rage when he heard the news and immediately flew part of his unit back to Darmstadt. He then threatened to machine-gun the Workers' Council unless the weapons were returned to his pilots at once. His threat succeeded. Then Goering led his planes back to Darmstadt and ordered them to crash land in defiance of French Air Force orders. In a final burst of bitter reaction to defeat, Goering and his pilots spent their last week or so together in the small Bavarian town of Aschaffenburg some 20 to 30 miles from Frankfurt. There they ate and drank the best the town could offer. Goering gave vent to a number of speeches which expressed his anger at the revolt of the German soldiers against authority and at the insults to German officers from civilians. Orator that he already was, he spoke emotionally about his love of Germany, of the glories of the Richthofen Squadron and of his belief in the future of the Fatherland. They say the mob in Aschaffenburg set upon him. But he stayed there till December and then went to Munich where his mother was living. He was now an unemployed man of 25 living in a strange new world. Wilhelm II, the Emperor of Germany, had fled to Holland and a German Republic had been acclaimed on 8 November. Many German soldiers in uniform regarded their officers as traitors. Civilians were trying to organise local socialist revolutions.

Goering could have stayed in Germany to fight for its revival. German officers had immediately set up a Free Corps to defend their caste and revive their cause. But he turned his back on his country for the more peaceful air of Scandinavia. He was to return within two or three years. Then the politician in him was to take over from the airman and Goering's potential for violent action against ordered civilian life was to become apparent.

CHAPTER TWO

Phoenix from the Ashes

1919—1935

AT THE turn of 1918-1919, Hermann Goering had no private means or pension and so he had to get a job. The immediate prospects of being employed as a pilot in Germany were poor. Had he been patient he might well have secured an important post in the early 1920s in the new German Defence Ministry under General von Seekt, as did his subsequent senior German Air Force colleagues, Kesselring, Stumpf and Sperrle. Goering was, in fact, invited to join the new post-war German Army of about 100,000 men. And so he might have played a leading role in hatching the secret German plans of the early 1920s for the revival of both civil and military aviation. But patience was rarely if ever a trait in Goering's mercurial make-up. He felt he had to do something quickly.

By the spring of 1919, he had become a commercial pilot in Denmark, where he also negotiated the sale of Fokker aircraft on behalf of this famous Dutch firm. Civil aviation was then in its infancy and a pilot with Goering's ability and experience could hope to make rapid progress in this field. In Denmark he flirted with the ladies and attended gay parties in the evenings after flying during the day, sometimes to and from Danish airfields, sometimes performing aerobatics as a stunt pilot to please the crowds and sometimes carrying passenger enthusiasts on brief air hops.

The photographs of Goering in this period show him to have been a slim, attractive and ardent-looking young man. His capacity for oral outbursts was well illustrated in June 1919 when the terms of the Treaty of Versailles were published. The air clauses were of course anathema to him. They stipulated that Germany was not to have army or naval forces, that over 15,000 aircraft and more than 25,000 aero-engines were to be surrendered to the allies. He happened to be at a Copenhagen dinner party when he learned the distasteful news. He shouted loudly and rudely at the guests 'One day we will write another treaty'. Later there were to be many other public outbursts of this kind during which he became transformed from a charming, amusing and intelligent person into a boaster, in whom the potential gangster and the ham actor competed with the man of vanity and ambition.

In the spring of 1920 he obtained a better job as a pilot for Svensk-Lufttrafik, a Swedish civil airline. In Sweden his fame as a stunt pilot grew. Thus *Svenska Dagbladet* reported him 'executing a series of loops and other aerobatics at between 1,800 and 3,000 feet' and added 'next Sunday, Stockholm's popular air chauffeur will continue passenger-carrying flights'. He also became the agent in Sweden for a new German parachute which opened automatically when the pilot baled out.

The sales leaflet for this parachute is of some interest. Goering wrote the text himself and made pointed comparison with American parachutes of that time which did not open automatically. He also struck a personal note. 'I made so bold as to state that in the many air combats in which I have taken part, I have shown that fear and slackness are not numbered among my qualities'. This was no more than the truth. Then he added this charming *non sequitur* : 'Of one thing one can never be quite certain—the workings of the human mind and soul.'

In Sweden, he became a friend of the wealthy van Rosen family. They had a passion for flying which extended from 1920 when they first met Hermann Goering to the Nigerian Civil War of the late 1960s when one of the van Rosens flew for the Biafran Government. It was the van Rosens who introduced Goering to his first wife Karin. Goering was then 27. She had been married for ten years to Baron von Kanzow, a Swedish army officer. Karin and Hermann met at van Rosen's estate north of Stockholm. It was love at first sight and the love lasted until well after Karin's death. Karin's family were not keen on her marrying Goering. But she soon separated from her husband and went to live with her mother and father. Karin von Kanzow was a tall, handsome woman who had protective and maternal qualities allied to intelligence and grace. She was to give Goering true love and deep loyalty sometimes in very difficult circumstances.

The divorce proceedings dragged on, and so Goering returned to Munich in the early summer of 1921 to tell his mother about his love affair and to look for a job in Germany. At the age of 28 he enrolled as a student of political science at Munich University. The course bridged the years 1921-22.

In this period Germany was in a state of major civil disorder. The German Reichswehr had made an abortive attempt to oust the Weimar Government. In Munich German Army officers were playing a game of bluff with the German Workers' Party which had bought the *Voelkische Beobachter*. This newspaper was already anti-Jewish and anti-Communist. A few days after Goering returned to Munich, Adolf Hitler became leader of the National Socialist German Workers' Party.

On 3 February 1922, at the age of 29, Hermann Goering married Karin in Munich. Amongst the guests was Karl Bodenschatz, now a Reichswehr officer. Goering's first home was a hunting lodge at Barischzell, near Munich. It was purchased with Karin's money.

She encouraged her husband to attend political meetings in Munich. But for the first few months of their marriage there was no suggestion that he would join the Nazi Party. Goering had still to find a political orientation and in the meantime he was a happily married man.

At his Nuremberg Trial, Goering gave what seems to be an authentic account of his first meeting with Adolf Hitler in Munich in November 1922. After hearing Hitler speak, Goering felt that the hopes and ideas he expressed corresponded to his own. Goering too urged that the Treaty of Versailles must be annulled and that Germany must be made strong again.

And so Goering made up his mind to offer his services to the leader of the N.S.D.A.P. party. The two men had met at a time when Hitler's political fortunes were rather low. Perhaps Hitler was flattered by the offer of help from a man who enjoyed a much higher educational and social status than himself and who could offer the glitter of being a former commander of the famous Richthofen Circus.

Nine months after his marriage to Karin, Goering joined the Nazi Party. Hitler soon appointed him commander of its brown-shirted thugs, the S.A. (*Sturm Abteilungen*) storm troopers. There was political and administrative trouble for Goering almost at once. His Chief of Staff, Ernst Roehm, wanted the storm troopers to be linked to the Reichswehr. Hitler wanted them to support the expanding Nazi Party against the Weimar Republic which he hoped to overthrow.

In January 1923, the Bavarian government allowed the Nazi Party to hold a major rally in Munich. Some 5,000 of Goering's storm troopers took part. On this occasion Hermann Goering played only a minor role and did not even speak on the Nazi platform. His main job at this juncture was to recruit and train S.A. brown shirts, while Adolf Hitler and Ernst Roehm schemed to get new political allies for the Nazi Party in order to oppose the central government of Germany.

Soon Goering was getting to know his new Nazi colleagues— Drexler, Heines, Eckart, Rosenberg, Streicher and others. With them he discussed the French occupation of the Ruhr. Nazi policy was to take no action and to keep the S.A. brown shirts in reserve for a putsch designed to take over Bavaria.

On 1 May 1923, thanks in part to Goering's persuasive eloquence, the Nazi Party was chosen to lead the May Day march in Munich. They hoped to take the town by storm with the support of von Lossow, the local Reichswehr army commander. Ernst Roehm, then Chief of Staff of the S.A. units, managed to obtain some guns for Hermann Goering's storm-troopers who were concentrated just outside Munich. But General von Lossow reacted firmly. He ordered Roehm to return the guns and then presented Hitler with an ultimatum which forbad him to cause any disturbance in Munich. Adolf Hitler meekly obeyed. But he prepared another coup for November 1923. It was a dark period for German domestic politics. The central government was in the hands of Gustav Stresemann who had to contend with disloyal army and police chiefs and a group of wartime generals who were trying to rally monarchist elements in Germany.

For Goering, November 1923 was a bad month. His mother died and his wife Karin, whose lungs were weak, was now ill with pneumonia. And on the political front in Bavaria, his attempt to persuade von Lossow to abandon his allegiance to the Stresemann government and to join forces with the Nazis had failed. Nor did he succeed in winning over Gustav von Kahr, the new state Commissioner of Bavaria.

8 and 9 November 1923 marked both the climax and the failure of the first Nazi major putsch. At the Burgerbraukeller in Munich, von Kahr called a public meeting attended by over 2,000 Bavarians. The chief Nazis present were Hitler, Hess and Goering. Von Kahr spoke of Germany's need to regain her former military strength. The audience drank beer but remained unmoved. Suddenly the strident adenoidal voice of Adolf Hitler interrupted the Bavarian governor's speech. The Nazi leader fired a shot at the ceiling and shouted 'The National Revolution has begun. This building is occupied by 600 armed men. No one is allowed to leave.'

Goering and Hitler cleared the platform of von Kahr and his political colleagues at the point of the gun. Hitler than made a wild speech which attempted to bluff the audience into the belief that the governments in Bavaria and Berlin had been overthrown, and that the German army and police had gone over to the Nazis.

When Goering realised that Hitler's speech had fallen on stony ground he managed to repair the tense situation by an injection of carefree cheerfulness. He shouted from the platform 'We are your friends . . . What are you complaining about? . . . You have your beer'. He then told the audience that a new government was being formed with the help of General Ludendorff who was about to arrive at the beer hall. Ludendorff himself then appeared, uncertain of the role he was to play. The audience cheered him and for the time being all was well. But the next day brought major disaster.

After pledging their support to Ludendorff and the Nazis, von Kahr and his ministers decided on an overnight *volte-face*. Meantime Roehm had occupied the army military headquarters in Munich with his brown-shirted S.A. troops. As dawn broke on 9 November there were posters all over Munich, which banned the Nazi Party and denounced those who supported Hitler. They were the work of von Kahr.

The Nazi march began at about 11 a.m. It consisted of some 3,000 storm-troopers, some of whom had no weapons at all.

Hitler, Goering, Hess and Ludendorff headed the advance. Ludendorff was convinced that the Bavarian police and soldiers would not fire on him, and indeed they did not. As the columns moved towards the centre of Munich they were stopped by a detachment of armed police at the Ludwig Bridge. Here Goering told the police that he held some Bavarian ministers as hostages and that they would be shot if the march was opposed. The police gave way and even surrendered some of their weapons to the S.A. It was first blood to Goering.

But at lunch time disaster fell upon the Nazis. In a narrow street near the Marienplatz the advancing columns were firmly opposed by a second detachment of Bavarian armed police. When Hitler called on them to surrender they began to shoot. Hitler fell to the ground, dislocated his shoulder and was hustled off in a car. Ludendorff walked calmly on and was unmolested. But Hermann Goering was hit and seriously wounded in the groin.

He was carried to the nearest house, where his wounds were tended temporarily by a Jewish woman, Frau Ilse Ballin, whom Goering helped later when the Nazis came to power. Under cover of darkness he was then moved to a Munich hospital where Professor von Ach prescribed morphia to relieve the pain. Meantime von Lossow issued a warrant for Goering's arrest. Hitler himself was arrested on 14 November and taken to Landsberg prison, where he wrote *Mein Kampf*.

Karin rushed from a sick bed to see her beloved husband whose spirit was depressed—indeed sliding downwards to a nadir of deep despair. Karin wrote to her mother at the end of November 'Deep in his heart he is desperately unhappy'.

Friendly elements in the Munich police smuggled Karin and Hermann Goering across the border into Austria. At the Innsbruck hospital the Austrian doctor prescribed morphia every day. Karin wrote to her mother in December, 'It is just a month ago today since he was shot and in spite of daily morphine the pain has not subsided'. Goering remained in the Innsbruck hospital until 24 December.

The Goerings spent Christmas and the New Year at the Tiroler Hotel in Innsbruck. To keep up his failing spirits and to alleviate the pain, Hermann Goering continued to take injections of morphine. To aggravate Goering's situation Karin caught a bad chill. His unhappiness was now very deep.

One has to admire the resilience of the man. By February 1924 things looked better. Karin's health had improved and the Goerings celebrated their second wedding anniversary with some joy if not with full gusto. But Goering's leg was still very painful and he continued to make use of morphine. Later that month he wrote to his mother-in-law, the Baroness von Fock, 'Thanks to you it was easier for me to overcome the crisis of mental depression. I did not care about the physical injury because it meant nothing beside the terrible hurt to my soul . . . we must count on a long interval before we return to Germany. I only want to return to a Nationalist Germany and not to this Jewish Republic.'

But at the turn of 1923-24, Goering was in fact a long way from overcoming the crisis of his mental depression. He had become, at any rate temporarily, a morphia addict. The problem for both the biographer and the psychiatrist is to link the effects of morphia with Goering's conduct and decisions; for he took this and other drugs such as paracodeine intermittently for the next twenty years or so.

Since the end of the Second World War studies of drug addiction have been considerably developed. In the period 1925-1945 they were relatively sparse. However by consulting psychiatrists and drug specialists, one can hope to relate Goering's drug-taking with at least some of his major decisions, for example at Dunkirk and in the Battle of Britain.

In the April 1924 elections the Nazi Party won a few seats in the Reichstag for the first time; this was in the absence of both Hitler and Goering. In that month, Goering wrote to his mother-in-law, 'We would like to go back to Sweden by boat via Italy . . . perhaps I can get some kind of work in Sweden'.

At the end of April, the Goerings moved on to Venice. During their stay Karin wrote to her mother, 'And as for my Hermann you cannot imagine how good and sweet he is to me. His one thought is that I should be happy'. Hermann Goering was certainly an affectionate husband, as his wives Karin and Emmy have attested at some length.

In the summer of 1924, the Goerings visited Florence, Siena and then Rome, where Hermann Goering met Mussolini for the first time and told him about the Munich putsch of November 1923.

Goering was now desperately short of money and both he and his wife were in ill-health. But they stayed on in Italy hoping perhaps that the Italian sun would give them comfort and healing. Early in 1925, Karin's mother became ill and so the Goerings decided to return to Sweden via Austria, Czechoslovakia and Poland. Back in Stockholm they rented a small flat in the Odengarten district.

Goering was 32 and rapidly becoming too gross to be a pilot. He was now a flabby unemployed man, subject to recurrent depressions, who injected himself, perhaps daily, with morphine. By the spring of 1925 he was in the hands of Swedish doctors who have reported that he was sometimes taking two or three injections a day.

In the summer of 1925 Karin began to suffer from epileptic fits and she had also developed a weak heart. There was worse to come for her husband. On 1 September 1925 he was taken to the Langbro lunatic asylum where he was certified as a dangerous, violent drug addict. His Swedish psychiatrist at Langbro has stated that he was hysteric, unstable, callous and sentimental, and that his violence was prompted by fear. Such a psychiatric verdict was not a judgement on the normal Hermann Goering, but on a man who was mentally ill. Goering's performance at the Nuremberg trials, when he was no longer addicted to drugs, and also his operational flying record in the First World War are ample testimony that the Goering who spent about three months at the Langbro asylum was a substandard edition of the true man.

How far did Goering's addiction to morphia and later to paracodeine over a long period affect his air leadership before and during the Second World War? After many consultations with psychiatrists and drug experts one comes to the view that some of his aviation decisions were punctuated by euphoria, by the kind of morphia-ridden optimism which fails to see difficulties even when they stick out like a sore thumb.

The real problem is to know the exact doses of morphia Goering injected and when. Without such precise knowledge the medical pundits say one should not even speak of true addiction. The fact that Goering later went over to paracodeine and pethadine tablets suggests that his drug-addiction was somewhat reduced in the 1930s and 1940s. Pethadine is a nonaddictive drug developed primarily for Goering's airborne forces during the war.

At the turn of 1925-26, Goering's Swedish doctors declared that he was mentally healed. He turned to his previous job as an aviation salesman. He began to develop fresh contacts in German, Dutch and Scandinavian air circles and also paid an abortive visit to London in the spring of 1926. He tried to establish contacts in the British Air Ministry and to effect sales of aircraft and parachutes in Britain. After a few days he returned from London to Stockholm without orders and with virtually no new business contacts.

When he got back to Sweden, Goering was not allowed any drugs to combat his acute mental problems. He turned temporarily to religion in this further period of distress. He attended the local chapel to pray with Karin and her mother. Later he wrote to his mother-in-law, 'You cannot imagine my feelings in that wonderful atmosphere. It was so calm and beautiful that I forgot all earthly turmoil and cares and felt as though I was in another world'. This burst of religion was only a temporary phase. When asked years later if he was religious, Goering replied that he believed he should go to church for marriages, births and deaths.

In Germany the political fortunes of the Nazi Party were still low. Hitler's *Mein Kampf* was not selling well and the *Voelkische Beobachter* had only a small circulation. But when the Socialist President Ebert died in 1927 and was succeeded by President von Hindenburg, a new era of Nazism began. In the autumn of that year he proclaimed a general political amnesty which legalised the Nazi Party.

When Goering heard the news he decided to return to Germany even though Karin was seriously ill. Hitler had not seen him since the Munich putsch of November 1923. There were now 14 Nazi members in the Reichstag and Adolf Hitler was looking for new blood for the Party.

When he returned to Berlin, at the end of 1927, Goering decided at first to concentrate on his aircraft business interests. To this end he went to see Erhard Milch, now head of what was called civil aviation in Germany; he also saw Ernst Heinkel and Claud Dornier, who were already designing military proto-type aircraft. They both had aircraft manufacturing facilities

outside Germany. Goering also resumed contact with the major
aero-engine plants of B.M.W. in Bavaria (the initials stand for
Bayerische Motoren Werke). He renewed his friendships with
Karl Bodenschatz and Bruno Loerzer. The latter was now
prosperously married. At this stage Goering had been out of
the main stream of German aircraft development for about five
years. He knew little about such things as low wing monoplane
design and navigational aids for night flying. And for five years
he had not known who was who in the middle ranks of civil
aviation and of the reviving clandestine aircraft industry in
Germany. He was also out of touch with the air department of
the Reichswehr. Perhaps in the long run this five years hiatus
was not crucial. If he had concentrated his mind on aviation in
the key period of 1933 to 1939 he could have picked up most
of the missing threads of the 1920s.

But, in 1928, Goering switched his main interest from aviation
to politics. New elections were due and he wanted to be elected
to the Reichstag. By now he was recovered in mental health,
for when he met Hitler in Berlin, in January 1928, the Nazi
Party leader took him once again into his full confidence and
spoke to him about his future political plans. To add to
Goering's growing happiness and confidence, Karin was now
well enough to leave Sweden and she joined him in Berlin.

In April 1928, Hitler told Goering that he was to stand as a
candidate for the Reichstag. Goering threw a dinner party to
celebrate. Karin, Erhard Milch and Paul Koerner sat at table
with him. Koerner was a German officer of the First World War
who had just become Goering's junior business partner, chauffeur
and secretary. There was hectic discussion at the dinner about
Goering's election campaign. Milch said to him, 'You must have
a policy of moderation and dignity'. Goering agreed, surprisingly,
and he spoke strangely of the Nazi S.A. brown-shirt thugs as
though they were some shocking element in his remote past. The
main theme of his campaign speeches was 'revolution without
radicalism', But he added the standard Nazi theme. The Treaty
of Versailles must be cancelled and Bolsheviks and Jews must
be eradicated from power in Germany.

At the 1928 elections the Nazi Party polled only 810,000
votes compared with over nine million for the Social Democrats.
This gave them 14 seats in the Reichstag and Goering secured

one of them. He took his place for the first time on 14 June 1928. As a deputy, he was to get about £28 a month which, at the time, was a fair living wage, of which he was in need. But soon he had the financial patronage of Fritz Thyssen, the Ruhr coal and steel magnate.

Goering began his Reichstag career in a sensible manner, concentrating his speeches on aviation and transport matters. Thus in a June 1929 debate on the air estimates he demanded more money for Lufthansa, the German civil monopoly air line. He praised Lufthansa as 'the stronghold of the German Air Force spirit during the years of darkness'. He went on, 'German aviation has a great patriotic task to fulfil. Why is there no Secretary of State for Air? We airmen, whenever it has been required, have fought in the open and we shall do so again. I hope that you will deal with this matter in the same spirit of frankness, so that the difficulties which are confronting the German Air Arm may be eliminated. Save the German Air Arm. If you don't, you will live to regret it'.

This implied threat of the revival of German military air power was largely discounted in Europe in 1929. The military potential of the Lufthansa planes and training facilities was not generally appreciated. British air intelligence was almost alone in sensing the threat, as subsequently appeared in the Second World War. The Junkers 52 was already a reality as a civil air liner. In the Spanish Civil War it was to be used as both a bomber and a military transport plane. Later Lufthansa was to use a Heinkel passenger plane, which became the Heinkel 111 bomber, also the four-engined Focke Wulf 200 Condor, which had bombing and reconnaissance successes against both British and American ships in the Battle of the Atlantic and which bombed the U.S. base at Casablanca in Morocco at the turn of 1942-43.

Goering was now back in touch with all the major aviation developments in Germany; but for the next ten years or so, up to the outbreak of the Second World War, he probably spent on the average no more than half of his time on air affairs. And so his air leadership inevitably suffered because of the competing claims of German politics, economics and diplomacy, which were his three major diversions. In such circumstances perhaps it was inevitable that his air planning and strategy lacked

C

symmetry and harmony. To achieve the best balance in air power between fighters, bombers, reconnaissance and transport squadrons called for more consecutive study than this hydra-headed career could permit.

By 1930, his mental and physical batteries seemed to be fully recharged. His relationship with Adolf Hitler had become very intimate. He was building a new reputation in Germany as Hitler's salon ambassador. In this role he appeared with August Wilhelm, brother of Crown Prince Wilhelm, on the same Nazi platform to applaud the young man's speeches and to develop friendship with him. Goering also entertained, on behalf of Hitler, people like Hjalmar Schacht, President of the Reichs-bank, and Thyssen, the Ruhr business magnate.

The 1930 elections brought a major success to the Nazi Party. Held on 17 September, they resulted in six million votes for the Nazis and 107 seats in the Reichstag for Hitler. The Nazis were now the second largest party after the Catholic Centre Party. Shortly afterwards, at a Party meeting in Berlin, Goering produced this gem in the course of a speech he made: 'We are fighting against this State and the present system because we want to destroy it utterly, but in a legal manner'. He continued to help Hitler to promote civil disorder in Germany through the brown-shirted S.A. forces.

On the domestic front Goering's genuine sadness continued. Karin had to go twice to a nursing home in the summer and autumn of 1930. But Goering continued to cultivate the influential and the rich on behalf of Hitler, people like von Schroeder, the banker, Walter Funk, the editor of an industrial paper, and von Schnitzler, of the giant I. G. Farben Industrie.

In 1931, Hitler bought a large Mercedes car for Goering, who was incidentally an erratic driver. He also loved to sound the horn rather loudly. In February 1931 he walked out of the Reichstag together with Hitler as a protest against the Bruening government. He did not resume his seat until September. In the meantime Hitler sent Goering to the Vatican in May. The mission achieved little, except some publicity for Goering. He was by now a leading Nazi figure and an ample one in every sense. He weighed more than 18 stone.

The death of Karin's mother on 25 September probably hastened Karin's own death. Goering went to Stockholm with her for the funeral but hurried back to meet President von Hindenburg to explain Nazi policies to him on behalf of Hitler. In mid-October Goering was battling in the Reichstag against the Bruening government which fell on 16 October. The next day Karin died in Stockholm and a new phase of Hermann Goering's personal life began. Though he mourned her deeply and genuinely he met his second wife six months after her death after a Nazi rally in Weimar. Her name was Emmy Sonnemann. She was a tall blonde actress and a divorcee. She became at first Goering's mistress. Unlike Karin she took little interest in German politics.

In the decade before Hitler and his Nazis came to power in Germany in March 1933, Hermann Goering must have had only a superficial knowledge of some of the important German aircraft developments taking place. How far this affected his early air leadership which began in 1933, when he became Minister for Aviation, is hard to say. But the gaps in his contacts and knowledge were considerable, quite apart from the period between the end of 1923 and the end of 1927 when he was away from Germany. He must have known very little for example of Lufthansa's detailed plans to train military aircrews on their civil air lines. Goering hardly knew Willi Messerschmitt in the 1923-27 period. He was almost out of touch with the production of Heinkel planes for export to Sweden, Japan and the U.S.S.R., and with the prototype construction of Claudius Dornier's flying boats and of Hugo Junkers' four-engined bomber-cum-transport plane, used by the Lufthansa and built later under licence in Japan as a military bomber. One could perhaps say that when, in the early 1930's, the phoenix of the German Air Force rose from the ashes of the Treaty of Versailles, Hermann Goering was frequently a remote witness of the revival. In the period 1933-1935 he had much leeway to make up on the German air events of 1923-1933. There was, for example, the air agreement with the U.S.S.R. which followed the Treaty of Rapallo in 1922, following which Hugo Junkers built an aircraft plant in the suburbs of Moscow; and there was the provision of German pilot training facilities in the Ukraine. When one considers Goering's political and public career from

1931-1935 the reason for the continued aviation hiatus becomes apparent. He was taking a major part in the election campaigns and the political manoeuvres of the Nazi Party. His personal stature as a public figure increased rapidly but it was inevitable that his knowledge of contemporary air developments in Britain, the United States and the Soviet Union suffered as well as of air events in Germany itself.

At the turn of 1931-1932 the internal situation in Germany was bad. The Wall Street crash of 1929 had dried up a major source of foreign loans; German industrial production fell by about half in the 1929-1932 period. Two major banks failed and there were soon to be about six million unemployed in the country.

In April 1932, the Nazi Party suffered a major setback when Chancellor Bruening persuaded his senile President, von Hindenburg, to sign a decree suppressing Hitler's S.A. storm-troopers. They then totalled nearly 500,000 men and so were numerically stronger than the Reichswehr. Hermann Goering's private plane which carried Nazi speakers to conferences and rallies was also banned. Goering expressed his pique at this move with typical vigour. Both in the Reichstag and on public platforms he counter-attacked the German Chancellor. 'The Bruening Cabinet must go so that Germany can live' he declared to the assembled Reichstag. And he went on, 'Bruening has lost every battle, and when generals lose battles they have to go'. He also said that the 'Nazis would fulfil their historic mission to reconcile all classes of German people'. This presumably excluded Jews.

Chancellor Bruening resigned on 30 May 1932. Early in June, President von Hindenburg sent for Hitler and Goering to tell them that von Papen was to be the new German Chancellor. On 15 June von Papen lifted the ban on the S.A. storm-troopers in exchange for the fragile promise of Nazi support in the Reichstag.

In the new elections of June and July 1932, Hitler, Goering and Goebbels were the chief Nazi speakers. In the voting on 31 July their Party secured over 13 million votes. This gave them 230 of the 608 Reichstag seats. Sensing the final political victory, Goering said exultantly to Goebbels, 'Now we are in the saddle'.

When the new Reichstag met in August it elected Hermann

Goering as its President. In this great moment of triumph he sent a note to Emmy Sonnemann which said simply, 'I love you'.

The oratory of politicians is not of course intended to stand up to the microscope of historians. In his first speech in August 1932 as President of the Reichstag, Goering naturally promised to perform his duties 'justly and impartially according to Reichstag rules'. He said he would be 'vigilant in protecting the honour and dignity of the German people' and he concluded, 'The safety of the nation and the freedom of the Fatherland will be the chief guiding stars of my actions'. But soon Goering was bending Reichstag rules to suit his purpose.

Hitler's paladin and right-hand man now had access to leading Germans of all kinds from the President downwards. Goering's political, financial and social status was rising rapidly. In September he helped to put Chancellor von Papen out of office by a trick of Reichstag procedure and he was aided and abetted by the Communist Party. But in the November 1932 elections which followed, Hitler's candidates obtained about two million votes less than in the July elections of that year. A contributory cause of this setback was the alarm among German industrialists at the continuing violence of the S.A. storm-troopers and the dictatorial trends in Nazi politics.

The next German Chancellor was General Schleicher who attempted to split the Nazi Party by offering the Vice-Chancellor's job to Gregor Strasser, a senior Nazi known to be in opposition to both Hitler's and Goering's political views. Schleicher was Chancellor of Germany for only 57 days. In the Nazi plotting to get rid of him, Goering was one of the chief schemers.

1933 was to be a vintage year of political progress for both Goering and the Nazi Party. 22 January 1933 was a day of special triumph for him. He was summoned from Dresden to Berlin to see Oscar von Hindenburg, the son of the President. He then went on to discuss Germany's future with the President. Together they and Joachim von Ribbentrop, aided by Otto Meissner, plotted to get rid of Schleicher. The latter tendered his resignation as Chancellor on 28 January 1933 after a series of Nazi and other pressures and threats. The next day Goering went to the Kaiserhof Hotel in Berlin and announced with a flourish to Hitler and his aides that the Nazi leader

would now become the next German Chancellor. It was a
surprise announcement. Goebbels, for example, noted in his
diary of January 1933 that he expected von Papen to be the
new Chancellor.

But on 30 January the Goering prophecy proved correct.
Hitler became Chancellor of Germany, even though the Nazi
Party had at the time only three of the eleven cabinet posts in
the Reichstag. Goering sensed the importance of the occasion
and spoke on the radio to the German people: '30 January
will go down in history as the day on which the nation found
itself after fourteen years of torture, sorrow, shame and disgrace.
Freedom and honour are fundamental to the coming state. Now
the future will, at long last, bring us that for which the Fuehrer
and his faithful followers have worked and fought—bread and
work for the German people, freedom and honour for the nation'.
This was stirring stuff from an orator who certainly knew how
to stir his audience. The new Reichstag elections were to be held
on 5 March.

Goering was by now also Minister of the Interior for
Prussia. Although barely two months in this office, he
removed, during February, a high proportion of the Prussian
police officials and replaced them by Nazi S.A. and S.S. storm-
troopers, ignoring von Papen, who, as Prime Minister of Prussia,
was in theory his superior. Goering now had the political bit
between his ruthless teeth. A Goering message to the Prussian
Police in February 1933 ran: 'We will employ every means at
our disposal without hesitation and utilise to the full our heaviest
weapons' . . . and he added . . . 'you can shoot down if necessary
those hostile to S.A. and S.S. personnel'. In this same month,
Goering expanded the Prussian police by a further 50,000 men
who were drawn mainly from the S.A. brown-shirts.

On 24 February, Goering's police raided the Communist
headquarters in Berlin. Goering publicly claimed to have
documents to show that the Communists were about to launch
a revolution in Germany, but he never produced any serious
evidence to support this assertion.

On the night of the 27/28 of February, the Reichstag was
set on fire, it is said with Goering's connivance. On 28 February
President von Hindenburg, in a moment of panic, signed a
new decree 'for the protection of the people and the state'. This

suspended the sections of the German constitution which guaranteed individual civil liberties. It allowed Goering and his policemen to arrest almost at will. Thousands of Communists and Social Democrats were imprisoned.

Early in March 1933, Hermann Goering, in a broadcast to the nation, again promised to produce full proof of the Communist conspiracy. But again he neglected to do so and in a speech at Frankfurt he said, 'I don't have to worry about justice . . . my mission is to destroy and exterminate . . . I shall use the power of the State and the police to the utmost, my dear Communists, so do not draw any false conclusions'. The crudities of this public utterance were no doubt soon forgotten by his German audience.

On 5 March 1933, the German people voted the Nazis into power. Taking into account the many terrorist actions of their S.A. storm-troopers in the previous weeks, the wonder is that nearly five million Germans voted for the Communists and over seven million for the Social Democrats. But as the German Nationalist Party, which won 52 seats, supported the Nazis, Hitler was now sure of being able to form a government of his own.

The new Reichstag, convened on 21 March 1933, immediately passed, by an overwhelming majority, the 'Law for Removing the Distress of People and Reich'. This made Adolf Hitler lord and master of the Third Reich, and later when he became Commander in Chief of the German armed forces he was also lord and master of much of Goering's air strategy.

Hermann Goering was now perhaps the most popular man in Germany despite his well-known terrorist tactics. There was a distinct dichotomy in his public image. Some called him 'der Dicke (the fat man)' and saw Goering as the laughing, happy-go-lucky clown who was easygoing and indulged his taste for his favourite Bavarian food, in which fattening dumplings featured frequently. Others called him 'der Eiserne (the Iron Man)' who created the Gestapo in 1933, who helped to organise the first German concentration camps and ruled the Prussian police with a rod of iron. A wide range of jokes were told about him in the night clubs of Berlin and Hamburg.

When Goering was appointed Aviation Minister in March 1933, Adolf Hitler created a special fund to meet his growing expenses. He was now entertaining foreign diplomats and statesmen lavishly and beginning his successful period of bluff about the air potential of Germany. He was offered and accepted free shares in two of the main aero-engine companies of Germany, Daimler-Benz and B.M.W. He acquired a share in the Ruhr newspaper *Die Essener Zeitung* and used it as a mouthpiece for his views and hobby-horses.

He also began to gather about him a number of aircraft and aviation specialists who were to be his counsellors in formulating German air policy. There was, for example, Ernst Udet, the flying ace and stunt pilot, who failed to convince Goering of the great potential aircraft production of the United States—a blind spot which remained until the 1942-1943 period. Udet was closely concerned with overall technical policy together with Erhard Milch and General Wever.

Goering was not all bluff. He told a meeting of the German Aero Club at the end of 1933 with great frankness, 'The aviation position is very bad. Do not let that worry you'. And he went on, 'You can take your pick from six million unemployed. We shall put them to work building new aerodromes, factories, aircraft and engines'. And he went ahead with his plans to expand the German aircraft industry in the next five years or so. But somehow the output of aircraft lagged far behind the commitments of Hitler's strategy, particularly after the summer of 1940.

Goering delegated most of the aviation planning of the period 1933-1935 to Erhard Milch, who was now Deputy Air Minister, and also to General Wever, who was earmarked to be Chief of Staff of the new German Air Force when it was created publicly in March 1935. But Goering was too feverishly busy with German domestic and foreign policy to lend an ear to his two senior and most competent advisers. General Wever was unfortunately killed in an air crash in 1936. As for Milch, he tried in vain to tell Goering that the German aircraft industry and air training organisation needed until 1942 to support an adequate Luftwaffe fully ready to go to war. But Goering was tied hand and foot by Adolf Hitler's war plans and by his undoubted loyalty to the Fuehrer who was also his Commander in Chief.

It seems odd to record that when Goering was urgently planning the vital new military airfields, a new Henschel aircraft plant near Berlin and a new Messerschmitt plant at Augsburg, he was also indulging in new diversities such as the Reichstag Fire trial and the new job of *Reichsjaegermeister* (Master of Hunting). Perhaps there was some inbuilt defect in his psychological make-up which prevented him concentrating his mind for very long on any one subject.

In 1934, Goering became deeply involved in a major rift betwen the Nazi Party and its S.A. storm-troopers. Ernst Roehm, now chief of the S.A. forces, wanted his brown shirts, who totalled over two million, to be both the army of the Nazi Party and of the Third Reich. It seems fairly certain that Roehm aspired to replace General von Blomberg as Defence Minister. In February 1934, Roehm openly presented a long memorandum to Hitler and his cabinet suggesting that the S.S., S.A. and Reichswehr forces should be combined and that he should be Commander in Chief of all these elements. Goering made two key moves against Roehm in the spring of 1934. He appointed Himmler chief of the Prussian Gestapo (Secret Police) and of the S.A. forces. He also created his own personal police force—the *Landespolizeigruppe General Goering*.

In May and June 1934, Himmler and Goering plotted the liquidation of S.A. commanders and others who opposed Nazism. In a speech delivered to the Prussian State Council, in June 1934, Goering attacked Roehm and reaffirmed his loyalty to Hitler. On June 21st, General von Blomberg told Hitler that he might have to declare martial law in Germany. Four days later Himmler and Goering brought their police forces to instant readiness and General von Fritsch, commander in chief of the German army, put his troops in a state of alert. What followed between then and the purge of Ernst Roehm and his S.A. leaders during the bloody week-end of 30 June and 1 July will never be known in full. It is believed that, as in the case of the Reichstag Fire trial, Goering suppressed some of the key evidence. When Hitler spoke to the Reichstag on 13 July he announced that 61 people had been shot, including nineteen S.A. leaders. At a Munich trial in 1957 a figure of more than 1,000 was quoted. Whatever the true figure, Goering had shown the touch of a ruthless gangster in working with Himmler in the S.A. purge. It was a ruthlessness born in part of loyalty to his Fuehrer.

When the S.A. purge was over in July 1934, Goering sent

his aide Pili Koerner with an S.A. Commando Unit to Sweden, to bring back Karin's remains to Germany. A personal loan from Thyssen had enabled him to buy a former imperial hunting lodge at Schorfheide, some thirty miles north-east of Berlin. He called it Karinhall in memory of his first wife, shortly before he proposed marriage to his second wife Emmy. Karinhall became a sumptuous estate and one of the air headquarters of the German Air Force, for it was often used for senior air staff meetings as well as for parties and receiving important foreign diplomats and royalty, including King Boris of Bulgaria and the Duke and Duchess of Windsor.

When President Hindenburg died, on 2 August 1934, Hitler abolished the title of President and made himself Fuehrer and Chancellor of the Third Reich. He also issued a decree which exacted an oath of unconditional loyalty from all members of the German armed forces.

When in March 1935 the new German Air Force emerged publicly, Goering became its Commander in Chief and was given the rank of Air General. He now commanded a force of about 20,000 officers and men and about 1,800 planes of which over half were trainer machines. Although its equipment was obsolescent by the standards of the Second World War, the operational aircraft were quite modern by 1934-35 criteria. They included the Junkers 52 three-engined bomber, the Dornier 23 twin-engined bomber, the Henschel 123 dive-bomber, the Heinkel 38 fighter and the Heinkel 59 seaplane which was in fact in service as a sea-rescue and coastal patrol plane until the end of the Second World War.

In the next ten years, the Luftwaffe was the means by which Hermann Goering exercised the greatest influence on foreign affairs. As General Carl Spaatz, then Commander in Chief of the U.S. Air Forces, wrote in 1946, 'It was the German Air Force which dominated world diplomacy and won for Hitler the bloodless political victories of the late 1930s'. This might be something of an overstatement but it has considerable substance.

CHAPTER THREE

Prelude to the Second World War

1936—1939

THE CHIEF events which involved Hermann Goering in major air policy and air planning decisions in the period 1936 to 1939 were the Nazi re-occupation of the Rhineland, the Spanish Civil War, the Austrian Anschluss, which added that country to Hitler's territory, the invasion of Czechoslovakia and finally the German Air Force preparations for the war against Poland. The strategic developments that might flow from the Polish campaign of September 1939 were, of course, not apparent at the time, either to Goering or to most contemporary air commanders, whether inside or outside Europe.

Some psychiatrists maintain that people who take morphia occasionally indulge in fanciful daydreams, in which difficult problems find easy solutions through the soothing euphoric effect of this hard drug. But even when Goering abandoned morphia and took to large quantities of less harmful paracodeine, he never made any serious attempt to cope with the full reality of German Air Force planning requirements during the crucial three or four years which preceded the outbreak of the Second World War in September 1939. At no time during this period did he, for example, in his air leadership of Germany, prepare seriously for, or anticipate, a two or three front war, in which the German Air Force would be opposed by major air forces, such as the Royal Air Force, the United States Air Forces or by Soviet air power. In this sense he was a total strategic failure as an air leader and may, in fact, have virtually lost the key air battles of 1939-1945 before the war itself had begun.

At the turn of 1935-1936 Goering was voicing his demand for equality for Germany's military air power. He plugged this line energetically and persistently, both in public speeches and privately to the many highly placed guests he received at his Karinhall estate. What he meant by equality was never defined. As German air intelligence was very weak at this juncture, especially on Soviet air power, Goering must have used the concept of equality rather vaguely and without chapter and verse.

At the turn of 1935-1936, the German aircraft industry was producing about 2,000 planes a year, that is of all types, military and civil. The Soviet aircraft industry was then turning out more than twice this number, and among other prospective opponents of the Luftwaffe were also the French and British Air Forces. Unless Goering could rapidly expand Germany's aircraft production and pilot training, numerical parity for the German Air Force in the late 1930s would merely be another of his manic verbosities. Politically, of course, the slogan of air equality was sound in 1935-36.

Now that the German Air Force was officially reborn and not, as before, developing like some secret underground movement, Goering was personally a happier man in both his public and private life. He would openly indulge his genuine affection for the new young generation of German Air Force pilots whom he loved with fatherly pride. Small wonder that one of his first public acts as Commander in Chief was to name a group of the new fighter squadrons the Richthofen Geschwader. This was the unit he had commanded proudly but without success in 1918.

And as he now knew that Emmy Sonnermann could be the kind of lover-wife he wanted, he married her on 10 April 1935. Their official engagement had been celebrated a few weeks previously, and was marked by a pleasant holiday in Greece in the company of Prince Philip von Hessen, a member of the growing circle of Goering's aristocratic friends.

Of course the Hermann Goering/Emmy Sonnermann wedding made banner headlines in the German press and also had world-wide coverage. Goebbels' radio reported to German listeners at about noon on the day: 'The wedding procession is on the way from the Chancellery to the Town Hall. The streets

are lined with people . . . thousands of people . . . It is raining
. . . Here comes the bride. She is wearing a beautiful dress.
Hermann Goering . . . our Hermann, is in the uniform of an
air general'.

What kind of an air general was Hermann Goering in the
spring of 1935? In the months that marked the beginning of
his second marriage and the first stages of the official revival
of the German Air Force, in the years which followed up to the
outbreak of the Second World War, there were probably no
really experienced air generals or air marshals anywhere in the
world.

In his writings Marshal of the Royal Air Force Sir
John Slessor, one of Britain's more expressive air leaders, has
pointed out that in the middle and late 1930s there was general
ignorance among virtually all air leaders about many aspects
of both strategic and long-term air warfare. In particular the
requirements of long-range bombing and strategic air defence
were not comprehended. There was for example no real use of
sustained large-scale bombing of strategic targets before the
Anglo-American attack on Germany from 1943 to 1945, or of
sustained fighter defence with modern equipment before the
Battle of Britain. 'The miracle', said Sir John, 'is that so few
mistakes were made'.

In the years 1935-1939, if there had been public debate on the
radio or in a television studio about the use and abuses of air
power with say Goering and Milch on one side of the table,
and on the other side their opposite numbers in the British,
American, Soviet or Japanese Air Forces, a cacophonous and
uncertain discord would surely have emerged. No one round
the table would have had practical experience of the large-scale
use of air-power, relevant to most of the major air battles of the
Second World War.

This inevitable lack of large-scale operational experience
cannot of course excuse some of the faults in the air leadership
of Hermann Goering in the period 1936-1939. These were the
key four years of build-up and expansion which decided Luftwaffe potential in the crucial period 1939-41. His mathematics
on the subject of future German air power in this period were
done largely by guess and by grope. He knew he was tied to the
fanciful strategy of Adolf Hitler, but he seemed unable to under-

stand the time-scale he needed to produce a modern air force sufficiently large to meet the requirements of Hitler's plans for the Wehrmacht. Not that there was anywhere in existence, in Germany or elsewhere, a firm body of doctrine or experience, which could tell air policy makers roughly how many bombers were needed to destroy or irreparably damage some aspect of enemy industry or how many fighters were needed to escort and protect the bombers under various combat conditions. Strategic air defence was also in a state of early adolescence in the period 1936-1939. Radar was a young aeronautical colt on trial. Night fighter defence without it was largely ineffective.

Hermann Goering must of course accept a large measure of personal responsibility for many of the German Air Force decisions taken in the three or four years after the re-emergence of the Luftwaffe. For some he must be given credit, and for others bear a large measure of blame. On the credit side there was the creation of a large force of Junkers 52 transport planes, which gave the German Air Force of the middle and late 1930s more mobility and fluidity in support of ground armies than any other contemporary air force. On the debit side there was his failure to build up adequate reserves of aircraft, a failure which limited German Air Force intensive large-scale operations to a few weeks, and resulted in some units being below strength even after a few days of combat, with no replacement aircraft readily available. Indeed the combat strengths of some German Air Force units oscillated erratically throughout the Second World War in both short and long periods of air operations.

The first public test of the new German Air Force came when Hitler decided to re-occupy the Rhineland. The plans were made only three weeks after Goering's happy marriage to Emmy Sonnermann. The code name used, *Schulung,* means training. It was highly appropriate. On 2 May 1935, when General von Blomberg issued the Rhineland directive to the Wehrmacht Chiefs of Staff, neither the German Air Force nor the German Army were ready for anything more fierce than training manoeuvres.

Goering's main role in the months before the German troops moved into the Rhineland, on 7 March 1936, was to huff and bluff in order to give an inflated impression, to Germans and foreigners alike, of the German Air Force front-line strength. In this political aspect of his air leadership he was highly successful both then and in the next two or three years. He succeeded in giving an exaggerated view of Luftwaffe operational potential to a wide range of attachés and other diplomats, as well as to foreign intelligence services.

Certainly the mystique and myth of German Air Force strength created by the personal counter-intelligence work of Hermann Goering played a considerable part in encouraging Anglo-French inertia when Hitler's forces marched into the Rhineland in 1936, into Austria in 1938 and into Czechoslovakia in 1939.

The German Air Force supported, without bloodshed, Hitler's march into the Rhineland in the spring of 1936 with a force of about a hundred planes, mainly Arado and Heinkel biplane fighters. Adolf Galland, then a young Heinkel pilot, and later a staff air general, who was one of the great combat leaders of the German Air Force, has stated that some of the German planes used over the Rhineland were unarmed and flown by only partially trained pilots. As it was then only about a year since the German Air Force had been publicly recreated, Galland's evidence in this instance would seem to be entirely credible.

It was the Spanish Civil War (1936-1939) which gave Goering the first major opportunity of trying out a large number of his air squadrons under combat conditions. It is to his credit as an air leader that he seized the opportunity in full measure. Goering's keenness to send his air squadrons to fight in Spain was later reflected at the Nuremberg Trials on 14 March 1946. Then he spoke proudly of his decision and testified, 'With the permission of the Fuehrer, I sent a large part of my transport fleet and a number of experimental fighter and bomber units and anti-aircraft guns'. Goering, of course, commanded and controlled German anti-aircraft artillery as well as the Luftwaffe squadrons. He went on to tell the Nuremberg trial, 'In that way, I had an opportunity to find out under combat conditions whether the aircraft and equipment were equal to the task. In order that the personnel too might gather some experience, I saw to it that there was a continuous flow of new personnel'.

This particular testimony given at Nuremberg was true except for one vital thing. The combat conditions in the Spanish Civil

War could tell the German Air Force Commander in Chief virtually nothing about whether his squadrons were equal to the task of facing well organised modern air forces, such as the Royal Air Force or the United States Army Air Forces. Nor did the Spanish Civil War help Goering very much to deal with a Soviet Air Force of over 10,000 planes in the months that followed Hitler's attack on the U.S.S.R. in June 1941. Nevertheless, the German Air Force gained its most valuable pre-war combat experience in Spain, and it stood Goering in good stead. The German Air Units used were called the Kondor Legion. Its operational strength in the Spanish Civil War varied from about 110 aircraft (a figure not achieved until the spring of 1937) to a maximum strength of 285 front-line planes in the period 1938-1939. In terms of support for General Franco's troops, Hermann Goering's most vital contribution was probably the twenty Junkers 52 three-engined transport planes which, in the period August to September 1936, air-ferried some 10,000 mainly Moroccan troops across the Mediterranean. For the first time in military history it could be said that an air lift of infantry had had a real impact on ground warfare. To Hermann Goering must go much of the credit for this aeronautical first.

The first German Air Force Commander of the Luftwaffe units in Spain was General Hugo Sperrle. He had at his disposal for supporting General Franco a moderate force of 30-50 twin-engined bombers, about the same number of dive-bombers and also of single-engined fighters, about thirty reconnaissance and patrol planes and eventually about 50 transport Junkers. Such moderate forces could not have had a really decisive influence on the ground battles in Spain. But the Spanish Civil War was, as Goering himself said at the time, an invaluable proving ground. He had pressed Hitler hard to let him send German Air Force units to Spain.

Goering made good use of the new operational training facilities in Spain to test both new crews and new aircraft types. Thus in the bomber squadrons, the obsolescent Junkers 52 was replaced by the early versions of both the Heinkel 111 and Dornier 17, the main twin-engined bombers used in the Polish and Norwegian air campaigns, in the 1940 battles over France and the Low Countries and in the Battle of Britain.

Perhaps the most important German aircraft tried out by

V. The Luftwaffe — an Early Flypast

VI. An Early Luftwaffe Review

Goering in the Spanish Civil War under combat conditions was the new Messerschmitt 109 single-seat fighter; this aircraft began to replace the Arado 68 and Heinkel 51 biplanes in Luftwaffe squadrons in the period 1937 to 1938. This low-wing monoplane fighter was the most extensively used single-engined fighter in the German Air Force in the next seven years or so, that is up to the end of the Second World War. The Junkers 87 dive-bomber, which had a long but chequered career in German air squadrons, also made its combat début in the Spanish Civil War, replacing the already obsolescent Henschel 123 biplane dive bomber.

Quite apart from trying out the latest types of operational aircraft, Goering took advantage of the opportunity of getting practical on-the-spot experience in the tactical use of modern air power in the Spanish war theatre. He absorbed some of the lessons but neglected others.

On the credit side, he consulted closely with von Richthofen, who was to become perhaps his ace tactical air leader in the Second World War, commanding the Luftwaffe's 8th Air Corps on many fronts, both western and eastern. Richthofen was the first German air commander to develop, to a high standard, the use of mobile wireless stations in transport aircraft and radio telephone communication between ground and air forces, to achieve quicker, closer and more mobile co-operation. The fruits of his Spanish Civil War experiences were to ripen in the use he and his fellow tactical air commanders made of German air squadrons in support of the German armies in Poland, the Low Countries, France, Yugoslavia and Greece in the period 1939-41.

The Spanish Civil War gave Goering himself little direct practice in the art and craft of air leadership for he was rarely on the spot in the theatre of operations to see for himself. Moreover, the aeronautical pace in Spain was slow, compared with the blitzkrieg air campaigns of 1939-1940 and very different from the hectic German disarray in the Battle of Britain or the later intensive air campaigns in the Balkans, the Mediterranean theatre or on the eastern fronts against the U.S.S.R.

Hermann Goering had shown initiative and imagination in the way he seized the experimental opportunities afforded by the Spanish Civil War. But perhaps the relatively easy successes of his air squadrons against moderate Soviet air and other

D

opposition, unsupported by any early warning radar, gave an impulse to his latent, innate optimism about German Air Force potential. As Spain presented few German air problems in combat, it probably stimulated an excess of confidence in Goering and even bouts of euphoria, for he was still taking morphia. As Stalin did not send his élite air regiments or latest planes to Spain, the Civil War there was probably a contributory factor to Goering's built-in tendency to under-rate Soviet Air Force potential.

The Austrian Anschluss of 1938 and the German occupation of Czechoslovakia about a year later were in themselves no test of Goering's air leadership. But the period during which these two operations were planned, prepared and executed by the German General Staff, cover a crucial phase in any overall assessment of the long-term planning capacity of the Commander in Chief of the German Air Force. It was from 1937 to 1939 that Goering and his staff formulated the air frame to support Hitler's war strategy. One might even say that, in aeronautical terms, Goering lost the prospects of victory in Europe for the Third Reich in these crucial three years.

One of the main reasons for his failure to plan adequately for major wars was his intensified pre-occupation with other portfolios. In September 1936 he had been made Commissioner for the German Four Year Economic Plan, and so wielded great new power in terms of Germany's raw material and manpower resources. As a result he obtained a high priority for German Air Force economic requirements in aircraft production. This was certainly a plus factor in the complicated ledger account of Goering's air leadership. Goering's work on Germany's Four Year Plan was yet another diversion which, like his political and police work in Germany and his foreign diplomatic activity, took up time and energy he could ill spare from the wide range of new German Air Force problems.

On 18 October 1936, Adolf Hitler formally gave Hermann Goering the authority to issue decrees in the general field of German economics. He was by this act, perhaps unwittingly, driving a large nail into the coffin of Goering's Air Force leadership. This further responsibility was yet another major diversion which was to divide Goering's mind and prevent him from managing his Air Force with persistent effectiveness.

Perhaps Goering's best known sally on German economics was the Hamburg speech in which he told the huge crowd that they needed guns and not butter. He added, 'What does butter do but make you fat?' The crowd roared its delight. At the time Goering tipped the scales at over twenty stone and had a serious weight problem. This and his glandular troubles were to upset his health intermittently in the period 1937-1939 and later. The effect of this on his air leadership was, however, probably not very serious.

As a doyen of German economics, Hermann Goering played his role with considerable verve and panache, at any rate in his public and private utterances. His desk-work, however, was less effective. At one meeting in October 1936 with Schacht and other senior Third Reich economists, he said, 'If we have war tomorrow, we must use raw material substitutes. In that case money will not play any role at all'. This was splendid theory, superbly neglectful of the fact that the German Air Force at the time needed large supplies of aluminium, rubber and oil from abroad to be paid for in foreign currency. German scientists needed many years to develop complete substitutes for these products in quantity. Perhaps Adolf Hitler had prompted Goering's optimistic statement for, about the same time, Goering told his senior Air Force colleagues, 'I have been deeply impressed by the Fuehrer, by his logic and the boldness of his economic ideas'. Goering's loyalty to Hitler sometimes had the touch of the sycophant.

Later in October 1936, Hermann Goering said at a Berlin press conference : 'I do not acknowledge the holiness of any law about economics . . . The German economy must always be the servant of the nation'. At another conference of senior German economists, including Schacht, held in Berlin in December 1936, Goering announced that he was taking over the business of placing all orders for the German armaments industry. Thus he had as free a hand as any air commander in aviation history, to develop the German aircraft industry on the lines he wanted for the future expansion of the German Air Force.

With what results? The output figures from German factories in the key five years from 1937 to 1941 were grossly inadequate to meet the air operational requirements imposed by Hitler's European strategy. In 1936 the German aircraft industry had

produced about 5,100 planes of all types, civil and military. The
increase in 1937 was small, the output total being only 5,600.
Because of the introduction of new types of planes there was a
moderate drop in 1938 to 5,235 planes, i.e. including operational
trainer and civil machines. The imminence of war brought a
big increase in 1939 to a total of nearly 8,300 aircraft. There
was a further increase in 1940 to about 10,250 machines and in
1941 to 12,400.

To put these figures in perspective, it should be pointed out
that Britain's aircraft production was substantially greater than
Germany's in the total number of planes in 1940, as was also
Soviet aircraft production in 1941. There are other factors to
be taken into account, such as the size and performance of
planes, radar developments, bombs, aircraft armament, Goering's
choice of air leaders and, of course, the question of training. In
some respects, e.g. standard of pilot and crew training, the
evolution of the 20mm cannon on fighter aircraft and the use
of the fuel injection aero-engine, Germany's progress was noteworthy. But in the development of early warning radar, the
Luftwaffe lagged badly behind the Royal Air Force in the
pre-war period, and Goering must take part of the blame for
this, as well as most of the credit or blame for choosing the
Luftwaffe air commanders.

To what extent can Hermann Goering be blamed for the
relatively moderate number of planes turned out by German
aircraft factories in those five key years? Did he, for example,
have enough advance warning of Hitler's solid strategic intentions, as opposed to the Fuehrer's vapid outpourings in *Mein
Kampf*?

Certainly by the end of 1937, Goering must have realised
that he needed to plan for the contingency of a major war in
Europe. On 24 July 1937 Field Marshal von Blomberg issued a
top secret directive to the Commands-in-Chief of the German
Army, Navy and Air Force on behalf of Adolf Hitler. It was a
call for preparedness for war on two fronts, though not neces-
sarily at the same time. The emphasis, said the directive, was on
the West. Presumably this meant war against Britain and France.
As an alternative, a two-front war was mentioned in the text,
the second front being South-East Europe, presumably meaning
the Balkan countries. Surprise attacks by France on Germany,

and by Germany on Czechoslovakia, were among the war situations also envisaged, as well as a German attack on Austria.

In pursuance of this 24 July directive, Adolf Hitler held an important meeting at the German Chancellery in Berlin on 5 November 1937 to discuss its contents. As Commander-in-Chief of the German Air Force, Goering attended, together with General von Fritsch, Commander-in-Chief of the German Army, and Admiral Raeder, the German Navy's Commander-in-Chief. Von Neurath, the German Foreign Minister, was also present. The meeting lasted four hours and Adolf Hitler did most of the talking. He spoke plainly enough. 'Germany's problems can only be solved by force', he said. He added that Britain and France were in Germany's way as they were opposed to any strengthening of Germany. Hitler also spoke of the danger in delaying action. 'Germany's military, naval and air equipment might become obsolescent', said the Fuehrer; 'and our strength would decrease in relation to the rest of the world'. Hitler said he wanted to solve the problem of Germany's expansion by 1943-45 at the latest.

Thus by the turn of 1937-1938, Hermann Goering had at least a broad picture of the likely future war commitments of his German air squadrons, at any rate for the next two or three years. It was surely at this stage of his varied career that Goering should have concentrated his personal effort on building up German air power until it could meet the needs of Adolf Hitler's proliferating strategy. But this he failed to do, and because of this failure he virtually lost the air war in Europe before it began.

The German documents state that, in 1938, 43 German firms were engaged in aircraft production or repair, and 16 in making or repairing aero-engines. But in 1938 the German aircraft industry made fewer than 5,250 planes. Already events in Austria and Czechoslovakia were signposting the way to the Second World War. Such a production figure for planes was absurdly unrealistic and inadequate for anything but a brief blitzkrieg of a few weeks. And it would have to be a blitzkrieg success for Germany. There was no catering for German air set-backs or even for protracted air warfare against strong opposition.

How did this happen? Why did Hermann Goering fail to gauge the air requirements of the Third Reich? The fact is that his mind was becoming a pot-pourri of economics, domestic politics, diplomacy and aeronautical *bric-à-brac,* not to mention his growing preoccupation with acquiring jewellery, pictures and pieces of sculpture. Then there was his hunting, which he loved dearly. And like so many other contemporary leaders, he blundered on believing that the worst would never happen.

At a German Cabinet meeting held in Berlin on 4 February 1938, Adolf Hitler announced: 'From now on I take over personally the command of the armed forces'. This of course left Goering with little strategic freedom in which to manoeuvre. At this same Cabinet meeting Hitler elevated Goering, who was present, to the rank of Field Marshal, dismissed von Neurath from his post as Foreign Minister and replaced him by von Ribbentrop. Ribbentrop and Goering were to be at loggerheads intermittently until Goering's death in 1946.

In the same month, February 1938, Schuschnigg, the Austrian Chancellor, met Adolf Hitler at Berchtesgaden. Goering, who at times had almost a compulsive habit of not attending key meetings, was represented on this occasion by General Hugo Sperrle, one of his toughest senior air commanders. In the meantime Goering himself received the Austrian Foreign Minister, Guido Schmitt, at Karinhall. There he showed his visitor from Vienna a newly printed map of Europe with no border marked between Germany and Austria. Meantime at Berchtesgaden, the Austrian Chancellor had accepted Hitler's ultimatum and appointed Seyss-Inquart, a Nazi lawyer from Vienna, as his new Minister of the Interior. This gave the Nazis in Austria control of the police and virtual control of the army.

The Hitler directive for 'Operation Otto', the codeword for the invasion of Austria, stated: 'The forces of the Army and Air Force must be ready for invasion on 12 March 1938 at the latest by 1200 hours'. Goering's air leadership was not put to any real test in the Austrian Anschluss. In fact, when the final German Air Force plans were being made on the days preceding Operation Otto, Hermann Goering was presiding over a court-martial trying General von Fritsch, the Commander-in-Chief of the German Army, who was accused of homosexual activities.

Goering's personal role in the Austrian Anschluss was political and diplomatic rather than aeronautical. Thus on the day before, on 11 March, he had nearly thirty telephone conversations about the invasion with Seyss-Inquart and other leading Austrian Nazis. All were duly recorded at Karinhall, for Hermann Goering was an enthusiastic monitor of both his own and other people's telephone calls. He was in a trenchant mood. He ordered Seyss-Inquart to 'tell Miklas that if the conditions are not accepted immediately, the troops which are already advancing to the frontier will march in tonight along the whole frontier and Austria will cease to exist'. At midnight President Miklas appointed Seyss-Inquart as his Chancellor and accepted the new Nazi Cabinet.

This was not enough for Hermann Goering. By 6.30 a.m. on 12 March he had washed and shaved and was on the phone to Seyss-Inquart again. 'You must dismiss the President . . . in five minutes the troops will march on my orders'. Goering was bluffing again. At 20.45 on the previous day Adolf Hitler had already given the order for the invasion of Austria.

During the month which preceded the Anschluss, Goering was already busily engaged in diplomatic manoeuvres about the future of Czechoslovakia. Thus he made a trip to Poland in February to see Beck, the Polish Foreign Minister, to discuss German policy on Czechoslovakia. And on 11 March, on the eve of the invasion of Austria, Goering threw a large party at the new show-piece club of the German Air Force in Berlin— the Haus der Flieger. Amongst the roughly 1,000 guests who went to the party was Dr Mastny, the Czech Minister in Berlin. Goering drew him apart from the guests and whispered in his ear, 'Czechoslovakia has nothing to fear. Indeed the Fuehrer wishes to improve relationships with Prague'.

The fleet of 750 German Air Force planes allocated by Goering for Operation Otto was not required. The most notable air aspect of the operation was the employment of a large force of over 100 transport Junkers 52's, which enabled both the German Air Force and the Army to secure their objectives at high speed, by flying in petrol, ammunition, wireless equipment and guns. As in Spain, air mobility was a cardinal feature of German Air Force operations. On 13 March the Anschluss was completed when Adolf Hitler became President of Austria.

The day after German Air Force squadrons flew in from Germany to occupy the airfields of Austria, Hermann Goering was again talking by telephone, this time to von Ribbentrop from Berlin. Even though the new German Foreign Minister must soon have had access to the truth from official records, Goering exaggerated once again the role and potential of the Luftwaffe in Operation Otto. He told Ribbentrop that he had 'landed hundreds of aircraft to seize the airfield at Vienna'. Its capacity in March 1938 would certainly not allow for such a large-scale operation. He also annoyed the new German Foreign Minister by offering his views on Czechoslovakia. 'In no way are we threatening the Czechoslovak Republic', said Goering to Ribbentrop, and added, 'It has now the opportunity of coming to a friendly and reasonable agreement with us'.

In assessing the extent to which Goering played a leading role in German foreign affairs, it should perhaps be borne in mind that traditionally German generals have had a rather greater say in foreign affairs than, for example, British generals. Even so, Goering's pre-occupation with diplomacy in the year or so which preceded the Second World War was *de trop,* in more senses than one. It was often confusing for the German Foreign Office and it was certainly energy diverted from his main task of German air leadership.

In April 1938 and in the months that followed, Goering had a series of talks at Karinhall with Sir Neville Henderson, the British Ambassador in Berlin. He, like other British politicians and diplomats, was temporarily seduced by Goering's charm and persuasive hospitality. Goering spoke frankly to Henderson and told him that 'Germany would be quite content to have the Sudetenland of Czechoslovakia'. 'The rest of the country', said Goering to Henderson, 'was an appendix to be divided up between Germany, Poland and Hungary'. There was a genial ruthlessness about Goering's approach to the problems of Czechoslovakia.

The new Hitler directive for 'Operation Green'—code name for the German attack on Czechoslovakia—was issued on 20 May 1938. Like other Hitler directives it had vague elements. 'It is not my intention to smash Czechoslovakia in the immediate future without provocation, unless an unavoidable development within Czechoslovakia forces the issue'. It rejected a 'sudden attack without convenient excuse'. Hitler of course would himself define the word provocation and decide what was a convenient excuse.

Hermann Goering played only a minor role in the German Air Force preparations for Operation Green. His senior aide, General Karl Bodenschatz, stood in for him at a number of key Luftwaffe staff meetings. It was Milch, Kesselring and Udet who did most of the executive planning. Among the reasons for Goering's absence from the meetings were his preoccupations with other German domestic problems, such as the treatment of Jews in Germany and the commitments of the Economic Four Year Plan. There was also a decline in his personal health. Once again he had weight and glandular problems. He was also not a little worried by the first pregnancy of his wife, Emmy, then in her forties. But when she bore him a daughter in June 1938, Goering became for the first time a proud and happy father.

Goering was, however, present at the German Chief of Staff meeting convened by Hitler at his Berlin Chancellery on 28 May. He told Goering and the others present that 'preparations for military action against Czechoslovakia were to be made by 2 October'. Goering then seemed unaware of the long-term implications. He followed his leader with blind loyalty along the path which led to the Second World War.

His mind in the period 1938-1939 seems to have contained an untidy array of dubious dichotomies. The Goering who made strenuous, even desperate, efforts to keep the peace in the summer of 1939 was also the Goering who boasted absurdly, both officially and unofficially, about the operational strength of the German Air Force and the security of Germany's air defences. At times he had almost a childish indifference to the bewildering honeycomb of papers, diplomatic, economic, aeronautical and political, which called for some personal attention from him. Outwardly Goering never seemed unduly perturbed by the weight of his many responsibilities. He exuded confidence in his public utterances. But he was also a man who frequently ignored his in-tray.

In a speech made at Linz in May 1938, Goering said to his Austrian listeners, 'We have great plans for Austria. There will be power stations, a new autobahn, armament works, new industries, new social measures. Unemployment will be banned completely'. And he added typically a sting in the tail, 'Now you must work hard'. But in contrast to such public confidence, one is inclined to stress some of the post-war evidence of Emmy

Goering, who declared that in the summer of 1938 her husband said to her that he was 'bewildered by the problems of the job of running the German economy'.

Goering's air planning in the period 1938-1939 showed clearly that he completely miscalculated the nature and scope of the coming war. When Ernst Udet tried to warn him about the great potential of the United States aircraft industry, Goering scoffed and said that the U.S.A. 'could only mass-produce cars and refrigerators'. On 8 July 1938, when Hermann Goering met a group of German aircraft manufacturers at Karinhall for a forward planning conference, he told them frankly that a war with Czechoslovakia was imminent. Then he went on to talk about an extension of the war and said with great confidence, 'The German Air Force is superior to the British Air Force'. He told the aircraft industry leaders present that the victory for Germany in the coming war would be followed by a 'domination of world markets and great riches for Germany'.

Two months later, in a speech at Nuremberg, in September, Goering again put an absurdly bold front on German air power. He said, 'Our Rhineland defences are impregnable'. They were at the time ill-organised and without the vital help of early warning radar or any force of specialist night fighters.

Goering's public pronouncements defy any attempt at serious consecutive analysis. Perhaps in this respect he was no different from other contemporary leaders in Europe. At times his speeches read like extracts from some twentieth century descendant of Falstaff, humorous, roistering but drunk with power rather than alcohol. The clue to his extravert optimism can perhaps be found in the moment at the Nuremberg trials when the prosecution said he was a fabricator and a diddler. Goering laughed heartily as though in assent. He was a conjuror who had too many balls in the air at once. Perhaps he was thinking of his Soviet judges

Even though he was intermittently preoccupied with diplomacy about Czechoslovakia for much of the year 1938, the German Air Force progressed in many ways in that year. It was the first year of large-scale production of nearly all the types of new German planes to be used in the period 1939-1941, machines such as the Messerschmitt 109 single-seater fighter, and the less successful Messerschmitt 110 multi-purpose twin-engined plane, which later had moderate success in the role of night-fighting and as a reconnaissance and strike aircraft, but which failed in daylight as a long-range escort plane. Then there were the two Junkers bombers. The Junkers 87 dive bomber had notorious success in the air campaigns in Poland, Norway, Holland, Belgium and France, but notorious failure in the climax of the Battle of Britain. The Junkers 88 twin-engined plane had more persistent operational success as a high-level bomber, a torpedo-bomber, a reconnaissance machine and finally as a night-fighter.

But against the achievement of modernising the German Air Force in the period 1938-1939 must be set a series of policy failures for which Goering must personally bear a large portion of the blame. These mistakes were in some instances so crucial that Goering might well merit the tag of the leader who lost the air war in Europe before it began.

In the period of the Munich crisis, when the prospect of war became imminent, Goering told the heads of the French and Italian Air Forces, General Guillemin and Marshal Balbo, when they visited him at Karinhall at the end of August, 'I have plans for an air force with an operational strength of 18,000 planes'. No doubt the Luftwaffe Commander-in-Chief made this statement with a view to bluffing and impressing both his prospective Italian ally and his likely French enemy. It was a piece of hyperbole which was nevertheless realistic. In the summer of 1941, when the German Air Force was fighting on three fronts, it needed a combat strength of some 18,000 planes to meet all its operational commitments. But because Goering had never planned in serious detail for the long-term future, its actual combat strength was less than a third of this total required figure, when the invasion of the U.S.S.R. was launched on 22 June 1941.

At the end of September 1938, when the Munich agreement was formulated, the operational strength of the German Air Force was just over 3,300 planes, of which the most impressive elements were the bomber, transport and reconnaissance squadrons. The fighter units totalled less than 850 planes, while the bomber and dive-bomber units had a combined strength of about 1,500. Since some fighters would have to be kept back for the air defence of Germany, it was clear that Goering must have believed that his bombers would get through to their target with only moderate fighter escort. Part of this operational

optimism derived from the combat experience in the Spanish
Civil War when the German Air Force units met no large-scale
modern organised fighter opposition. At this stage he had no
serious thought in his air planning for such operations as the
Battle of Britain or the protracted air defence of Germany
against Anglo-American attack, in which very large numbers
of fighters were indispensable to German success in the air.

Goering also had no place in his pre-war planning for the
long-range four-engined bomber and he has been frequently
criticised as an air leader on this account. The German aircraft
industry produced three long-range four-engined prototype
bombers, a Junkers, a Dornier and a Focke-Wulf. Only the
latter went into small-scale production in the military version
towards the end of 1939. When Goering commented to his
senior colleagues on this long-range bomber issue he said, 'The
Fuehrer does not want to know the number of engines our
bombers have but merely how many bombers we have in
squadrons'.

There was a measure of commonsense in Goering's point of
view. To have gone in for four-engined bombers in the period
1938-1939 would have reduced the output of German aircraft
in the bomber category. Even though Goering and his advisors
decided on single and twin-engined bombers, the expansion of
German aircraft output was inadequate. Total production in
1939 was only 8,295 planes, i.e. only 300 more than British
aircraft production in that year. And in 1940 German aircraft
output increased by less than a third to 10,286 planes while
British aircraft output had doubled to over 15,000 planes.

Did Goering realise at the time of Munich that he might
have a long war on his hands? There are good grounds for
believing that he held this view at least at one stage. Thus, at
a meeting of the German Chiefs of Staff in Berlin on 28 September 1938, he said to his colleagues, 'A great war can hardly be
avoided. It may last seven years but we shall win it'.

Did Goering think the German Air Force would be ready to
fight a war in Europe which might begin in 1939? The balance
of evidence shows a mixture of confidence and groping uncertainty. Milch and Udet, the two German air chiefs, urged on
Goering the wisdom of keeping the peace until 1942, when
large-scale expansion would have been achieved. And Goering

himself when he met Mussolini in Rome in April 1939 told the
Duce that he hoped to 'postpone the war until 1942 when the
combined forces of Germany and Italy would be so strong that
they would be invincible'. But apart from some desperate last-
minute moves mainly made in August 1939, Hermann Goering
followed his leader in provoking the war in Europe, knowing
that his Air Force was mainly prepared to fight relatively short
and short-ranged wars on a single front. He prepared optimistically for the best and quickest result. Reality, caution, due
allowance for unforeseen contingencies had little or no place in
most of his air leadership.

During the growing crisis in Europe in the autumn of 1938,
Goering again suffered from bad health. After a visit to Karinhall
on 17 September, the British Ambassador in Berlin reported to
London on Goering's indisposition, adding that he was 'restrained
in his language'. Now surely was the time for Goering to
concentrate on his functions as air leader and to cut his political
and diplomatic commitments; but he had too much power and
too little self-discipline to draw back. And so at the Nazi Party
Rally at Nuremberg in September 1938 he provoked a war
atmosphere by thundering at the Czechs, calling them 'a petty
segment of Europe' and 'a miserable pygmy race'. The British
Ambassador in Prague reported to London, 'Goering has been
making no secret of his intention to liquidate Czechoslovakia'.
A few days before Goering had told the British Ambassador in
Berlin, 'If the Czech Government does not accept the Fuehrer's
terms, mobilisation of German armed forces and an attack on
Czechoslovakia will follow'.

All this in the month of September 1938, when incidentally
the U.S.S.R. still had a pact of mutual assistance with the
Czechs. It was a month in which the situation called for
complete concentration by Hermann Goering on the high
priority task of building up German air power for the war
which, according to all accounts, he now realised was virtually
inevitable.

But there was a demon in Goering's mind which prevented
him from concentrating on the main matter in hand. What, for
example, was he doing in September 1938 in the odd role of
translator working on the Italian and French texts of the Munich
agreement with the Italian Ambassador in Berlin, Bernardo

Attalico, or arranging meetings on foreign affairs between Hitler and the British and French Ambassadors in Berlin? And a month or so later, on 12 November 1938, Goering found himself chairing a large meeting at the Air Ministry, not on aviation matters but on anti-Jewish measures which amounted to a pogrom.

The year 1939 began badly for Goering. In January and February he again suffered from ill-health, this time an inflammation of the jaw, and the familiar weight problems plagued him. The abscess in his jaw needed three weeks' treatment. He ran high temperatures and again had glandular trouble. By 18 February, Goering could receive the British Ambassador at Karinhall. He told Sir Neville Henderson that 'he was extremely tired, had taken off forty pounds in weight and would like to have taken off sixty'.

At the end of February, Goering and his wife went to San Remo for a much-needed holiday. He had wanted to go to Spain to meet General Franco, but Ribbentrop intervened and with the Fuehrer's backing cancelled the visit. Before Goering could react, the Fuehrer ordered him back to Berlin where he was again plunged into the diplomacy of the final dismemberment of Czechoslovakia.

Emil Hacha, an elderly judge, had succeeded Benés as head of the Czech state in October 1938. On 10 March 1939 he had dissolved, perhaps somewhat rashly, the troublesome autonomous governments of Slovakia and Ruthenia and proclaimed martial law. When Hacha was called to the Berlin Chancellery on 12 March, Hermann Goering was given the job of bullying him into signing away Czech independence.

At the Nuremberg Trials, Hermann Goering admitted that on this occasion he threatened to bomb Prague in order to speed up the matter. Hacha, who had a weak heart, collapsed on hearing this threat. Dr Morell, Hitler's physician, was called in to revive the Czech leader and borrowed a hypodermic needle from Goering to make the required injection.

On 15 March 1939, Hacha signed the required document and German troops invaded Czechoslovakia. As in the case of the Austrian Anschluss, a year previously, Hermann Goering left the air planning for 'Operation Green' in the hands of Udet, Milch, Kesselring and Bodenschatz. When Hitler went to

Prague to survey his new conquest, Hermann Goering did not go with him. Goering's current concern was to acquire the gold reserves of the Czechoslovak National Bank and to placate the Polish Ambassador in Berlin on the subject of German policies about Poland. But he also made plans with Udet to incorporate the Czech Air Force planes into the Luftwaffe pool of trainer aircraft and to set up facilities to make Messerschmitts in factories near Prague. Goering also commented to Udet at this time that the Slovakian airfields would be 'useful for operations in the East'. It looks as though he saw the possibility of a war with Russia even in the spring of 1939.

By the end of March 1939, the relations between Poland and Germany on the subject of Danzig and the Polish Corridor were so strained that Britain and France gave Poland public assurances of their support in the event of a threat to Polish independence. Hitler's reaction was to issue a top secret order on 3 April for 'Operation White', the invasion of Poland. One would have thought that Hermann Goering would now at least concentrate on preparing the German Air Force as best he could for the coming war. But on 14 April he was in Rome dabbling again in foreign affairs. With Count Ciano and Mussolini he discussed the implications of the Italian invasion of Albania on 7 April, the French and British guarantees to Greece and Rumania made on 3 April, and the future of German and Italian policies towards the U.S.S.R.

He was back home at Karinhall by the end of April, but early in May his health again took a turn for the worse and he returned to San Remo to convalesce. At this juncture it may be worth recalling the post-war evidence of Albert Speer, who knew Goering personally throughout the 1935-1945 decade: 'Until 1939, Goering was in good mental shape and showed a great deal of energy. After 1939 his energies slumped'. One wonders to what extent Goering was intermittently the sick man of European air warfare. Outwardly he remained ebullient and energetic. But he certainly found the growing number of air problems too much for him at times and his public behaviour and the irrational elements in many of his air decisions and orders suggest that Albert Speer's view has substance. Goering was certainly lacking in balance, realism, judgement and a sense of proportion as an air leader at the outbreak of the Second

World War. His mind was perceptive and vigorous but usually only in short bursts. In the longer haul of serious strategy and planning, there was often an illogical hiatus in his decisions and viewpoint which boded ill for German Air Force prospects.

In the summer of 1939, the German Air Force was far from ready to face a major war in Europe, though in some respects it was superior to any other Air Force in the world. In the previous year it had expanded, particularly in transport and reconnaissance units. On the day of the invasion of Poland, 1 September 1939, it had an operational strength of some 4,250 planes. Perhaps the most significant aspect of its composition was the fact that it was a shop-window air force lacking reserves. Even though it had had no major operational commitments since its official inception in March 1935, a number of bomber and fighter units were still below the statutory establishment strength of 39 planes per Gruppe. In the period September 1938 to September 1939, the overall rise in operational strength was about twenty five per cent. The main increases in this period were in Junkers 52 transport planes, dive bombers and short-range reconnaissance planes. Thus it was clear that, in September 1939, Hermann Goering saw the coming air war mainly in terms of the use of airborne forces, in air lift and tactical ground support on behalf of the German army. His failure to expand the Me 109 fighter units to any great extent suggest, first, that he had an illusory view of the future requirements of the air defence of Germany and, secondly, that he had no idea of the kind of fighter opposition he would encounter in the Battle of Britain.

Goering's concept of the role of naval air power in September 1939 exemplified some of the features of his erratic air leadership in the Second World War. His relations with senior members of the German Navy were not happy. He was slow to realise that, in the coming war, his force of floatplanes and flying boats would have to be replaced by land-based Junkers, Heinkel and Focke-Wulf planes for bomber, reconnaissance, mine-laying and torpedo attack operations. Goering's failure to see that a satisfactory aerial torpedo was developed by the outbreak of war meant that he had to draw on Italian resources for this air weapon. The torpedo came from a factory near Fiume and the training facilities from an Italian Air Force base

VII. Emmy Goering

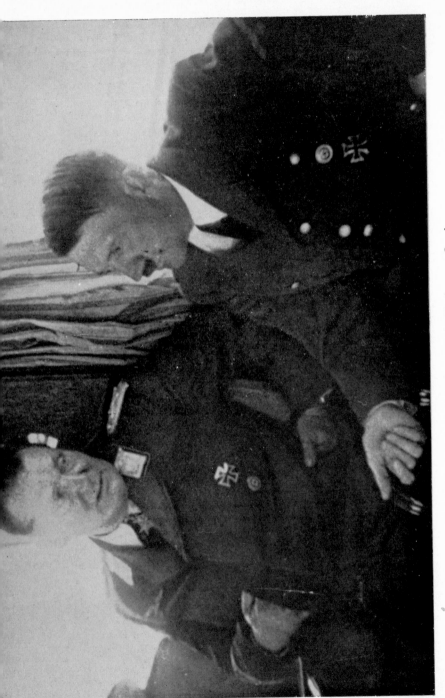

VIII. Hitler and Goering in a Train Conference, October 1939

near Grosseto. On the other hand, the anti-shipping operational training of German Air Force bomber units in 1938-39 was systematic and thorough. It bore fruit in the operations from Denmark and Norway in the spring of 1940.

It is strange that a man who had been the commander of the Richthofen fighter aircraft squadrons in the First World War failed to follow fully a major evolution of fighter aircraft needs in preparation for the Second World War. Goering certainly was slow to appreciate the vital role of early warning radar and this became a crucial failing in the Battle of Britain. In the middle 1930's, German scientists and technicians had developed early warning radar. But Goering was unaware of its key importance until he saw a full demonstration with Hitler in June 1939 at Rechlin, where there was a major Luftwaffe technical development centre. In July 1939, he signed an order for 800 Wurzburgs and 200 Freyas and some of the equipment came into successful use in the first months of the war, when British Wellington bombers were intercepted by Messerschmitt fighters. But Goering left the study of the strategic implications and tactical use of radar to his signals chief, General Martini, who was unfortunate in his early efforts to monitor and assess the growth of the British early warning radar system.

Like most Commanders-in-Chief, Hermann Goering had mixed fortunes in the choice of his senior aides. Had he allowed more scope for the tough brilliance of Erhard Milch, his Secretary of State for Air, the aircraft production expansion programme of 1938-1939 might have been more successful. Instead, Goering stripped Milch of some of his power and transferred it to Ernst Udet, who became Director General of Equipment in 1939. Udet had been a first-class pilot and was the life and soul of any party; but he was no organiser of an aircraft industry and loathed office work and meetings. He allowed too many modifications in 1939 to combat aircraft and too many gifted technicians to be transferred to the armed forces. Under the aegis of Albert Speer's energetic direction, the German aircraft industry produced about five times as many planes in 1944 as it did in 1939, despite the Anglo-American bombing. For the production limitations of the 1938-1939 period Goering had a major responsibility, because he chose Udet to steer German aircraft production.

E

Hermann Goering presided over a Reich Defence Council meeting in Berlin on 23 June 1939 when the final plans for the conquest of Poland and the total mobilisation of German manpower were fully discussed. He was already aware that some new treaty between the U.S.S.R. and Germany was in the air for, in the first week of May, he had sent Karl Bodenschatz to talk on this theme to the French and British Ambassadors in Berlin.

The die was now fully and truly cast. Goering knew that his Fuehrer was determined to execute Operation White, the attack on Poland. He was present at a German Chiefs-of-Staff meeting on 14 August when Hitler announced that 'Poland must be defeated in a week'. As so often, Goering played two roles simultaneously. First the resolute war leader determined to follow his leader loyally. Then the desperate diplomat seeking to keep the peace.

Thus in July and August he toured the Rhineland and inspected the air defences and boasted stupidly that they were impregnable. 'If an enemy bomber reaches German soil, my name is not Hermann Goering. You can call me Meier', he declared. This assertion made the headlines and was to stick in Goering's throat and in the minds of Luftwaffe pilots and of the German public.

Why did Goering boast so openly when he knew the air defences of Germany were weak? He certainly had too much faith in the protective powers of his anti-aircraft batteries and was both ignorant and contemptuous of the potential of prospective enemy air forces. His intelligence chief, Major Josef Schmid, was a bad choice. Goering accepted Schmid's view of April 1939 that the 'English and French air fleets were out of date and that British air defence was weak'.

Even after the pact of alliance between Germany and the U.S.S.R was signed on 21 August, Hermann Goering turned desperately to a wealthy Swedish friend, Birger Dahlerus, through whom he contacted British Government circles and British businessmen in a last-minute attempt to keep the peace, by arranging a four-power conference between Britain, France, Germany and Italy.

But shortly after midnight on 31 August, Hitler issued his final order for the invasion of Poland at dawn on 1 September.

On that day Hermann Goering attended the Reichstag Assembly at Kroll Opera House in Berlin and heard Hitler announce officially that the German Air Force Commander-in-Chief was his rightful successor, and therefore Deputy Fuehrer. The appointment encouraged Goering to be even more high-handed in defence matters outside the orbit of German air affairs.

At the outbreak of the Second World War Hermann Goering had too many different tasks in hand and too many balls in the air to keep his roving mind on the current *Schwerpunkt* of German aviation. His many duties frittered away the sharpness of his mind. His air leadership which needed to be sharper in war became diffuse and blunt. He was a confused practitioner of a military art which so far had offered few major precedents to guide him. Coming air events were to show that he was often misguided.

CHAPTER FOUR

Blitzkrieg Successes

THE FAMILIAR dictum of Lord Acton, that all power tends to corrupt and that absolute power tends to corrupt absolutely, fits some aspects of the air leadership of Hermann Goering. When the Second World War broke out, on 1 September 1939, he had certainly acquired a wide range of powers, some of them virtually absolute. He was Hitler's official deputy, both Air Minister and Commander-in-Chief of the German Air Force, Head of the Four Year Plan for Economics, President of the Prussian Council and of the Reichstag and he was also responsible for hunting policy in the Third Reich (*Reichsjaegermeister*). After the war I asked a number of ex-German Air Force officers to sum up their view of Goering in a sentence or two. One of them gave the snapshot reply: 'He was like your Henry VIII, but Henry had the wives and Hermann had the jobs'.

Hermann Goering was not only powerful but also very rich. His various incomes amounted to over a million marks a year and there were additional generous expenses for each of his jobs. Further money flowed into his account from the thousands of shares he held in German aircraft companies, from the books of his collected speeches, from his newspapers, and from the Hermann Goering factories making steel and other products. His great private estate, Karinhall, was continually being expanded and embellished.

The heavy strain of Goering's multifarious career interests, particularly those dealing with Germany's manpower and raw material problems, undoubtedly diluted and so corrupted his powers of air leadership. Goering also suffered recurrently from bouts of nerves and exhaustion and relied fairly heavily on drugs to recover from them. He still had grave weight problems, tipping the scales at about twenty stone. He loved fattening foods and good wines. Among those he enjoyed were the Steinberger Riesling, Mouton Rothschild claret and the Chambertin burgundies.

The main criteria by which Goering's air leadership can be judged are the ability to organise and maintain a comprehensive flying training system, his awareness of current and future aircraft and weapon developments, of current and future air tactics and strategy, his ability to judge the size and nature of the aircraft industry required for current and future German needs, and, one might add, the knack of choosing good senior air commanders. One of his greatest failings was the inability to create an intelligence organisation capable of being both knowledgeable and objective about enemy and potential enemy air forces. A good Commander-in-Chief should also have the flair to judge the right occasion to intervene personally, either on general policy matters or in the ebb and flow of day-to-day battles. Goering's interventions were sometimes followed by failure and disaster, for example at Dunkirk and in the Battle of Britain.

In drawing up the balance sheet of Goering's air leadership, it is difficult to gauge the extent to which Hitler's over-ambitious war strategies should be brought into account. Goering had a tough, independent, courageous mind of his own; but he seemed to have shown at times a sycophant's loyalty to Hitler's war plans and directives. He was not as myopic and unrealistic as the Fuehrer became, particularly from the end of 1941; but he followed his leader's war strategy with an energetic patriotism which was highly uncritical. That the German Air Force was so often asked to do too much with too little, in the period 1941-1945, can often be attributed to Hermann Goering's inability or unwillingness to foresee the consequences of Hitler's strategy or to protest at its absurdities.

To begin with all was well. The Polish air campaign began on 1 September 1939. On this day Goering issued a kind of trumpet call to his air squadrons, telling them they were 'born of the spirit of German airmen of the First World War'. He went on: 'Inspired by our faith in our Fuehrer, the German Air Force today stands ready to carry out every command of the Fuehrer'. In Poland this was possible. The campaign quickly produced the kind of tactical blitzkrieg air success for which

Goering and his senior air colleagues had been planning since 1935.

Goering allocated two of his four air fleets for Operation White, as the German attack on Poland had been code-named. One was commanded by General Kesselring, previously Chief-of-Staff of the German Air Force, and a man with a mind of his own. The other Air Fleet Commander was General Loehr, a relatively meek Austrian. The two Air Fleets had a combined strength of about 1,750 planes. This figure was reduced to about 1,400 in mid-September, when Goering decided to withdraw some of his fighter and bomber squadrons to rest and refit for 'Operation Yellow', the German code-name for the planned attack on France and the Low Countries. In September 1939 Adolf Hitler was again forcing the pace. He wanted Operation Yellow to be launched 'on 12 November at the latest'. But the German Army Chiefs-of-Staff persuaded Hitler that his armoured and infantry divisions were not yet ready. Goering, the vain and pompous, remarked triumphantly, 'the Luftwaffe is always ready'. He chose to ignore the problems of intensive air operations under adverse weather conditions. Euphoria was always at his elbow, and the quick successes of the first fortnight of the Polish campaign had no doubt heightened his pathological optimism, which chose to disregard the details of many air problems.

During the first fortnight of the Second World War, Hermann Goering divided his working time between his headquarters operations train, code-named ASIA, then located east of Berlin, his home and air headquarters at Karinhall, Hitler's Chancellery and the German Air Ministry, both in Berlin.

The air operations in Poland were going according to plan, but the entry of France and Britain into the war on 3 September seemed to take Goering temporarily out of his stride. On that day he was at Karinhall listening to the news on the radio. When he heard the announcement of the French and British declarations, he turned to his wife, Emmy, and said: 'If we lose this war, God help us!' Goering made similar remarks to senior colleagues in the next day or so. But his public mood soon changed to one of defiance, and in a broadcast to the German nation on 9 September from a munitions factory, he threatened terrible retaliation if British or French planes tried to bomb

Germany. At the same time he added soberly: 'I think it will be a long war'. His moods did not last long.

In Poland the Wehrmacht continued to prosper. Cracow had fallen on 7 September, and by 21 September Warsaw was encircled. So far Goering had not intervened in the day-to-day detail of the German air operations. He had ordered the two air fleets engaged 'to concentrate on airfields and road junctions' and 'to give maximum support to the armoured forces'. His orders continued to be of a broad general nature.

But on 21 September, Goering flew from Berlin to Kesselring's headquarters in East Prussia to confer with him on the problem of bombing Warsaw. The targets agreed upon were the railway junctions and airfields close to the Polish capital. Inevitably the German air attacks killed and injured civilians, as they had done in the Spanish Civil War during the attacks on Barcelona and other cities. For these and later attacks, Hermann Goering has been labelled a bomber of civilians. But bombing in general is so often an inaccurate form of military assault. Looking at the record of U.S., British, Japanese and Soviet bomber attacks in the Second World War makes one feel that any indictment of Goering because of Guernica, Warsaw, Rotterdam or London needs to be shared by other air leaders who attacked other towns and cities.

Warsaw fell on 27 September 1939, but it was another week before Adolf Hitler formally announced the end of the Polish campaign. Operation White had not been a serious test of Goering's operational air leadership. Polish air opposition was brave and determined, but the Poles lacked modern planes and equipment, for example radar. However, Goering must take some credit for this first demonstration in the Second World War of German Air Force effectiveness and mobility. In September 1939, the Luftwaffe had the largest air transport lift of any air force in the world. Goering and his air leaders had also demonstrated that the German technique of giving air support to armoured forces was, at the time, the best in the world.

In the first week of October, Goering was still dabbling in what he thought might become fruitful negotiations for peace with France and Britain. Dahlerus, Goering's Swedish friend, returned from London on 1 October. He told Goering, who was at Karinhall, that Britain and France would negotiate only with Hitler's successor. The next day, Admiral Canaris, head of one of the main branches of the German Secret Service, joined Goering and Dahlerus at Karinhall to discuss the dim prospects of peace. But there was nothing practical to be done. When Goering attended the next meeting of the Reichstag assembly in Berlin on 6 October, he heard Hitler make yet another speech offering peace to France and Britain. He applauded his Fuehrer like the others. The next day, he came again to Berlin from his Karinhall estate. This time it was to sign a decree which gave the Third Reich the power to Germanise Poland and take over the property and persons of Polish Jews. 'We must get a million Poles to work in Germany', said Goering at the time.

Before he could implement the new and ruthless Polish decree, he had to leave Berlin, on 8 October, for his sick-bed at Karinhall. There he was tended by his wife, Emmy, and his nurse, Christa Gormanns, who did her best to limit the tonics, pills, medicines and morphia injections to which Goering was still prone.

Perhaps this was the moment when Goering should have dropped his responsibility for the German Four Year Economic Plan, stopped dabbling in diplomacy, which was really Ribbentrop's affair, and concentrated on the many new German aeronautical problems which called for detailed long-term planning and carefully-reached decisions.

It is true that the basic flying training scheme of the German Air Force was adequate and efficient. In the period 1939-1940, the annual capacity of the air training schools to turn out fighter, bomber, transport and reconnaissance pilots increased from about 10,000 to about 15,000. But some forms of specialist training were being neglected. Because Goering believed too much in the air defence capability of his anti-aircraft batteries, he neglected to develop the night-fighter arm in the period 1939-1940. He realised his mistake later, when the weight of Royal Air Force Bomber Command attacks increased. Then Goering held one or two desperate conferences at the Air Ministry in Berlin and issued a personal plea to the Air Fleet Commanders for 'volunteers from reconnaissance and bomber units to transfer to the growing night-fighter formations'.

Goering was also slow to organise the training of torpedo-bomber units, though he was pressed to do so more than once by Admiral Raeder, Commander-in-Chief of the German Navy. While it is true that Junkers 88 torpedo-bombers had successes in 1942 and thereafter, for example against the Anglo-American P.Q. convoys sailing to Murmansk, this was due in part to training facilities and torpedoes provided by Italy. In the autumn of 1939 the German Air Force had no land-based torpedo-bomber units.

Goering was also slow to recognise the importance of creating reserve operational training units. These enabled pilots under training not only to fly the same planes used in front-line operations, but also to learn something about the particular battle tactics and experience of individual front-line units. This training scheme was barely under way at the time of the Battle of Britain, when it could have been valuable because of the heavy German air losses. Hermann Goering was, however, still living in a world of the autumn of 1939, when heavy German Air Force losses were simply not part of his planning schedule. At this stage he did not prepare long-term safeguards.

Perhaps the most serious charge which might be made against Goering is that, although he foresaw the possibility of a long war, he did nothing fundamental about it until the end of 1941 when it was virtually too late. Those in British air intelligence who were jointly responsible for assessing Goering's air plans and intentions in 1939-1940 had great difficulty in persuading their seniors that Goering had no great plans for expansion, that his Air Force was lacking in reserves and depth and that Goering only looked at the air future in a vague, uncharted way. But so it proved to be.

Goering and his aircraft production chief, Ernst Udet, were slow to realise that the Luftwaffe's squadrons of certain types of planes would become quickly obsolescent as well as vulnerable in combat. For example they did not foresee that, by 1940, their force of about 150 float-planes and flying-boats was already obsolescent in the roles of reconnaissance, mine-laying and torpedo-dropping. Much more serious was the German failure to foresee the obsolescence of the short-range tactical reconnaissance plane, the Henschel 126. It had done well in Poland, acting as the eyes of the German armoured divisions, and it was to repeat its reconnaissance successes in the May-June 1940 campaign against France and the Low Countries. But when the German Air Force came up against strong fighter defences in the Battle of Britain and later, the Henschel 126, slow and ill-armed, could not be used with safety.

It was not until early in 1942 that Goering and his air staff realised that special versions of Messerschmitt fighters would be needed in areas heavily defended by enemy fighters, if photo-reconnaissance planes were to bring back the pictures required. Then, but only then, did the reconnaissance version of the Messerschmitt become part of the 'Goering Programme' for future aircraft production.

In the first week of September 1939, Hermann Goering had told the German Chiefs-of-Staff the war might last seven years. But his aeronautical plans of the period 1938-40 rarely looked forward more than a few months. There was no contingency planning for a war between Germany and the Soviet Union, even though this had become a near possibility by the end of July 1940. Perhaps this was why Ernst Udet, Goering's aircraft production chief, committed suicide on 17 November 1941. He knew by then that he had failed to do his job and probably thought that the air defeat of Germany was inevitable.

But it was Goering himself who was the main source of false optimism about the future of the German Air Force. In particular he raised false hopes about the future of the Messer-schmitt 110 long-range escort fighter which he called 'the strategic fighter élite of the Luftwaffe'. In the Battle of Britain it was a major failure and was diverted thereafter mainly to the role of night-fighting in the air defence of Germany.

Goering certainly made mistakes, in the crucial 1938-1940 period, in assessing the fighting value of German aircraft. Other Air Force Commanders did the same : the British Battle bomber was to show death-trap vulnerability against Messerschmitt fighters in the air combats over France and the Low Countries in May 1940, and the Defiant fighter had to be quickly phased out of the main stream of daylight combats in the Battle of Britain. But no other leader had such enormously misplaced confidence about the efficacy of his air defences.

One aspect of air power, with which Goering had only a nodding acquaintance at this stage, was the defensive potential of well-organised day fighters, supported by both radar early warning and by sector controls advising fighters by radio about enemy attack patterns. This basic system of fighter defence helped to win the Battle of Britain.

It would be easy to blame Goering for failing to grasp the growing defence capability of Royal Air Force Fighter Command. At least two German Air Force officers were in duty bound to spell out to the Luftwaffe Commander-in-Chief the details and the importance of what was going on in Britain's air defences. These were Beppo Schmid, the head of German Air Force intelligence, and General Wolfgang Martini, Head of Signals in the German Air Force. As some of the evidence required could best be obtained by monitoring Royal Air Force radar signals and radio telephone voice traffic, it was clearly a job for Martini and his staff. He did make attempts to monitor R.A.F. radar and warned Goering about its growth, but he seems to have missed the importance of assessing the flexibility of Royal Air Force Fighter Command from the radio telephone conversations which were there to be monitored before the outbreak of war.

Nevertheless, if Goering and Martini missed out on this aspect of electronics, they were in 1939-1940 ahead of the rest of the world in other aspects, for example navigational aids to bombing at night or in bad weather. From 1935, the first year of the Luftwaffe's official existence, General Martini, with the backing of Goering, began to develop beam systems for blind bombing. They were used for the first time against British targets in June 1940 and in the blitz on Britain in the winter of 1940-1941. In addition, Goering lent an attentive ear and gave paternal blessing to a wide range of new technical projects, for example the fuel injection pump used instead of a carburettor and the 20mm aircraft cannon. These were but some of his pre-war preoccupations with the technical aspects of air power.

When Goering chose Hans Jeschonnek to be his Chief-of-Staff at the time of the Munich crisis, he made a cardinal error, though Jeschonnek was a handsome, intelligent and devoted staff officer. He needed men about him who were critical, even aggressively critical, like Erhard Milch, his Secretary of State for Air, or like Albert Kesselring who had preceded Jeschonnek as Chief of Air Staff. Part of Jeschonnek's job was to balance the euphoric, ebullient vanity of Goering about German air potential with some more realistic account of what needed to be done. From the summer of 1940 onwards Jeschonnek realised the growing air problems of the future and they assailed his young mind. His sense of failure grew and grew. He committed suicide in August 1943.

November 1939 was not a happy month for Goering. During the first week he was again unwell and confined to his estate at Karinhall. When he recovered he went to Berlin to attend a tedious series of Chiefs-of-Staff meetings on the much postponed 'Operation Yellow', the planned attack on France and the Low Countries, and on German Air Force co-operation with the German Navy. They were partly tedious for Goering because he tended to utter hasty interservice indiscretions which he probably regretted shortly afterwards. Thus at the Chiefs-of-Staff meeting of 20 November Goering spoke in offhand fashion about 'the low morale of the army compared with the high morale of the Luftwaffe'. This was when the German Army again asked for more time to train infantry and armoured divisions for Operation Yellow. At other meetings, Goering's relationship with Admiral Erich Raeder, head of the German Navy, verged on open hostility. Raeder had for some time fought a losing battle with Goering, at Chiefs-of-Staff level, on three main subjects: first, a higher priority for building German submarines, then more air protection for the German fleet, and finally a bigger say for the German Navy in the anti-shipping operations of the German Air Force.

Hermann Goering was governed in his anti-shipping attacks by two directives on the subject issued by Adolf Hitler. The first was dated 31 August 1939, that is the eve of the outbreak of the war. It was wordy and suggested a much greater scale of air attack than Goering was able to supply. It stated: 'In conducting the war against England, preparations are to be made for the use of the Luftwaffe in disrupting British supplies at sea, the armaments industry and the transport of troops to France. A favourable opportunity is to be taken for an effective attack on massed British naval units, especially against battleships or aircraft carriers'. But Hitler's vision had dwindled into caution within a few days, when France and Britain were both in the war against Germany. In his Directive No. 2 of 3 September he said: 'The German Air Force is not to attack even

British naval forces unless the British open similar attacks on German targets'.

Goering's anti-shipping air policy of the first few months of the war reflected his Fuehrer's caution. He did however base about 100 twin-engined bombers on the Island of Sylt with a view to launching a series of attacks on the British Home Fleet which, under the threat of the Luftwaffe attacks, withdrew from Rosyth and Scapa Flow to the west coast of Scotland. Because of bad weather and cautious leadership, the German Air Force scale of attack was limited to twenty sorties or less per day. Their successes were few and Goering began to get worried. At a meeting held at the German Air Ministry in Berlin on 10 October he said expansively. 'We have got to have success. Everyone who helps to destroy enemy ships will have all the medals he wants and a house of his own'. But it was not so easy to discover if enemy ships had been destroyed. At this early stage of the Second World War, Goering came up against the very difficult problem of correctly assessing enemy casualties and damage sustained in battle. It is a problem which has plagued all air forces since the inception of military air power. It was brought to Goering's attention in October 1939 by the repeated claim of the German Ministry of Propaganda that German Air Force Heinkel bombers, based on Sylt, had sunk the British aircraft carrier *Ark Royal*. The Commander of the Heinkel units concerned was so indignant at the absurdity of the claim that he sent Goering a copy of a notice he had put up and circulated to all air crew members in his units. It ran: 'Any member of my squadrons who claims to have sunk or damaged an enemy ship will be court martialled'. Goering roared with laughter when he read the words. He would have done better to emulate the British who put some tough lawyers on to the damage and casualties question, but he did not. In the coming Battle of Britain, Goering's ignorance of the damage and casualties which his air force was inflicting proved to be a genuine Achilles heel. His indifference to this serious problem resulted in deep incomprehension and confusion.

Perhaps Hermann Goering preferred not to know, so that he could utter with greater confidence. This was how it seemed at a Soviet Embassy reception held in Berlin on 7 November, when the Luftwaffe Commander-in-Chief, recovered from his recent

indisposition, spoke confidently about the anti-shipping operations of his air squadrons. Admiral Raeder was there but he did
not speak to the assembled journalists. One of them chose to
ask Goering why the German Air Force was not bombing ports
as well as ships. Surprisingly Goering replied : 'We are humane.
Do not laugh, I am serious. I am humane'. Hermann Goering
was certainly capable of humane acts; but his record as per-
secutor of the Jews, Prussian police terrorist and head of Hitler's
storm-troopers disqualified him from ever assuming a humane
pose with any conviction.

Goering had a split personality without being schizophrenic.
When dealing with German pilots he was often benign and
paternal, as he was to individual Jews and to some British pilots,
for example Douglas Bader, the legless R.A.F. fighter pilot, shot
down over the Pas-de-Calais in the summer of 1941. But Goering
was also the man who stripped Poland of its machinery,
raw materials and workers, Jews and Gentiles alike. It was
he who helped to set up the first concentration camps in
Germany.

On 8 November, Goering was again unwell and so could not
be present at the anniversary ceremony of the Nazis' putsch,
held in Munich. When on that day Adolf Hitler spoke to the
German people on the radio, he said : 'I asked Goering to
prepare for a five-year conflict on the day Britain and France
entered the war'.

Goering was fatally slow to adjust his air thinking to such a
long-term proposition. He was a sprinter in terms of air leadership, not a long-distance runner. The quick, victorious dash of
a few days or, at most, of a few weeks was his favoured approach.
Long-term study and planning only found favour with him at
the end of 1941 when he had suffered air defeat and encountered
new problems created by inadequate air power. 'Too little and
too late' is a criticism which has been made of British planning;
but the tag fits the air planning of Hermann Goering in the
first two years of the Second World War.

However, the German Air Force Commander-in-Chief did
ask his intelligence staff to produce studies on air warfare against
Britain. Beppo Schmid produced on 22 November a paper
called 'A proposal for the conduct of air warfare against
Britain'. It was a plan to strangle Britain by cutting supply

lines, sinking warships and merchantmen and attacking British
ports. Goering also commissioned a study on a landing in
England following the defeat of France. The study was circulated to senior Luftwaffe officers in mid-December 1939.
Goering took it home to Karinhall to read and commented on
his copy: 'The planned operation can only be considered under
conditions of absolute air superiority. A combined operation with
a landing in England as its object must be rejected'.

And so, for Goering in December 1939, as in July 1940, the
essential condition for an invasion of England was the destruction
of the Royal Air Force. But at no time and nowhere can one
find a record of how many squadrons of bombers and fighters
the German Air Force estimated they might need to obtain air
mastery over or destroy the Royal Air Force. While Royal Air
Force Fighter Command fought to get a precise number of
squadrons—at least 45—for the air defence of Great Britain,
Goering seemed strangely indifferent to the elementary mathematics of air power and incapable of detailed forward planning.
Only when he had to face the problems of a three-front air war
in 1941 did he pay detailed attention to forward planning of,
for example, the expansion in the aircraft industry and the air
defence of Germany.

His main worry about the future, in December 1939, was
Germany's relationship with U.S.S.R. The Soviet Union had
just invaded Finland and had occupied Estonia, Latvia and
Lithuania. How far did Stalin intend to go in Western Europe?
How long would it be before the Fuehrer would want to
implement his *Mein Kampf* anti-Soviet strategy? Goering
expressed his forebodings about German-Soviet relations to his
wife Emmy but not yet, as far as one knows, to his senior Air
Force colleagues.

In the first week of January 1940 an incident occurred which
led to the dismissal of one of Goering's ablest Air Fleet commanders, General Helmut Felmy, and in effect postponed
Operation Yellow, the attack on France and the Low Countries.
One of Felmy's officers was flying to an Air Force meeting in
bad weather. His aircraft, which had on board the plan and
maps for Operation Yellow, had to force-land in Belgium. The
plans fell into Belgian hands. Hitler, Goering and Keitel conferred in the Fuehrer's Chancellery in Berlin on 13 January and

decided to postpone Operation Yellow to the spring. A week later Goering attended the Chancellery and suffered the indignity of a lecture on security from Hitler.

The dismissal of General Felmy was a typical example of Goering's illogical haste, and his compulsive need to do something definite, even if it was not justified. Felmy was in fact recalled to active air staff duties in the spring of 1941. He had previously incurred Goering's displeasure at the time of the Munich crisis by a report on 'The problems of bombing Britain'. Goering disliked the realism of Felmy's memorandum and wrote tartly on the report: 'I have not asked for a memorandum weighing the existing possibilities of success and pointing out our weaknesses. These things I know best of all'.

But he did not know them. He needed more men about him like General Felmy, men capable of serious misgivings about German air power, who were willing to underline weaknesses where they existed. Men like General Adolf Galland as he later became.

Hermann Goering played less than a secondary role in Hitler's next strategic move, the invasion of Denmark and Norway. Perhaps his greatest personal success, in March 1940, was to plead with the Fuehrer not to invade Sweden, where Goering had friends and relations. The code-name for the new operation was *Weseruebung* (Weser Exercise) and the first directive was issued by Hitler on 1 March. At a Chiefs-of-Staff conference at his Chancellery in Berlin on 2 April he announced that the invasion was timed for 9 April at 0515 hours. At this meeting, Hermann Goering named the new Commander-in-Chief of a new Air Fleet (No. 5) created for the attack on Denmark and Norway. He was General Hans-Juergen Stumpff. Stumpff had to get his air squadrons from the other four air fleets, as there were almost no reserve or new units. He was responsible to General Falkenhorst, who was made Commander of all German forces engaged, army, naval and air, and also to General Erhard Milch, Goering's deputy in the Luftwaffe.

There are at least two reasons why Goering did not assume direct command of the German Air Force engaged in the Norwegian campaign. The first is that Operation Yellow, the attack on France and the Low Countries, was fairly imminent and he wished to give it his undivided attention. Secondly, he was again

unfit and needed a rest before the new responsibilities of
Operation Yellow.

There was gossip at the time that Milch had been going over
Goering's head to see Hitler on air matters. At one meeting of
the Luftwaffe senior air staff, Goering said jokingly to Milch:
'Everyone thinks you are head of the Luftwaffe'. But the suggestion that Milch should have operational responsibility in
Norway came from Goering himself. Goering probably felt that
Milch would benefit from the experience. If Goering played
little direct part in the Norwegian campaign, he may at least be
given credit for choosing good air leaders. General Stumpff
made an excellent Air Fleet commander; General Harling-
hausen, an ex-naval pilot, was a good choice as Chief-of-Staff
of the Tenth Air Corps, newly created for Operation
Weseruebung.

Although Hermann Goering took no direct part in the air
operations in Norway in April and May 1940, the effectiveness
of German air operations illustrated some of the positive aspects
of his air leadership and policies. In general terms, the Fifth
German Air Fleet of less than 1,000 planes, including bombers,
dive-bombers, fighter and reconnaissance machines, gave the
first demonstration that land-based air power can secure
superiority over naval power. In fairness it should be added that
Goering's Air Force failed to protect the German Navy from
suffering heavy losses at the hands of the British Navy. Ten
German destroyers and three cruisers were sunk. Admiral
Raeder's fleet was gambled off the coasts of Norway and the
game was lost.

These German naval losses off Norway imposed an extra
responsibility on German Air Force forward planning. To offset
the losses, Goering needed to increase mine-laying by his land-
based bombers, hurry the formation of land-based torpedo
bomber units and expand the use of the new four-engined
Focke-Wulf long-range anti-shipping bomber. But although a
Battle of the Atlantic air organisation was created in the German
Air Force and a special Air Corps for anti-shipping operations
by the summer of 1940, the number of squadrons permanently
assigned for these anti-shipping operations by Goering was
small, sometimes totalling only about 50 aircraft.

Whatever else he may have been, Goering was not an orthodox

air leader. His use of Junkers 52 transport planes to ferry troops to General Franco in the Spanish Civil War had no military precedent and in the planning of the Norwegian campaign Goering decided to use his flying-boats and float-planes in an air-lift role to supplement the Junkers 52's, because there were many suitable anchorages for float-planes and flying-boats in Norwegian fjords. Later, in both the Mediterranean and Eastern Front campaigns, he was to use bombers for air transport emergencies. This unorthodoxy was not always effective, either in the air supply of Rommel's desert warriors in North Africa or of the German Army in their plight at Stalingrad.

In the Norwegian compaign, German parachutist airborne troops were used effectively and with panache for the first time. General Student's parachutists flourished on Goering's personal patronage. In the Polish campaign German parachutists had failed to capture the target bridges; but in Norway, where German airborne forces were used more extensively, they helped to secure at top speed the key air-base at Stavanger and at Christiansand in Southern Norway. They were also dropped to strengthen small groups of the German Army near Stavanger, Bergen, Trondheim and Narvik. The Norwegian campaign justified the Goering policy of having both the aircraft and the airborne forces together in the Luftwaffe. It was more common in other national forces for the army to control and train the airborne forces and for the Air Force to fly them to their drop zones.

In the third week of April 1940, Hermann Goering became more directly concerned with operations in Norway. On 17 April Adolf Hitler produced a burst of nervous hysteria when he had the news of heavy German naval losses at Narvik and of the withdrawal of German ground forces in that area commanded by General Dietl. The Fuehrer called a series of conferences at his Berlin Chancellery during the next week and demanded that the German troops be evacuated by air. Hermann Goering was quite cool and firm. He said: 'Impossible, my Fuehrer. There are no local airfields'. And he was supported this time by all the Wehrmacht commanders present, by Halder, Keitel, Jodl, Raeder and others. Goering could not have failed to notice how easily his Fuehrer might crack under the strain of a minor setback in battle. Goering himself was often unaware of them.

In Operation Yellow, the attack on France and the Low Countries, launched on 10 May 1940, Goering's airborne forces had their most spectacular success so far, and the use of tactical air power in support of an army was demonstrated on an unprecedented scale. The number of operational planes deployed by the two Air Fleets (Nos. 2 and 3) was initially 3,824, out of a total Luftwaffe front-line strength of 4,850. Allowing for the aircraft needs of the occupation of Denmark, Norway, Poland, Czechoslovakia and Austria, and the token air defence of Germany, Hermann Goering was committing, for the first time, almost the maximum available German air power. After the successes in Poland and Scandinavia, he was naturally in a more than buoyant mood. He had taken to his bed at Karinhall in the first week of May, but with the help of his pep pills he revived fairly quickly. Indeed, by 9 May, he had returned to Berlin to bring himself up to date, and then had taken his operational headquarters train, ASIA, to the Belgian frontier, where it was shunted alongside the Fuehrer's headquarters train.

The German Air Force sorties in support of Operation Yellow brought both success and failure. In terms of air leadership and preparation, Goering must be given credit for the rapid air superiority which the Luftwaffe achieved over the French, Dutch, Belgian and Royal Air Force squadrons engaged. German Air Force single-engined fighter strength had been nearly doubled since the outbreak of war from 777 Me. 109's to 1,346. But Goering failed to foresee the heavy wear and tear on the Luftwaffe which Operation Yellow would cause. Much more important, he failed to learn the air lessons of the Dunkirk operations. He had, incidentally, been irritated by an air incident early in the campaign in which the Luftwaffe bombed the German town of Freiburg by mistake. Goering said to his air colleagues who met in his train ASIA: 'That's a splendid way to start the operations. Both the German Air Force and myself now look quite ridiculous'.

Hermann Goering's directive to the two Luftwaffe Air Fleets circulated on the day before Operation Yellow was of necessity broad, indeed all-embracing. He ordered them 'to achieve the destruction of enemy air forces and their sources of supply, to give direct and indirect support to the army, and to attack enemy ports and shipping'.

Goering followed up this general directive with a series of signals to the two air fleet commanders, Kesselring and Sperrle, urging them to put out a maximum effort in support of the German Army. The German Air Force responded by launching a devastating series of air attacks on 10 May on Dutch air bases near the Hague and near Rotterdam and on French air bases near Dijon, Lyon, Metz, Nancy and Romilly. And in the tactical air operations launched in support of the German Army, the five Air Corps deployed reached an unprecedented level of close co-operation with the armoured forces which promoted the quick breakthrough on the ground. Effective use of Luftwaffe glider-borne assault forces was of special importance in the early stages of the attack on Belgium and Holland.

In discussion with General Student, commander of German airborne forces, and General Jeschonnek, the Luftwaffe Chief-of-Staff, Goering had helped to plan the airborne assault on the Moerdijk bridge near Rotterdam and the large-scale parachutist attack on the Waalhaven airfield in the same area. Other German airborne forces were landed at Ypenberg and Valkenburg where they met strong Dutch resistance. The Dutch shot down some 25 Ju 52 transport planes and took nearly 100 German prisoners. In Belgium, Goering's gliderborne forces successfully assaulted the key fortress of Eban-Emael and seized key bridges across the Albert Canal. Goering was the first military leader to use airborne forces in modern war successfully both in the Norwegian campaign and in the May 1940 assault on Belgium and Holland. He must have learnt how vulnerable airborne forces can be; but he was always willing to accept casualties as the price of success.

In the period 10 May to 17 June, the day France asked for an armistice, Goering's Air Force achieved unprecedented results as an instrument of army support. Over 600 German Air Force reconnaissance planes were available on 10 May to act as the eyes of the German Army, over 2,000 bombers and over 400 transport planes gave tactical support. The latter were soon helping to move German air bases forward into Belgium and Holland so that German air squadrons could operate over France with maximum bomb loads or at maximum range.

In the fortnight of 10 May to 24 May, Hermann Goering probably reached the peak of his success as an air leader. Behind him was the political effect of German air power on the Austrian Anschluss, the occupation of Czechoslovakia, the successful intervention in the Spanish Civil War and the blitzkrieg successes in Poland, Denmark, Norway and now France and the Low Countries. But, on 24 May, there came a crucial day of high-level confusion in the German High Command. Fearing that German armoured units were pushing too hard and too far towards the Channel coast, Adolf Hitler ordered the German tanks to stop their swift advance. The documentary evidence on how this happened is conflicting. General Halder, Chief of the Army General Staff, has said that Hitler had a *crise de nerfs* as he did in the Norwegian campaign. He became frightened at the rapid success of his armoured units, suspected a trap and called a halt. Sir Winston Churchill's *War Memoirs* say that the initiative for the halt came from von Runstedt, the German Army Commander.

But the real question was 'What next?' as the British forces retreated to Dunkirk. At this crucial stage, Goering's arrogance and vanity intervened. He gave Hitler the definite answer he was groping for in his neurotic state. 'The Luftwaffe can destroy Dunkirk and so prevent the evacuation', said Goering, and went on extravagantly: 'My Luftwaffe will complete the encirclement and will close the pocket at the coast from the air'. Then, in a mood of almost drunken optimism, he added: 'I will not only take Dunkirk, but Calais as well if necessary'.

Goering had discussed the air attack on the Dunkirk evacuation with General Kesselring, the Air Fleet Commander concerned. He refused to see any of the problems that Kesselring underlined. The Luftwaffe Commander-in-Chief pointed out that Kesselring now had air bases in Belgium and Holland and so his dive-bombers and fighters could operate over Dunkirk. Kesselring warned Goering that many of his air squadrons were tired and under strength, and that he could only operate about 300 bombers and dive-bombers and less than 500 Messerschmitt fighters to crucially limit 'Operation Dynamo', the Dunkirk evacuation of 27 May to 4 June. In that period, 338,000 men, nearly all Englishmen, got away.

Dunkirk was Hermann Goering's first major failure in combat leadership. The bad weather on two days was no excuse, for the largest number (68,000) were evacuated on 31 May, when the weather was fine. There were many reasons for his failure. He overestimated what the German Air Force could do in its assault on shipping. The Norwegian campaign had produced a burst of anti-shipping optimism which blended with the euphoria of the blitzkrieg successes in Holland and Belgium. Goering now really believed in himself and his Air Force. How could it fail? But for the first time he had to reckon with British home-based Hurricanes and Spitfires. Goering was new to the reality of Spitfires and indeed to any kind of strong fighter opposition. And, because he tended to discount the air enemy, he badly underestimated the power of Royal Air Force Fighter Command to disrupt German bomber attacks. After the war, Luftwaffe General Adolf Galland wrote: 'Dunkirk should have been an emphatic warning to the leaders of the Luftwaffe'. This was wisdom after the event. In any event, Hermann Goering could not afford to dwell on the German Air Force failure at Dunkirk. There were other air fronts in France of major importance.

At German General Staff level the final collapse of France was not predictable in the first week of June. Strong opposition from the French Army was still expected. And so, on 3 June, Goering ordered the German Air Force to carry out a new wave of heavy air attacks on French air bases and aircraft factories within fifty miles of Paris. And when, on 5 June, the German Army launched a major offensive along the entire French front, using over a hundred divisions, Goering moved his train to forward headquarters at Sovet in Belgium and supported the offensive with over 2,000 bomber, fighter and reconnaissance planes.

Goering's air squadrons responded superbly to the German Army needs of the next two weeks. In some instances, requests to bomb new targets were met within half an hour. German fighter pilots flew up to six sorties a day. Goering's air transport units flew ammunition and fuel to forward bases for the army and then flew back their wounded to Germany. The dark patch of distress and discontent about Dunkirk was soon forgotten. Goering was once again proud of his Luftwaffe. He made a defiant public announcement that 'all captured French airmen would be put in chains if German Air Force prisoners are ill-treated', and he went on: 'For every German airman shot, I will shoot five French prisoners and increase this to fifty if a

German pilot is shot while parachuting to earth'. Goering did not carry out his threat. Perhaps he was simply telling German air crews that he cared about them, as he certainly did.

Goering's train moved forward with the tide of battle, to a tunnel near Calais on 5 June and to a siding near Compiègne on 18 June. There he again met Hitler, who said to him : 'The war is finished. I'll come to an understanding with England'. Goering replied : 'Now there will be peace'.

Goering may have said this without conviction for he was already considering an urgent plan proposed by Erhard Milch, Goering's deputy in the Luftwaffe, to make an immediate air attack on the airfields of South-East England, followed up by waves of parachutists and airborne troops flown in by Ju 52 transport planes. These would then ferry across more troops, fuel, food, ammunition and supplies. Goering discussed the Milch plan with Kesselring and Sperrle, the two Air Fleet commanders, and neither was keen on it. And so Goering turned it down. He said to Milch: 'This is impossible. It makes no sense at all'. Sir Winston Churchill in his *War Memoirs* supports Goering's decision, adding that the Luftwaffe had been engaged to the utmost limit in the Battle of France and required a period of some weeks to recover.

Luftwaffe combat wastage in May and June 1940 totalled 1,469 planes, that is the equivalent of the whole output of operational aircraft for these two months. The heavy losses were mainly due to the intensive all-out effort which exceeded 5,000 sorties on some days and stretched the air squadrons to the full. It produced an extra crop of crashes on take-off and landing, and more accidents in ferry flights. At the end of June 1940, the front-line strength of the Luftwaffe was just below 4,000 planes, compared with 4,850 early in May. Clearly there was no prospect of any major expansion for the coming air attack on Britain. Goering had kept his Air Force in the shop window of the Battle of France. There was little new up his sleeve for the very different Battle of Britain.

Five days after the conclusion of the Franco-German armistice, Goering issued a general directive on the conduct of the air war against Britain. It was dated 30 June 1940, and began : 'As long as the enemy air force is not defeated, the first requirement for the air war is to attack the enemy air force on every possible opportunity in the air and on the ground without consideration of other tasks'. It went on: 'There are to be firm targets and firm dates of attacks so that not only the most effective results will be achieved, but the well-developed defence of the enemy can be split and he will be faced with a maximum form of attack'.

The compliment to Royal Air Force Fighter Command is noteworthy. Perhaps Goering had learnt a lesson from Dunkirk; but his intelligence on Royal Air Force fighter strength was uncertain. Goering's directive said hopefully: 'By means of reconnaissance and combat against small formations it should be possible to draw out smaller enemy formations and ascertain the strength of groupings of enemy forces'. Heaven help the air commander who has to rely on such combat intelligence for his enemy order of battle!

Hermann Goering's air plan of 30 June 1940 was splendid as a concept; but in practice it was over-ambitious for the resources he had at his disposal. He was simply not the leader required for a new type of strategic air battle in which, because margins were narrow, extra attention had to be paid to target intelligence and to obtaining the most accurate assessment of how the battle was going. Goering was a good air leader when there was a wide margin of success. In sterner battle conditions his leadership tended to be ineffective. In the next three months of July, August and September, he had to face tough aeronautical combat conditions for the first time.

CHAPTER FIVE

The Battle of Britain

THE BATTLE of Britain was one of the decisive battles of European and perhaps of world history. Winston Churchill expressed such a view, with trenchant emotion, when he said to the British Parliament on 4 June 1940: 'May it not be that the cause of civilisation will be defended by a few thousand airmen?' and a few days later wrote to the Prime Minister of South Africa, his friend General Smuts, 'I see only one way through now, to wit, that Hitler should attack this country and, in doing so, break his air weapon'. This was, in essence, the result that the air leadership of Hermann Goering produced in July, August and September 1940. It might be fairer to say that the German Air Force was heavily battered in the battle rather than broken; and thus, the vital expansion of squadrons, needed for the 1941 campaigns in the Mediterranean and on the Eastern front against the USSR, was crucially slowed up.

At no period in those three vital months was Goering fully aware of the difficulty of the task that his air units had undertaken. Nor did he show any outward sign of being conscious of the strategic importance of the Battle of Britain, in relation to the future of German air power, or to the future course of the Second World War. In the summer of 1940, he was still taking morphia and paracodeine. This, once again, may have aggravated his natural predisposition to be confident to the point of arrogance. He never seemed to see the detail of air problems. Perhaps he did not want to.

He certainly had a persistent tendency in the summer of 1940 to overestimate the German Air Force potential, and a disastrous knack of underestimating Royal Air Force opposition. For the latter fault, part of the blame attaches to German air intelligence and part to Goering's bland, over-confident leadership. But if he developed a personal mythology, which overestimated the effect of German air power, he was in parallel with British and US air leaders who later on, in 1943 and 1944, assessed the effects of their bombing of Hitler's Third Reich too optimistically. However, the British and US air leaders were at least subject to criticism from various members of their staffs. Goering's vanity and euphoria fused into a more dangerously explosive fall-out, which led to a neglect of reality and of long-term planning, at this vital juncture in German air history. Goering was an air leader of personal accomplishment and intelligence, but his leadership accomplished much too little for his brave and highly-skilled pilots. In the Battle of Britain, his indifference in July produced incomprehension, and then bewilderment in August and September. He neglected the detailed study of day to day air operations as he neglected the diet sheets proffered by his private nurse, Christa Gormanns, who was vainly attempting to reduce his corpulence and his intake of pills.

After the Battle of Britain, Royal Air Force intelligence was asked to produce a paper on why Goering's air leadership had failed. He was compared with an examination candidate trying to cope with a difficult mathematics paper. It was beyond his talents and so he bumbled on from one problem to the next, without finding any solution to any one of the problems. He failed because he did not seriously recognise the complex nature of the operational problems he had set himself.

He managed to develop what amounted to indifference, especially during the important preparatory month of July 1940, to the detailed German Air Force tactical and intelligence difficulties raised by the first-ever German air attack on an enemy territory defended by modern fighters supported by modern electronic equipment.

Goering in fact spent nearly half the month of July either on holiday with his wife and daughter at Bad Gastein, or sightseeing in Paris, or resuming futile diplomatic efforts to secure peace with Britain, or discussing the economic future of Europe with German economists. He was also diverted from German Air Force affairs by his art deals with Herr Rosenberg, through whom he acquired additional paintings for his large collection at Karinhall; they were culled from the art galleries of France, Belgium and Holland, which were now there for picking.

Goering had not lacked warning about the coming invasion of Britain or of the role the German Air Force was to play. On 2 July, the German Chiefs-of-Staff issued a directive that 'a landing in England is possible, provided that air superiority can be obtained'. The keynote of the conference which produced the statement was pessimism from the German Navy, which was then weak and ill-equipped to protect German ships carrying invasion forces, optimism from the German Army chiefs, fresh from blitzkrieg triumphs in France and the Low Countries, and routine euphoria from Goering. His optimism at this stage was as unimpaired as it was unrealistic.

At a German Air Force Chiefs-of-Staff meeting, held at Goering's home at Karinhall on 11 July, the Commander-in-Chief of the German Air Force said, 'When the time comes, the enemy aircraft industry and air force must be destroyed at the earliest possible moment by the first blows of the attack. The defence of Southern England will last four days and the Royal Air Force four weeks. We can guarantee invasion for the Fuehrer within a month'.

In both August and September, Goering was to repeat his view that the RAF defence of Southern England would last only four or five days. It is impossible to see any serious basis for such an over-confident assessment. As a perceptive German Air Force officer, Heinz Loechner, once said quietly and cynically to me: 'Goering's pronouncements were intended to have the stimulating effect of a rousing after-dinner speech'.

At the 11 July conference at Karinhall, Goering asked his three Air Fleet Commanders, Sperrle, Kesselring and Stumpff, to work out plans, between then and 21 July, for the final air assault on Britain. The date for this had not yet been fixed, but the code name for the first day was decided. It was to be 'Eagle Day' *(Adlertag)* and the overall air campaign was to be coded 'Eagle Attack' *(Adlerangriff)*.

The new Hitler Directive No. 16, of 16 July 1940, sealed the responsibility of Hermann Goering's air leadership for the Battle of Britain and for the planned German invasion which was to follow. Hitler's reasons for 'Operation Sea Lion', as the invasion was code-named, were clearly set out in his directive: 'This operation is dictated by the necessity of eliminating Great Britain as a base from which the war against Germany can be fought; if necessary the island will be occupied'. The conditions required for Operation Sea Lion were, first and foremost, 'the elimination of the Royal Air Force', then the clearing of mines in the path of the invading ships, due to land between the Isle of Wight and Ramsgate in Kent, and finally, 'neutralising the British fleet and Britain's heavy coastal artillery'.

Goering said, on 16 July and later, that Sea Lion would not be necessary, as Britain would have to surrender to the violence and effectiveness of German Air Force attacks. This was taking the air theories of Douhet to extremes. Not that Goering is known to have been an addict of Douhet's air theories; he was simply prone to an addiction which made it difficult for him, at times, to distinguish between fact and fancy.

Goering's operational intentions for July 1940 were clear. He himself said he regarded Luftwaffe operations during that month as 'largely training exercises' designed to probe and test the air defences of Great Britain. He gave orders for a secondary, moderately scaled attack on British shipping on 10 July, which involved only two of the five main available air corps to any great extent.

There is interesting evidence to show that, at this preliminary but important stage, Goering's intelligence on Royal Air Force Fighter Command's combat capability was vitally defective. For this he must be only partially to blame. However, his Chief of Air Staff, Jeschonnek, had suggested to him that air intelligence officers should be appointed at the lower levels of air operations, such as the Gruppe, a unit of thirty to forty planes, to get better combat intelligence. Goering replied to this suggestion 'The work can be done by the adjutants or signals officers as a part-time job'. Thus vital intelligence on Royal Air Force tactics, losses and the damage inflicted by German Air Force attacks, was to be left to the vagaries of part-time intelligence amateurs.

Beppo Schmid, Goering's air intelligence chief, produced an overall estimate of Royal Air Force potential in a key paper dated 16 July. It was duly read by Hermann Goering and his senior air colleagues. This important report was misleading in several aspects, as many military intelligence papers are; but Goering accepted all its findings without probing for vital details or the reasons for the assessments made. He knew what he wanted to know.

Thus in the comparison between the British Hurricane and Spitfire planes and the Me 109 and Me 110 fighters, Goering accepted the finding of Schmid that 'the fact that they (the Hurricanes and Spitfires) are not yet equipped with cannon-guns (20mm calibre) makes them inferior to the Me 109E and particularly to the Me 109F'. Goering and Schmid however conceded that 'the Me 110 is inferior to skilfully-handled Spitfires'.

In the light of Battle of Britain experience, these were absurd views, which only served to fan the flow of Goering's extraordinary optimism. In any event he must have known by 16 July that the new Messerschmitt Me 109F would not take part in German Air Force operations on any scale for several months. And so the comparison with the Hurricane and Spitfire was largely, if not entirely, irrelevant. The point about the 20mm cannon equipping Messerschmitts was pertinent. But a statement might have been made, which does not appear in the report of 16 July. It is that the eight-gun Hurricanes and Spitfires had a fire-power advantage over the Messerschmitts currently equipped with only four guns and not with cannons.

The really misleading feature of the key German Air Intelligence report of 16 July was its failure to take account of British early warning radar plus the spoken ground control by radio of RAF fighters. These were a vital addition to the technical potential of the Hurricanes and Spitfires. The Luftwaffe intelligence report of 16 July expressed the view that Royal Air Force fighter squadrons were 'rigidly attached to their home bases'. In contrast, the quick switching of the next two months demonstrated their flexibility. It was a flexibility which Goering could have foreseen if someone had studied the raw data of General Martini's listening service during the month of July. It could have been easily deduced from Royal Air Force voice traffic, and in fact it was deduced by some of Martini's signals officers. But their views never reached Goering.

The Beppo Schmid intelligence appreciation, signed, sealed and circulated by Hermann Goering, went badly astray in other respects. It said, 'The German Air Force is clearly superior to the Royal Air Force in strength, equipment, training, command and location of bases. In the event of an intensification of air warfare, the German Air Force, unlike the Royal Air Force, will be in a position, in every respect, to achieve a decisive effect this year'.

The Schmid report made the obvious recommendation that the period of operations should be July to October. Perhaps its most misleading statement was its estimate of British fighter aircraft production during the key months of Operation Adlerangriff, i.e. the Battle of Britain. This was assessed broadly at between 180 and 300 planes a month, dependent no doubt on the success or otherwise of Luftwaffe attacks on the centres of Hurricane and Spitfire assembly and production. The German intelligence estimate proved to be a gross underestimate. The figures were 496 British fighter aircraft in July, 476 in August, and 467 in September.

Goering had, more than once, said to Hitler and other Nazi colleagues that the British should not be underestimated. This is precisely what his 16 July intelligence document on Luftwaffe and RAF comparison succeeded in doing, in no uncertain fashion. The claim to superior air leadership was particularly ill-founded. The combination of Air Chief Marshal Sir Hugh Dowding, Commander-in-Chief of Fighter Command, and of Air Chief Marshal Sir Charles Portal, as Commander-in-Chief of Bomber Command, could hardly be matched for intelligence, integrity and professionalism anywhere in the upper ranks of the German Air Force, certainly not by the Commander-in-Chief of the German Air Force.

Goering held his next important air staff meeting on 18 July at Karinhall. Virtually all his senior air colleagues attended—Milch, Udet, Jeschonnek, Bodenschatz, his senior air aide and the operational commanders of the three air fleets engaged in the Battle of Britain—Kesselring, Sperrle and Stumpff. Goering again radiated superb confidence and spoke of 'a first victory in four or five days, and the final air victory, at most, in two or three weeks'. He again emphasised the importance of using the secondary July operations, which consisted mainly of daylight attacks on British convoys in the English Channel, 'for training new air crews'. Other matters discussed were the replacement of the heavy aircraft wastage suffered in May and June, which may have persuaded Goering to limit the July operations, and also the introduction of an Air-Sea Rescue Service.

Goering's early sponsoring of the Air-Sea Rescue Service in

July—the Royal Air Force equivalent came into being only in February 1941—to help his pilots compelled to ditch in the English Channel, is but one of many examples of his paternal care for his air crews. He allocated a force of about 30 He 59 sea-planes for air-sea rescue. In this respect and others he was a positive air leader with a humanitarian touch. He was also generous with his awards of medals; the provision of creature comforts included a major distribution of liberated French claret and burgundy for his air crews. He also saw to it that they had good brothel facilities. Indeed there was a special transport unit to fly the ladies from one country to another.

Many other detailed criticisms could be made of Hermann Goering's leadership during the vital weeks before Adlerangriff. Thus he saw practically nothing of his Fuehrer, who was at his Berghof retreat in Southern Germany. Hitler, for his part, chose not to visit Goering's air headquarters or the German Air Ministry, to see how the air plans for the proposed invasion of Britain were developing. Yet Adolf Hitler repeated to his senior staff officers who came to see him at the Berghof that 'Sea Lion was off, unless the RAF could be driven from the skies'. He knew that the Luftwaffe was his chief strike weapon against Britain, but he chose to ignore its state of readiness for the tasks ahead. He was then inclined to leave all air matters to Goering.

Goering had agreed in his directive of 30 June that he must first destroy the enemy air force. But the July operations could have given him little comfort about the prospects of achieving this aim. But he was inclined to whistle in the dark. Instead of accepting—as he did—the inflated July claims of his pilots and planning a vital air campaign at long range from Karinhall, he would have been better advised to spend more time at his advanced headquarters train, which was now situated in a tunnel near Beauvais, north of Paris. The train was fully equipped with wireless, telephone and teleprinter facilities. There was living accommodation on the train for his chief air aide and long-standing friend, General Bodenchatz, and his personal military aide, Colonel von Brauchitsch, as well as for Robert, his valet, Christa Gormanns, his nurse, and Fedor Radmann, his cook. There were also facilities for air staff meetings. The lavish hospitality of Karinhall could not be reproduced in a train, but

Paris was near enough and Goering enjoyed his trips to the French capital.

The great advantage of using the ASIA train headquarters in July 1940 would have been its proximity to the air battles over the English Channel and the coastal areas of Great Britain. From Beauvais it was a quick, short run by road or train to many of the bases and regional headquarters of the key German Air Force units and the regional advanced heaquarters. Thus Field Marshal Hugo Sperrle (he, like others, was promoted in mid-July) had his Air Fleet headquarters in Paris, Messerschmitt fighter units were located in the Pas de Calais and there was a circle of German Air Force bomber bases within fifty miles of Paris.

From his headquarters train, Goering could have looked more easily into vital aspects of the July preliminary operations. For example, the evolution of Royal Air Force Fighter Command tactics and efficiency, as observed by General Martini's special listening units, monitoring the voices of both British fighter pilots and the ground controllers who directed them towards the raiding German formations. This would have given Goering a first-hand impression of what the British air defence system might achieve. By talking to General Martini and his signals specialists on the spot Goering could have learnt more about the potential vulnerability of the Royal Air Force air defence to low-level attacks. There would have been time to train some Luftwaffe units for this then relatively rare form of bombing.

Perhaps more important would have been an on-the-spot examination of the fighter escort problems which the German Air Force was already encountering in the month of July against the interception thrusts of RAF Hurricanes and Spitfires. He could have spoken to such Luftwaffe specialists as Osterkamp, Moelders and Galland, who would have put him wise to some of the problems. They could have brought some realism, perhaps, into Goering's aeronautically snobbish mind. For the Luftwaffe leader tended to judge his air contemporaries by his own peculiar standards, which inevitably flashed back to the irrelevances of the Richthofen squadrons in the First World War.

Goering was too much swayed by the privileged viewpoint of a remote Commander-in-Chief and too little aware of the grass-root details of unprecedented air operations, with all the detailed snags and difficulties especially in the growing electronic air age. The distinction between wishful thinking and the reality of air operations were thus blurred in his undoubtedly intelligent mind.

However, at a meeting at the German Air Ministry in Berlin on 19 July, there was a touch of realism and a typical outburst from the German Air Force Commander-in-Chief. He said on this occasion to the three German Air Fleet commanders engaged in the Battle of Britain: 'Our fighters must wake up! We are losing too many bombers and dive-bombers. The Messerschmitt 109 fighters should clear enemy fighters out of the way before the bombers arrive'.

Goering did not mention the inadequacy of the twin-engined Messerschmitt 110 at this meeting. This machine had not prospered so far in the July operations over the English Channel. Thus on 10 July, thirty Me 110's, escorting a formation of Do 17 bombers in an attack on a British convoy near Dover had to break off escort and form a defensive circle when attacked by Hurricanes. Of course, the whole story of the Me 110, and its successor the Me 210, provides a splendid example of the ancient tag that none are so blind as those who won't see. Goering had been very eloquent in his public claims for the combat qualities of this twin-engined multi-purpose aircraft. It was to be a major failure in the Battle of Britain, because it was asked to assume a role for which it was not suited, that is the protection of bombers against strong air defence. Its losses in August and September were to be over 200 compared with a total Me 110 strength in German air squadrons in that period of less than 300. It took such heavy punishment because it was a part of Goering's aeronautical pride.

Goering took time off from his cares on 20 July to give a press conference in Berlin for a group of US journalists. He was in his element on such occasions. Answering questions on the Nazi threat to USA, he said: 'The United States cannot be invaded. The German Air Force has no planes of sufficient range for transatlantic operations. Even if you don't like us, give us some credit for commonsense and reason'. The myth of a German air threat to USA died hard. When I first visited the Pentagon and the White House in June 1943, it was still absurdly alive and one had difficulty in quashing it.

Goering held further German Air Force staff meetings at

G

Karinhall on 20 July and 21 July. The first was little more than a social gathering to celebrate the promotions publicly promulgated on 17 July. Not only had Goering been made Reichsmarschall to celebrate the victory over France, but some half-dozen of his air chiefs were promoted to the rank of Field Marshal. This certainly called for a celebration of considerable size. The meeting on 21 July moved on to the Air Ministry in Berlin. Once again, as at the meeting of 19 July, Goering showed that he realised all was not well in the July operations over the Channel and over the coastal areas of Britain. He again emphasised, 'We are losing too many bombers. The Me 109's must clear the way before the bombers get to the target area'.

Goering missed a vital Chiefs-of-Staff meeting, held on that day at Hitler's Chancellery in Berlin, to which he sent General Jeschonnek, his young Chief of Air Staff. At this gathering, Adolf Hitler declared, 'Our attention must be turned to tackling the Russian problem. Thoughtful preparations must be made'. The German Fuehrer went on to say that General Halder, Chief of his Army General Staff, had, in a preliminary planning estimate, found that 80 to 100 divisions would be required for an attack on the USSR. The air strategy behind the move was that 'the attack would relieve the pressure of the air war against England while the German Army was to penetrate far enough to allow the German Air Force to smash Russia's strategic aims'. Jeschonnek duly reported to Goering on this meeting.

For the next ten days, the German Army planners worked intensively on a special staff study for an invasion of Russia. It was sent to Hitler at Berchtesgaden on 30 July and he summoned his Chiefs-of-Staff to his villa there on 31 July 1940, to discuss both Operation Sea Lion and the preliminary decision to attack the USSR. The Army and Navy Chiefs-of-Staff turned up, but not Goering.

Even allowing for his growing habit of not attending important Chiefs-of-Staff meetings, the absence of Goering from the vital conference of 31 July 1940 is difficult to condone. True, he would have been subjected to another strategic monologue from the German Fuehrer which, on this occasion, rambled widely over relations with Japan and the strategy of the Far East, Britain's links with the United States and, above all, the destruction of the Soviet Union. 'The sooner Russia is crushed the better', said Hitler to his naval and army Chiefs-of-Staff. The Fuehrer, at this meeting, took a preliminary decision to attack the USSR in the spring of 1941, to increase the strength of the German Army to 180 divisions and to use 120 of them for the proposed assault on the USSR. Hermann Goering's absence from this meeting was surely a vivid example of his strategic indifference.

And yet he had some kind of excuse. In the last week of July he was busy studying the staff memoranda from his Air Corps and Air Fleet commanders dealing with the way the coming Battle of Britain should be fought. Remembering that both he and Hitler expected Adlerangriff to be launched in the first week of August, it was rather late in the day to make any major modifications in German air planning for the battle.

Only three of the eight memoranda submitted to the Commander-in-Chief of the German Air Force are thought to have survived the Second World War, though others may be extant. The three available produced no fresh inspiration of any combat moment. Thus Richthofen, the 8th Air Corps Commander-in-Chief, after a windy introduction on air superiority, strongly recommended that his Junkers 87 dive-bombers should attack Royal Air Force ground targets. Because of their vulnerability to Royal Air Force fighters, especially in the case of inland targets, this proved to be an unhelpful point. Richthofen's mind was probably still on his tactical air successes in May and June, over France and the Low Countries, when combat conditions were vastly different.

The second Air Corps paper, interestingly enough, recommended attacks on London. Back in June, the Commander-in-Chief of Royal Air Force Fighter Command, Air Marshal Sir Hugh Dowding, had foreseen such a plan and said it would be 'the end of German Air Force hopes of victory'. However, this paper from General Bruno Loerzer, Goering's friend of more than twenty years, also warned of the impossibility of sending German bombers in daylight into the Midlands and North of England, where much of the Spitfire production was now concentrated, well beyond the range of escorting Messerschmitt fighters.

The First Air Corps gave four major objectives in its memorandum. First, the winning of air superiority by destroying the

Royal Air Force and its aircraft industry; secondly, the protection of the German Army as it crossed the Channel for the invasion and also the protection of Goering's airborne forces of two divisions allocated for the invasion; thirdly, the use of German air power to blockade England, by making its harbours unusable, and finally terror attacks against the major cities of Britain.

Goering's air victories so far had been quick and tactical. Now, for the first time in his air career, he was engaged in a strategic air battle calling for up-to-date knowledge on enemy airfields, enemy aircraft production and repair of planes as well as enemy tactics and other capabilities. His crass ignorance of Royal Air Force Fighter Command potential was to be the Achilles heel of his air leadership in the important months of August and September 1940.

The early days of August 1940 gave Hermann Goering further time for reflection, because the weather forecast for South and South-East England and for Northern France was unfavourable. On 1 August he held a major meeting of air commanders at the Hague where he again dined with his old friend General Christiansen, then Commander-in-Chief of German forces in Holland. Goering wore a new white uniform for the occasion and was in a wildly confident mood. He loved his uniforms.

He told the assembly of senior Luftwaffe officers: 'The Fuehrer has ordered me to crush Britain with my Luftwaffe. By means of hard blows I plan to bring this enemy, who has already suffered a moral defeat, down on his knees in the nearest future, so that an occupation of the island by our troops can proceed without risk'. Goering went on: 'For the first time in modern history the people of England are now to feel the full and direct impact of war on their own soil. Their morale is expected to deteriorate in consequence'.

What made Goering tell the Hague conference that the Royal Air Force had suffered a moral defeat in July 1940? He was clearly out of touch with reality. RAF Fighter Command had 708 fighters on 3 August 1940, compared with 587 on 30 June and in the same period its combat fighter pilots had increased from 1,200 to 1,434. In the operations of July over the English Channel and the coastal regions of South and South-East England, Luftwaffe losses had been about twice those of the Royal Air Force—270 planes against 145. Perhaps, if one knew

Goering's drug dosage for the last week in July, one could hazard a psychological reason for this extraordinary claim of a moral victory over the Royal Air Force.

At the Hague Conference on 1 August, the German Air Force orders, plans and directives were fully discussed and estimates were made of the time required to destroy RAF Fighter Command in the air and on the ground. For units based within 100 to 150 kilometres, south-west, south and south-east of London, it would take five days. A further three days would be needed for units further inland, within 50 to 100 kilometres of London. Finally, five days would be needed for RAF fighter units based within 50 kilometres of London. The plan, of course, bore no relationship to the reality of the trend of Luftwaffe operations in August and September. But Goering told the Hague meeting, 'This plan will irrevocably gain for us an absolute air superiority over England and fulfil the Fuehrer's mission'. When Theo Osterkamp, a senior fighter specialist, intervened at the Hague Conference to say he considered Spitfires were equal in quality to German fighters, Goering cut him short angrily and retorted, 'Nonsense. I am perfectly well aware of the situation. Besides, the Messerschmitt is much better than the Spitfire'.

The Fuehrer, at this time, felt somewhat thwarted about the delay in the execution of Adlerangriff. He had, on 30 July, issued from the Berghof his Directive No. 17, 'The conduct of Air and Naval Warfare against Britain'. The next day he told Hermann Goering that 'the preparations for the Luftwaffe's great attack must be completed immediately, so that it can begin within twelve hours after my orders'. Adolf Hitler was obviously out of touch with the pessimistic long-range weather forecast for Southern England and the English Channel for the first week of August.

During that week Hermann Goering prepared for his last conference of senior Air Staff officers before Adlerangriff. It was held at Karinhall on 6 August and was attended by the Air Fleet Commanders and his Chiefs of Air Staff. At this gathering, Hermann Goering modified his previous directive of 1 August, issued to the three Air Fleet commanders, Kesselring, Sperrle and Stumpff, after the Hague conference. He now ordained that Adlerangriff should 'achieve air mastery and the destruction of enemy naval units in the invasion area'. Meanwhile, added

Goering, 'harassing attacks on ports, communications, factories and airfields all over Britain were to be carried out'.

Such a counsel of dispersal of effort was the reverse of sane leadership. Goering himself obscured the directive at the 6 August conference when he also said, 'the attacks must in the first instance be directed against flying formations, their ground organisation, the aircraft production industry and the industry engaged in anti-aircraft production'. He told Milch, Sperrle, Stumpff, Bodenschatz, Kesselring and other air leaders present, that Adlerangriff would begin on 10 August. Adverse weather again postponed the air assault which went off at half-cock on 12 August, partly because of a failure of radio communications, and partly because of the weather intelligence which made the situation uncertain.

Whichever August date is taken for the beginning of Adlerangriff, two things are certain: Hermann Goering had failed to produce adequate fighter forces for the air assault on South and South-East England and both his planning and combat intelligence were inadequate for the job in hand. He must share the blame for this with the senior air officers who were there to advise and inform him. On the supply of fighters, it may be more than pertinent that, in 1939 and 1940, the German aircraft industry was working a one-shift system, based on 40 hours a week. It changed to two shifts only in 1943, when the air war was virtually lost.

One of the great weaknesses of Goering's air leadership, in the summer of 1940, was his lack of systematic attention to the problems of target intelligence. It was a weakness of major strategic importance. The target planning for Adlerangriff was superficial and slipshod. Perhaps similar criticism could be made of other air force planners in the Second World War. Economic intelligence on the enemy tends to be a universal Achilles heel.

Goering and his air staff appear to have made little or no allowance for the loss on operations of reconnaissance aircraft which, because they were unescorted twin-engined Dornier or Junkers planes, were bound to suffer casualties from Hurricane and Spitfire radar-aided interception. Logically, some duplication of sorties was needed in the case of vital reconnaissance of key airfields and aircraft factories; but Goering made no such allowance as far as one can trace—on some days in July and

August reconnaissance aircraft casualties were heavy. Again, German Air Force photographic interpretation in the summer of 1940 was crude and not linked to all other intelligence sources, as it needed to be. There was no real system of checking combat claims of enemy aircraft shot down or of targets damaged or destroyed. There was no detailed Luftwaffe plan for attacks on airfields. Should bombs and cannon fire be directed primarily at enemy planes, runways or buildings, and, if buildings, which buildings? The German air records do not answer this question satisfactorily.

On the eve of the Battle of Britain Hermann Goering deployed some 900 serviceable twin-engined bombers and about 250 serviceable dive-bombers. To escort and cover this attacking force he had roughly 800 Me 109 serviceable single-seater fighters and about 200 twin-engined Me 110's, the latter ill-suited for fighter cover and used partly in a bomber role. To get some impression of the total inadequacy of this degree of Messerschmitt fighter cover in the Battle of Britain, one has only to cross-refer to the extent of RAF Spitfire cover in 1941, when the combat situation was reversed and RAF bombers attacked targets in Northern France. Then it was considered that roughly two fighters per bomber were needed to escort and cover against moderately strong German fighter defence, supported by early warning radar and ground control by radio. And so in the Battle of Britain, it can be fairly said that the Messerschmitt fighter squadrons were much too few for the job.

By 8 August 1940, Hermann Goering should have seen a warning red light. In a series of attacks on a convoy sailing from the Thames Estuary, a force of Ju 87 dive-bombers, escorted by Me 109's, was badly mauled by intercepting Hurricanes and Spitfires. Even if Goering believed the inflated Luftwaffe claim of 49 RAF fighters shot down, an exaggeration of nearly three to one, the German Air Force lost 31 planes on that day. For the next day or so the German Air Force Commander-in-Chief was diverted by concern about the weather; but on 8 August he flew to see Hitler at the Berghof and said, 'Mein Fuehrer, when I get three days of clear weather, I will give the signal to attack'. On 11 August he again conferred with Hitler, by telephone, and they agreed to issue the final order for Adlerangriff 'as soon as there was a prospect of three days of good weather'.

Meanwhile, on 10 August, the Luftwaffe's attack in daylight on a Rolls Royce aero-engine factory was totally abortive, while the attack on the previous day on a Boulton-Paul aircraft factory near Norwich was both unsuccessful and irrelevant, for the plant was still turning out Defiant fighters of secondary importance.

Nor did the major operations by Field Marshal Sperrle's Third Air Fleet on 11 August suggest that Goering did anything to ensure that his Air Force was adhering to his directives laid down at the Karinhall meetings. What, for example, were German bombers doing on the eve of Adlerangriff attacking, as they did on 11 August, barracks, gasworks, docks and oil tanks in the areas of Portland and Weymouth near the south coast of Britain? The 850 sorties of Sperrle's air squadrons on that day were largely ineffective. The three fighter air bases attacked, Manston, Hawkinge and Lympne, were not main RAF fighter stations. They were all badly hit, but were ready for operational use on the next day.

And so, from the very beginning of the Battle of Britain, Goering's air leadership and direction was not being translated into effective, realistic operational terms. He also lacked the combat intelligence facilities to know what was going on. He was to accept the inflated claims of British aircraft casualties and of damage to RAF bases. His knowledge of the results of the German Air Force attempt to secure air superiority over Southern England in the next few weeks was to be erratic and incomplete. Because he was Hermann Goering, he preferred to accept false evidence that he was winning, or could win, the air superiority indispensable for Operation Sea Lion, the planned invasion of Britain.

One can either suppose that Adlerangriff started prematurely on 12 August because of uncertain weather and a failure of radio communication between Goering's headquarters and the Air Fleet commands, or that it was in fact launched on 13 August. Except for historians, who may insist on precise dates, the matter is of no great moment.

The day-to-day course of the Battle of Britain has been well and often plotted in the last three decades. If, during the battles, there were no consecutive trends in Goering's air leadership, it is because his planning and reaction to the German Air Force changes of fortune in August and September 1940 revealed his utter lack of logical thinking.

Rather late in the day, at the end of August, Goering began to make more frequent use of his advanced headquarters train, ASIA, still located near Beauvais, north of Paris. From here, he could have seen earlier how the battle was going at the tactical level more often and more intimately. On-the-spot talks with commanders of units would, perhaps, have revealed something of the absurd inflation of the claims of German Air Force bomber crews and of the fighter units. But Goering preferred to entertain at Karinhall, his splendid estate north of Berlin, to offer his air chiefs the best of his growing wine cellars and to show them his expanding collection of liberated pictures and antiques taken from the art galleries of France and Holland.

On 13 August, the German Air Force put out its first major air effort of 1,485 bomber and fighter sorties. From the first, Goering was personally closely involved in Adlerangriff, more than in any other German Air Force campaign. Thus, on the day of this first major assault, he postponed air operations by personal signal until the afternoon. But already there were ominous cracks in Luftwaffe staff work and leadership. The fact that Luftwaffe claims on 13 August were inflated by over 600 per cent—88 RAF fighters against a reality of 13—boded ill for Goering's future knowledge of the state of the battle. It is true that RAF fighter claims were also inflated in the Battle of Britain, but RAF intelligence worked out an accepted formula, at the time, for reducing them to realistic proportions. Hermann Goering was, of course, happy to accept uncritically the inflated Luftwaffe claims, for they maintained his euphoric belief in the mythology of German air superiority; but in the harsh reality of the mathematics of air power the claims can only have confused his decisions.

Goering was not helped by the rosy picture presented by his senior air colleagues. Thus, on 14 August, the German Air Staff reported to the German Chiefs-of-Staff that 'the rate of loss is three to one in favour of the Luftwaffe and five to one in the case of fighters'. The report went on : 'We have no difficulty in replacing losses. The British are probably not able to replace them'.

15 August was another major Adlerangriff day. The Luftwaffe

carried out 1,786 sorties. This was the only day on which
Goering made full tactical use of the three air fleets available.
It was a day of mixed fortune for Adlerangriff. The Fifth Air
Fleet attacked what Goering and his staff had called 'the weak
air defence of North-East England', but the Luftwaffe squadrons
sustained a bloody nose in these operations. Further south they
were more effective in attacks on aircraft factories in Kent. The
production of Stirling heavy bombers was set back by the
damage, but not the more crucial Spitfire production near
Rochester. The hits on radar stations in Kent produced no
practical operation dividend and the damage to RAF fighter
stations was soon put right.

Much more crucial than the German Air Force operations of
15 August was another conference held at Karinhall, with the
usual lavish attendant hospitality and a conducted tour of
Goering's private collection of art treasures. At this 15 August
conference of senior air force officers, Goering produced his first
major sign of operational sobriety in the Battle of Britain. He
said, 'The enemy is concentrating his fighters against our Junkers
87 dive-bombers. It appears necessary to allocate three fighter
units to protect each dive-bomber unit. It will also be necessary
to escort dive-bomber units returning from air combat.'

It was a logical move to step up fighter cover for the Ju 87
squadrons, which had suffered heavy losses so far. But the
proportion of three-to-one fighter cover for them suggests that
Goering was temporarily unaware of how many twin-engine
bomber squadrons he had which also needed fighter cover, and
how few Messerschmitt squadrons he had left to afford this
cover. His dive-bomber decision if implemented would have
left something like a mere 200 to 300 fighters for a force of well
over 500 twin-engined German day bombers. Once again the
German Air Force Commander-in-Chief tended to believe his
own private dream of German air power because the reality of
its limitations was too difficult to contemplate.

At the conference of 15 August Goering also said: 'It is
doubtful whether there is any point in continuing attacks on
radar sites, in view of the fact that not one of those attacked so
far has been put out of action'. In fact, a key radar station on
the Isle of Wight had been knocked out. Perhaps Goering should
not be more than partially blamed for this defect in German

damage assessment. But it was a defect which could have been crucial in the Battle of Britain for British radar, more than anything, made economic use of RAF fighter units feasible.

There was an element of panic in Hermann Goering's further decision of that day, to prohibit more than one German officer per air crew. But if he ever felt the panic, he probably did not recognise it as such. The psychological overlay of bombast and aeronautical vanity was too thick, at this stage, to allow him to probe the realities of Adlerangriff. If he had serious misgivings, he did not yet express them fully, perhaps not even to himself.

Once more Goering stressed at this Karinhall conference that 'operations are to be directed exclusively against the enemy air forces'. In less than three weeks he was to reverse this policy fatally. Once again he repeated to his air force colleagues, 'Our night attacks are essentially dislocation raids made so that enemy defences and population shall be allowed no respite'.

From 16 August, the Luftwaffe Fifth Air Fleet in Norway was virtually out of the Battle of Britain. But its squadrons moved south to France and the Low Countries to join the major air battle fought mainly over South and South-East England.

It was clear from the first week of Adlerangriff that many of Hermann Goering's squadrons were not hitting their primary targets. Thus, in attacks between the 16 and 18 of August, hangars at Fleet Air Arm bases were destroyed at Lee-on-Solent, a number of trainer planes were burnt out at a flying training school in Oxfordshire and another Fleet Air Arm base in Sussex was bombed. But it was the key RAF Fighter Command stations like Tangmere, heavily and successfully bombed on 10 August, which should have been more persistently subjected to Luftwaffe attention. Goering's defective machinery of target intelligence, target briefing and assessment of damage could not cope with the situation. While one must perforce blame his air leadership for these vital lacunae, one must also put some of the onus on his Air Fleet commanders and his Chief-of-Staff, Hans Jeschonnek, as well as on the timid inadequacies of Major Beppo Schmid, Goering's air intelligence chief.

18 August was another day of difficult decision about the vulnerable German dive-bombers. The overall effort of 750 sorties, mainly directed against RAF fighter bases, produced a loss rate of nearly 10 per cent—in fact 71 Luftwaffe planes of

all types. On this day it was again noticed that low-level attacks were missed by the British radar screen, for example in the attack on the Kenley air base near London; Goering missed this point because he was worried by the German air losses. On that day he pulled the Ju 87 dive-bomber units out of the Battle of Britain and later moved them to Pas de Calais bases, in readiness for the air support of the invasion of Britain—Operation Sea Lion. He and his air staff also decided that low-level attacks were too costly and were to be discouraged. In the light of subsequent low-level operations in daylight by German planes in 1941, and thereafter against targets in Southern England, one feels that Goering's views on low-level attacks were hastily acquired at a time when he was tense and perhaps already beginning to be worried by the outcome of the battle. But on the surface, his ebullient confidence remained.

When he held his next major conference at Karinhall, on 19 August, he opened his statement on the Battle of Britain in this way: 'We have come to the decisive period of the air war against England'. He read out the German Air Staff's estimate of RAF losses and strength in fighter aircraft. It was wildly astray, but neither Goering nor the assembled Air Fleet commanders and other air staff officers raised any query on the figures. They were taken as read. The latest complete data were up to 16 August. Luftwaffe estimates were that, since 1 July, 770 of 900 available RAF fighters had been destroyed and 300 of them replaced, leaving about 430 fighters, of which 300 were operational and ready to go. In fact, RAF Fighter Command had more than replaced all its fighter aircraft losses in the period 1 July to 16 August.

Unfortunately one cannot always provide firm figures for the day-to-day exaggerations of both German pilot and German Air Staff claims of RAF fighter losses in the Battle of Britain. On the Luftwaffe combat forms, some British planes, claimed as shot down, are classified at 'unidentified', others are of types which simply did not fly in RAF squadrons—Curtiss Hawks and the odd Morane for example. But a really major snag, eluding the most ardent fact-finder, is the clash of figures of RAF fighters claimed destroyed between the document evidence provided by Luftwaffe Air Operations Staff and Luftwaffe Intelligence. It is hard to find out which Goering finally accepted.

In the period 1 July to 16 August both sets of figures destroyed exaggerated the six weeks total by an average of about three to one. On some days they agreed. Thus on 13 July both Operations and Intelligence claimed six Hurricanes and two Spitfires shot down (only one Hurricane was lost in combat on that day). On 8 August the common claim was 49 RAF fighters destroyed in combat (the loss that day was only 20). One of the largest gaps between claims and reality was on 13 August, when Luftwaffe claims were more than six times greater than the combat reality. Thirteen RAF fighters were lost in battle. Both Luftwaffe Operations and Intelligence Staffs claimed 88 British fighter planes destroyed, including 70 Spitfires or Hurricanes. There were isolated Luftwaffe Staff officers, e.g. Major Osterkampf, who expressed a healthy scepticism about the claims in Goering's presence. But the latter was not inclined to adjust the figures. He needed them to justify his promises of a quick victory.

And so Hermann Goering blundered on to his next mathematical problem and to the disappointment of the next few days of restricted operations through bad or uncertain weather conditions.

He against stressed that the main task of the German air squadrons was 'to inflict the maximum damage on enemy fighters' and added, 'with this are to be combined attacks on the ground organisation of enemy bombers, conducted, however, in such a manner as to avoid unnecessary losses'. Presumably Goering put emphasis on the attacks on bomber bases partly as a sop to the German Navy, which feared that the landing craft assembled for the invasion of England might be vulnerable to RAF Bomber Command assault. In fact, Goering's air squadrons rarely attacked Bomber Command bases in Britain in the next few weeks, if only because they were out of range of Messerschmitt escort capability, and at night they could not be located and attacked with any persistent degree of accuracy.

There were two further signs, at the Karinhall conference of 19 August, that Goering's optimism had been somewhat punctured. The first was his directive that 'British aircraft production must be disrupted even if single aircraft in cloudy weather are used'. The second was his complaint about 'the lack of aggression of Luftwaffe fighter units'. The reproof was in general entirely unmerited. In difficult combat conditions Luftwaffe fighter pilots had been flying with bravery, dash and skill. There were simply not enough of them, and of the Messerschmitts, to go round.

Rather late in the day, 21 August, Goering paid his first visit to the forward headquarters of the Second Air Fleet near Cape Gris Nez, where he looked at the radar masts near Dover across the Channel, enjoyed Field Marshal Kesselring's hospitality and dispensed Iron Crosses to fighter units based in the Pas de Calais area.

The period 24 August to 6 September was crucial, both for Goering and for the Commander-in-Chief of Fighter Command, Air Chief Marshal Sir Hugh Dowding. Goering's air policy during this key period was ill-conceived and erratic. His directive of 20 August to the two German Air Fleets had been clear and sane—'to continue the fight against the enemy air force until further notice'. The enemy was 'to be forced to use his fighters by means of ceaseless attacks'. The main targets were to be the aircraft industry and ground organisation. New tactics were to be devised to deceive British radar. So far so good.

But air directives, German or other, rarely take account of the difficulties of air combat. Thus, on 24 August, in good weather and in daylight, a force of some 50 German bombers jettisoned their bombs in broadcast fashion on the city of Portsmouth while groping for an aircraft factory in the area. And on the night of 24/25 August, German bombers inadvertently attacked London, though this was expressly forbidden at the time by both Hitler and Goering. This time the bombing error was to have major repercussions. The next night RAF Bomber Command attacked Berlin, using what was for them a major force of 81 twin-engined bombers. Night attacks on the German capital were again made 48 hours later.

There is little doubt that these RAF Bomber Command raids had a major effect on Goering's air policy and Hitler's hysteria at a time when the Battle of Britain hung finely in the balance. Goering's air squadrons were doing quite well at this juncture. Thus in the period 24 August to 6 September the Royal Air Force lost more fighters than the Luftwaffe. Moreover, because of pilot casualties and battle fatigue, RAF Fighter Command was subject to very great strain. At the beginning of September the margin of victory or defeat for both attackers and defenders was indeed narrow.

On 31 August, in the wake of the RAF attacks on Berlin, Goering issued a staff instruction to his two air fleets 'to prepare a daylight reprisal raid on London and to make plans for night raids'. His mind at this stage must have been in a temporary state of potential schizophrenia, for on the next day, 1 September, he issued another directive to the same two air fleets, telling them 'to destroy if possible 30 factories making aircraft, engines, propellors and other equipment'. The German Air Force reacted well to the new directive and hit a Wellington bomber factory in Surrey and a Stirling bomber plant in Kent.

It was on 3 September that Hermann Goering called perhaps his most fateful conference of the whole of the Battle of Britain. It was held at The Hague. All the German Air Force air corps and air fleet commanders attended as well as Goering's senior air staff officers, including Milch, Udet and Jeschonnek. It was to be the final review of the air situation before Sea Lion, the planned invasion of Britain. The divergence of views was so great that part of the discussion sounded almost like extracts from an aeronautical *Alice Through the Looking Glass*. While Field Marshal Sperrle thought RAF Fighter Command had 1,000 planes, a number greatly in excess of the truth, the other senior Air Fleet commander, Kesselring, thought 'they were finished as a fighting force'. The optimistic Kesselring view prevailed in Goering's confused mind. It was based rosily on a very inflated series of Luftwaffe combat and damage claims. In August, the aircraft claimed to have been shot down by the Luftwaffe outnumbered the true losses by about five to one. The German claims of RAF airfields destroyed or heavily damaged were even more widely inflated. Goering preferred optimistic mathematics to reality.

A further factor which turned Goering from his main objectives, that is Royal Air Force targets, was that on the eve of The Hague conference, Adolf Hitler had phoned Goering and given his personal blessing for the start of reprisal raids on London. Goering announced to The Hague conference and later on the radio to the German people that 'he had decided to command the assault on London personally'.

On the day that the German Air Force launched its first major daylight air attacks on London, 7 September, Goering's personal train, ASIA, was brought up from the Beauvais area to the Pas

de Calais. There he and his senior staff officers were duly photographed watching the German air armada flying overhead on
the way to London. There was another spate of the kind of
radio and press publicity that Goering loved. He rang his wife
Emmy to tell her that 'London was in flames'. He flew back to
Berlin to broadcast to the German people about the attacks on
London. Goering said: 'In this historic hour, the German Air
Force has for the first time delivered its blow right into the
enemy's heart'. He telephoned Hitler to discuss Sea Lion and
told him, 'Any day now, mein Fuehrer'. But his nurse Christa
Gormanns said that in early September Goering was in a state of
nervous exhaustion and was torn by doubts and anxieties. These,
of course, had to be hidden from Hitler and his senior air
colleagues.

Goering's surface exuberance was completely misplaced. As
Dowding, his British air opponent, had predicted, his decision
to attack London meant major relief, victory and survival for
RAF Fighter Command. The 1,147 Luftwaffe sorties flown
against London on 7 September 1940 marked the beginning of
the end of the Battle of Britain. Goering had now completely
lost control of the situation. He had forgotten his previous pre-
scriptions for achieving air superiority. It was probably now too
late for him to achieve any of the major purposes of Adlerangriff.

On 8 September he ordered that London should be bombed
over a wider area. On the same day, the German radio announced, with unwitting irony, that the Reichsmarschall had
assumed command of the operations for the first time since the
outbreak of war. It is certainly true that Hermann Goering gave
more personal and direct attention to Adlerangriff than to any
other air campaign of the Second World War; but it was now
much too late to save the situation.

Within two or three days, he seems to have lost faith in the
overriding importance of the air attacks on London. Thus, on
9 September, he said in an air directive, 'Along with major
attacks on London, raids will be carried out as far as possible
on many sectors of the armaments industry and harbour areas
of England'. Obviously Goering was not a believer in the vital
strategic dictum about maintaining the aim.

The effect of the German bombing of London was modest in
terms of damage to civilian morale or buildings, compared with

IX.   Hitler and Goering in Berlin, October 1939

H.M.S. _____ (with his Staff) looking towards England, January 1940 the value of the important respite it gave to RAF fighter airfields. Goering of course refused to recognise this. He preferred to believe highly-coloured intelligence reports such as the one from the German military attaché in Washington who stated: 'The morale of the British population is strongly affected. Signs of great weariness. Optimism has disappeared. Effect on the heart of London resembles an earthquake'. Goering must have enjoyed the earthquake and swallowed it whole.

As late as 14 September, Goering had been able to maintain the illusion that victory was still round the corner. On that day he sent his Chief-of-Staff Hans Jeschonnek to stand in for him at a German Chiefs of Staff lunch given by Hitler. At that lunch the German Fuehrer said: 'The accomplishments of the Air Force are beyond praise. With four or five days of good weather a decisive result will be achieved'. The Goering formula of four or five days for basic victory died hard.

The next day was crucial in Goering's air career, though no doubt he was unwilling to recognise it at the time. On 15 September his Luftwaffe received a rough handling which virtually decided Hitler to put off the invasion altogether. That Royal Air Force claims on that day were inflated by three to one (185 claimed shot down against a real loss of about 60) did not matter. Official German air reports of the day referred to 'large air battles and great losses for the German formations'. The Luftwaffe effort of about 1,000 fighter and 320 bomber sorties was officially described by Goering as 'unusually disadvantageous'. Within a day or so, on the evening of 17 September, Hitler decided to postpone Sea Lion and for all practical purposes the Battle of Britain was over, though some chroniclers take it on through the night blitz on Britain to the spring or early summer of 1941.

Goering had been out of touch with reality as an air leader during Adlerangriff. This can be illustrated in many ways, not least by the 16 September conference held in his headquarters train near Boulogne. Once again the Air Fleet and Air Corps commanders were invited to give a review of the situation. One would have imagined that, so soon after the great air battle of 15 September, some permanent dose of realism would have been injected into Hermann Goering's veins. But the euphoria and the morphia remained. Goering said: 'In line with our estimate of

H

the enemy, it follows that we should keep at him with all our means, as, with four to five more days of heavy losses, he ought to be finished off'. The legend of four to five days persisted to the end. Goering promised his air colleagues fresh tactics, but the text of the meeting shows nothing new, except Goering's significant agreement that his squadrons in France and the Netherlands should begin to build winter quarters.

Although Goering's air squadrons had days of successful sorties later in September against aircraft factories near Bristol and Southampton, the Commander-in-Chief knew that the game was over and the Battle of Britain was lost. When the war was over and Goering was a prisoner-of-war, he told his US captors that the Battle of Britain was the turning point of the 1939-1945 war. But at the time of the battle he seemed entirely unaware of this.

On 20 September Hermann Goering left France for his hunting lodge at Rominten in East Prussia. There he shed his air force uniform and put on the silk blouse and green suede jacket which he wore as the Chief Hunter of the Third Reich (*Reichsjaegermeister*). He received some of his ace pilots, like Moelders and Galland, and hunted stags with them. Further bad news of the air battles came in. Perhaps, away from it all, Hermann Goering knew that he had underestimated his British opponents and their aircraft industry. But there is nothing to suggest that he realised at this stage that much worse was to follow. 1941 was to be a bad year for the direction of the Luftwaffe.

CHAPTER SIX

Multi-Front Problems

HERMANN GOERING could not, in September 1940, confess that the failure of Adlerangriff had been a personal strategic setback of the first water for his air leadership. To bolster the illusion that all was well, he issued this resounding order of the day to all Luftwaffe air crews, on 18 October 1940: 'German airmen, comrades. You have, above all in the last few days and nights, caused the British world enemy disastrous losses by uninterrupted, decisive blows. Your tireless, courageous attacks on the heart of the British Empire, the City of London, with its eight and a half million inhabitants, have reduced British plutocracy to fear and terror. The losses which you have inflicted on the much-vaunted Royal Air Force in determined fighter engagements are irreplaceable.'

This was a vintage Goering communiqué designed to boost morale in German Air Force units. However, in the night bomber blitz on Britain, the German aircraft crash rate was going up. In a despatch of 12 October to his air chiefs, Goering wrote: 'There have been many accidents in Luftwaffe night bomber landings'. But the Reichsmarschall was prepared to accept these losses, though their military purpose was not always very clear. On 20 October he issued an explanatory directive to his air commanders in France, Holland and Belgium, which ran: 'The purpose of these attacks is to destroy civilian life . . . 150 bombers of the Third Air Fleet have as their target the population of London'.

The directive also went on to give bombing orders to the squadrons of the Italian Air Force, now operating from Belgian air bases under the command of Goering's Second Air Fleet. They were to attack RAF night fighter bases and other targets near the English coast.

By the end of October 1940, Goering's use of German air power on the Western Front was becoming blunt and defensive. His Junkers and Heinkel twin-engined bombers were no longer attacking targets in daylight; Me 109 fighters, which used to escort these bombers in daylight attacks, were now being used as fighter-bombers. But their bomb-sights were crude and the results they achieved were poor. Me 110 squadrons, which had bombed Britain, were now being pulled back to bases in Western Germany and Holland and used as night-fighters to meet the threat of RAF Bomber Command night attacks. By December 1940 the German air attack on Britain was becoming little more than a sideshow in Goering's future air accountancy. Before the end of 1940 the Reichsmarschall had to begin planning seriously for new air campaigns in the Mediterranean and on the Eastern Front.

At his trial at Nuremberg in 1946, Goering testified that 'he was deeply troubled about the war with Russia, and that he was told nothing about it until he visited Hitler in Berchtesgaden in November 1940'. He must have forgotten that Adolf Hitler had sent for him on 14 August 1940. When Goering arrived at Hitler's Berlin Chancellery on that day, the Fuehrer asked him to stop deliveries of goods to the USSR by the spring of 1941. Hitler also requested Goering to make plans for the future administration of the USSR by the Third Reich, and to bring Luftwaffe target intelligence up to date by a new survey of Soviet industry and oil centres.

The memory of a man on trial for his life is apt to be erratic, and six years later, at the Nuremberg trials, Goering might well have had only a dim recollection of his other discussions of the period July to October 1940 with his air chiefs. Then he had conferred with Udet, Jeschonnek and Milch about forward planning for the air attacks on the USSR, and by the end of October 1940 Goering had issued instructions to expand German Air Force airfield and radio communication facilities in Western Poland, East Prussia, Northern Norway and Finland. The preliminary air moves for the German attack on the USSR were already in train by November 1940.

By the end of December 1940 Goering knew that his future air plans had to meet the needs of two new major air campaigns in 1941. In addition, he had to stiffen the night-fighter and anti-aircraft defences of Germany to balance the growing threat of RAF Bomber Command attacks.

Goering was enthusiastic about the new strategy in the Mediterranean. In September 1940 he had discussed with Admiral Raeder, head of the German Navy, ways and means of drafting a planning note for Hitler. At the end of the month it was sent to the Fuehrer. It said: 'The British have always considered the Mediterranean to be the pivot of their empire. Italy, surrounded by British power, is fast becoming the main target of the attack. For this reason the Mediterranean must be cleared up during the coming winter months.' Adolf Hitler needed little prompting to intervene in the Mediterranean, as the military fortunes of Italy deteriorated. On 13 December 1940, the Fuehrer issued a new directive for a German invasion of Greece, code-named 'Marita'. On 18 December he ordered Goering to set up German Air Force units of fighters, bombers and dive-bombers at air bases in Sicily for operations against Malta. Goering despatched his Tenth Air Corps to Sicily from Norway and Denmark. To bring its strength up to 350 planes, he had to draw on front line squadrons in France and Belgium. In the period October to December 1940 Goering was also building up his Fourth Air Fleet in Rumania, Hungary and Bulgaria to meet the commitment of Operation Marita, the planned attack on Greece.

On 18 December 1940, the day on which the Fuehrer had asked Goering to set up a new strike force in Sicily, Hitler issued a top secret directive for the attack on the USSR, now to be code-named 'Operation Barbarossa'. 'Preparations are to be completed by 15 May 1941,' said the text, and added, 'The German armed forces must be prepared to crush Soviet Russia in a quick campaign before the end of the war against England'.

And so on one day, 18 December 1940, it was impressed on Goering that his air force must now provide for the battle needs of the great new campaigns in the south and in the east. His failure to act quickly to meet these needs adequately showed a monumental unawareness of what the new 1941 air commitments might mean. Goering seems to have had a mental mechanism which substituted aviation molehills for the reality of mountains. His ebullient, brash optimism remained undiminished at the turn of 1940-1941.

He was still giving Hitler fulsome promises of easy victories. Thus at a two-day Council of War conference, held at Berchtesgaden on 8 and 9 January 1941, Goering agreed the German Chiefs of Staff view that 'Barbarossa would lead to the defeat of the USSR in about six weeks' and that the 'Mediterranean campaign could be ended in a few months'. At the conference, Goering spoke at length and optimistically about the Battle of the Atlantic. He told the Chiefs of Staff : 'By July or August 1941, German naval and air attacks on British shipping will lead to victory by cutting off supplies'. He was still master of the easy definitive statement.

At this stage of the war the relationship between Hitler and Goering was still very warm and close. At Christmas 1940 the two men had paid a joint visit to German Air Force units in France and Belgium. All was merry and bright. It was in 1941 that the shadows began to fall between them.

Perhaps the greatest failure of Hermann Goering's air leadership in the Second World War was his ineffectiveness in meeting the planning needs of the new air campaigns of 1941, and thereafter. His failure to expand German Air Force front-line strength and German aircraft output to any appreciable extent, is one of the most puzzling aspects of his air career. By the late summer of 1941 it must have been clear that the German Chiefs of Staffs' predicted programme of short victorious campaigns was behind the clock; Goering himself had doubts about the outcome of the attack on the USSR before it began.

German aircraft production statistics for 1940 and 1941 speak loudly for Goering's operational euphoria. In 1940 the industry produced 10,247 planes, in 1941 the figure rose to 12,401, and in 1942 to only 15,556. Then both the USSR and USA were in the war. Of course, Milch, Udet and Jeschonnek, Goering's three senior air aides, must share some of the blame for the failure to expand sufficiently and to meet the needs of training, general aircraft wastage and equipping and creating new squadrons; but it was Goering who then personally approved the aircraft production programmes, which were thereby subject to his whims and idiosyncrasies. One of Goering's faults was an inability to establish friendly relations between the technical department of his Air Ministry and Germany's aircraft designers and technicians. It was a crucial hiatus. When Albert Speer extended his influence on German aircraft production in 1943 and 1944, things took a turn for the better. By then it was too late.

Not that Goering was indifferent to the 1941 problems and responsibilties of the German aircraft industry. In that year, as the records show, he was personally concerned with the increase in supplies of aluminium from France, Switzerland and Norway, and in the development of aircraft production facilities in Holland, Belgium, Czechoslovakia and Poland. But he entirely ignored the potential of the Heinkel and Messerschmitt jet fighters, which had already flown. Indeed, new prototypes were being built at the Heinkel plant at Rostock and the Messerschmitt plant at Augsburg by the summer of 1941. It is true that the new and faster Focke-Wulf 190 fighter and fighter-bomber came into German Air Force units at this time; but the small increase in the production of German aircraft in 1941 was entirely inadequate for the greatly expanding operational needs, both in the Mediterranean and on the Eastern Front.

There is a touch of historic irony about the date on which Goering issued to his air staff a 'Special decree to restore the supremacy of the Luftwaffe'. It was on 22 June 1941, the day on which Hitler's Wehrmacht launched its attack on the USSR. Goering, who was in Berlin, declared, 'All measures required are to be taken to increase the performance of the aircraft industry, so that the objective can be reached in all circumstances. The High Command of the Wehrmacht has agreed that the necessary orders be given. The Reichsmarschall, as Chief of the Four Year Plan, agrees to the ordering of raw materials and power resources to be put in train.' But the measures called for were never taken. The phrase 'too little and too late' aptly describes what became known as 'The Goering Programme' in the files of the German Air Ministry. Until the full impact of Albert Speer's stewardship on Germany's aircraft production was felt in 1944, Goering's attempts to expand and reform had relatively little success. His mind was all too often elsewhere. Aircraft production was only a minor item among Goering's professional interests.

When Goering's Air Force opened its air blitz on France, Belgium and Holland, on 10 May 1940, it had a total operational strength of about 5,000 planes. This figure included the units of floatplanes, flying boats and Junkers transport planes.

And German Air Ministry records show that on 22 June 1941, the Luftwaffe's operational strength was again about 5,000 planes. There were differences in the strength of some of the aircraft categories and the number of reserve planes had increased slightly compared with the previous year.

Three aircraft categories had increased in strength. First and inevitably, the twin-engined night-fighter units, commanded by General Josef Kammhuber. These formed the main aircraft equipment of the new Air Defence Command of Germany, Luftflotte Reich. Between the summer of 1940 and the summer of 1941 there were also increases in air transport squadrons and in reconnaissance units. These Goering intended to meet the expanding requirements of mobility and operational intelligence on the new air fronts. But the expansions were offset by reductions in Goering's single-engine fighter and fighter-bomber units, and in his twin-engined bomber squadrons.

Goering's philosophy of air leadership—that attack is the best form of defence—was gradually sliding to ruin. The realities of 1941 were forcibly altering his path of leadership towards new concepts. He clung to a belief in bigger and better bombers. However, his latter-day attempts to produce a force of strategic heavy assault aircraft suffered from a mixture of bad luck and bad management. Thus the four-engined Heinkel bomber, the He 177, ran into a clutch of technical teething troubles. The Focke-Wulf 200 four-engined bomber, a major requirement for Goering's contribution to the Battle of the Atlantic, was produced in limited numbers of less than half a dozen a month, in part because the Focke-Wulf firm was committed to increasing its output of fighters from July 1941 onwards. The new twin-engined Me 210, which Goering hoped to use as a new tactical bomber, had trouble in 1941 with both its electrical and hydraulic equipment.

In Britain, there was a top-level divergence of view about Goering's ability and intention to expand the German Air Force in 1941. In his *War Memoirs* Sir Winston Churchill records that on 2 December 1940 he sent this note to his Chief of Air Staff, Air Chief Marshal Sir Charles Portal: 'One cannot doubt that the Germans will be making tremendous efforts to increase their air force this winter, and that a far more serious attempt must be expected against us in the spring. I would be glad if your

Intelligence Branch would let me have a paper—not more than two or three sheets—upon this matter; and it would be convenient if they could keep in touch with Professor Lindemann, while they are preparing this.'

When the raw data on Goering and the German Air Force had been examined, there was a wide divergence of view between Air Intelligence and Professor Lindemann, who was Churchill's adviser in this matter. Lindemann had his own intelligence methods, based largely on personal interrogation of Luftwaffe prisoners-of-war in Britain. But he was not well versed in the necessary techniques. In the event he failed to carry his conviction as far as he hoped. Churchill did not accept his view that Luftwaffe operational strength would double and perhaps treble by the end of 1941. Air Intelligence had already taken note of the reckless element of Goering's air leadership in previous years. There was his failure to provide adequate aircraft reserves, the blind undiscerning belief that he could win the Battle of Britain's first stage within a few days, and his failure to profit from the lessons of Dunkirk. We could scarcely see how a new strategic logic could be born in his mind from the elements of manic disorder noted in the past.

Winston Churchill asked Mr Justice Singleton to adjudicate. It was a fascinating experience to appear before the learned judge. After pooling the evidence and considering the rival views, he was inclined to think that the estimate of Air Intelligence— that the German Air Force would increase in operational strength to only a minor extent in 1941—was probably closer to the truth. For me Mr Justice Singleton's enquiry had happy consequences. Our intelligence unit was called on to provide daily appreciations on Goering and his Air Force direct to Winston Churchill. I later had the joy of briefing Winston Churchill personally on German Air Force matters. He would tease me with the question, 'And how is your friend Mr Goering today?'

In terms of German Air Force leadership, one never knew how to assess Goering from day to day. He could be engaged in so many other things entirely divorced from aeronautical problems. As a result, according to Milch, Bodenschatz, Koller and others, he was acquiring the habit of signing major air documents without reading them, and leaving important Luftwaffe signals, addressed to him, unanswered for weeks. His diversions were a mixture of business and private pleasure. Goering was still an active diplomat on behalf of Hitler, and as Head of the Four Year Economic Plan had to take executive action on many questions dealing with the use of manpower and raw materials. What was really unforgiveable was the undue time he spent on fostering his private collection of paintings, statues and antiques. He must have had more important things to do for the Third Reich, on 5 November 1940, than to issue a decree on the subject of 'ownerless Jewish art collections' in France, Belgium and Holland. And on 21 November 1940, he wrote personally and at length to a Dutch art dealer about the purchase of a Van Dyck portrait. Goering went so far as to detail a squadron of Ju 52 transport planes to bring back his pictures and *objets d'art* from the galleries of France and the Low Countries. He is known to have paid at least twenty visits to the art galleries of Paris in the period 1940-1943. Some of them lasted a week and some two or three days. Sometimes Goering would stay at the Ritz Hotel in Paris and sometimes he would use his headquarters train ASIA. His valet Robert and his nurse Christa usually went with him and he also had his own *cordon bleu* cook. Goering usually combined his art interests with a visit to the headquarters of his Third Air Fleet in Paris. He would talk to Air Marshal Sperrle about the needs and problems of the air war in the west.

The main diversion from Goering's job as Commander-in-Chief of the German Air Force was undoubtedly his duties as Chief Plenipotentiary of the German Four Year Economic Plan. He tended to drive hard and astute bargains with German manufacturers. He could be a down-to-earth practical business man. This contrasted with his generosity in many aspects of his private affairs and his bouts of casual indifference in some phases of his air leadership.

In April 1941 Hitler extended the area of Goering's economic interests. He had appointed Alfred Rosenberg Commissioner for the East European Region, as part of the forward planning for Operation Barbarossa. He asked Goering to plan with Rosenberg the economic exploitation of Soviet Russia. There was friction between these two Nazi leaders about the best way to exploit Soviet manpower, food and raw materials. In terms of Luftwaffe needs, it was a further diversionary bout of wasted time and energy. In April 1941 German air problems in North Africa were already becoming serious; but Goering was intent on playing a major role in the ruthless exploitation of the wealth of the USSR.

And so, in the period April to July 1941, he worked with his staff of economists on the planned seizure of Soviet assets. In a report of 23 May 1941, signed by Goering, it was stated that 'Many people will become redundant and will either die or have to emigrate to Siberia'. Later in July he reported to the German Chiefs of Staff, 'The war can only be continued if all the armed forces are fed by Russia in the third year of the war. There is no doubt that, as a result, many people will be starved to death if we take out of the country the things we need'. Goering went on to propose that the population of Moscow and Leningrad be dispersed or left to starve.

Goering's commitments to the developing German Four Year Plan were more than sufficient to affect adversely his capacity to lead the Luftwaffe at a time of growing air problems and potential crisis. But this was not all. Adolf Hitler also saw fit to make use of Goering in the dual role of strategist and diplomat to explain Germany's war aims and prospects. In particular the Fuehrer saw Goering as an important link between Berlin and Rome.

At a two-day conference at Hitler's Berghof, on 19 and 20 January 1941, Mussolini and his Foreign Secretary, Count Ciano, were present with the German and Italian Chiefs of Staff. The main theme was Axis strategy in the Mediterranean and on the Russian fronts. Goering beamed and approved when his Fuehrer said: 'I don't see any great danger coming from America, even if she should enter the war. The much greater danger is the gigantic block of Russia'.

Hitler subsequently sent Goering on a number of missions to Rome, partly for diplomatic purposes and partly for reasons of military strategy. When on 10 August 1941 Rudolf Hess flew to Scotland from Augsburg, 'on a mission of humanity' and to explain that the Fuehrer did not want to defeat England and wished to stop the fighting, Goering was despatched by the Fuehrer to Rome to explain away the Hess *démarche* to Mussolini and Ciano. In conference at the Palazzo Venezia, with the two Italian leaders, Goering said, 'We were amazed when the news reached us. It is the action of a madman. Hess has been suffering from a disease of the gall bladder'. Goering added that he was glad to be back in diplomacy and invited Ciano to attend a grand diplomatic reception in Berlin.

In the previous month of April, Goering had had a number of talks with the Japanese Foreign Secretary, Matsuoka, who was paying a long visit to Berlin. Goering entertained him lavishly at Karinhall on four or five occasions during the month. Goering spoke with arrogant confidence about the outcome of the German attack on the USSR. He decried the capacity of the United states aircraft industry. He told the Japanese Foreign Secretary what he had told Erhard Milch and other German air leaders: 'The Americans can make Fords and Chevrolets but they cannot build aircraft'. This was typical of Goering's deliberate blindness. He had had a series of hard intelligence reports in the previous months to show that the US aircraft industry was expanding and modernising rapidly.

It was in the Mediterranean operations of 1941 that the hard signs first emerged of the limitations of German air power, and therefore of Goering's air leadership potential. True there were blitzkrieg successes in Jugoslavia, Greece and Crete; but over Malta and the Central Mediterranean, in North Africa and the Eastern Mediterranean, the deficiencies and shortages were soon apparent. The qualities and courage of German air crews were in contrast, first-rate.

When Goering switched his Tenth Air Corps from Denmark and Norway to Sicily at the end of 1940, he told them that their first priority was 'the eliminating of Malta as an air and naval base'. He was at the time also conferring with General Student, the commander of his airborne forces, about a plan for an attack on Malta by German parachutists. The Luftwaffe attacks on Malta and on British shipping in the Central Mediterranean began with a successful flourish in January 1941. German bombers and dive-bombers helped to sink the British cruiser *Southampton,* and damaged the aircraft carrier *Illustrious.* But it was significant that in the first attacks on Malta's docks and air bases, German Ju 87 and Ju 88 bombers were often escorted by Italian Macchi and Fiat fighter squadrons. An even more trenchant illustration of the limits of the Luftwaffe was Goering's decision, in the first week of February 1941, to strip General Geissler, the Tenth Air Corps Commander, of half his Sicilian based air squadrons and transfer them to the new North African Air Command of General Froehlich (Fliegerfuehrer Afrika). Froehlich's desert air force then had a strength of about 200 planes. Its Ju 87 dive-bombers were also to be escorted by Italian fighters. Both Geissler and Froehlich signalled the German Air Ministry in Berlin for fighter reinforcements. In the middle of March 1941 a further 50 Me 109's reached Sicily.

Rommel was the first German general of the Second World War to conduct an important land campaign for Hitler without adequate tactical air support. Froehlich commanded a Desert Air Force of about 200 planes or less to support Rommel's ground operations, during most of 1941, in Tripolitania and Libya. He needed more fighters to cover his vulnerable dive-bomber units and more transport planes to meet the needs of the rapid advances or retreats which occur in desert warfare. Rommel was a quick mover of ground forces.

And so even before Operation Barbarossa the inadequacies of Germany's air resources were becoming apparent. But Goering had fresh blitzkrieg successes in the spring of 1941. Rommel's air requirements in North Africa became of secondary interest in German Mediterranean affairs. Operation Marita, the attack on Greece, was imminent. Goering was present at the final planning conference for it, held at Hitler's Chancellery in Berlin on 27 March 1941.

The original date of Operation Marita, 26 March, had been changed to 6 April. This was because the overthrow of the pro-German Prince Paul of Jugoslavia and the accession of young Peter to the throne, had, said Hitler 'endangered Barbarossa'. The Fuehrer then announced that Barbarossa would 'have to be postponed for up to four weeks' and he ordered Goering 'to destroy Belgrade in attacks by waves of bombers'. The Luftwaffe Commander-in-Chief nodded his assent and outlined his plans for the rapid reinforcement of his air forces in Austria, Hungary, Rumania and Bulgaria in the next week or so.

In the fortnight which preceded the German Air Force attacks on Jugoslavia and Greece, Hermann Goering produced a burst of vigorous leadership. He knew that air opposition in the coming campaigns would be very modest; in the case of Jugoslavia, it was almost non-existent. The positive note in

Goering's air leadership revived. He had not yet conferred personally with either General Geissler in Sicily or General Froehlich in Africa. But he was now in close, almost daily touch with General Loehr, the Austrian commander of the German Fourth Air Fleet, entrusted with the air attacks on Greece and Jugoslavia. In the fortnight before 6 April 1941, German air units based in the Balkans doubled their strength from about 500 to 1,000 planes; in addition air transport units were strengthened.

In his *War Memoirs* Sir Winston Churchill reports that the Royal Air Force in Greece totalled seven squadrons with a strength of 80 planes. In opposition to them was Goering's force of about 500 tactical support planes of which the spearhead was the Eighth Air Corps, commanded by General von Richthofen. And when the further force of 500 aircraft used against Jugoslavia were no longer required, some of the units were switched to the attack on Greece before the end of April.

During the preparatory period of Operation Marita, there was little to suggest that Hermann Goering was hatching a serious plot for an airborne attack on Crete. Thus his main discussions with General Student in the period December 1940 to January 1941 had been about a plan for an airborne attack on Malta. But by mid-April, a German airborne attack on Crete seemed likely. The fighting on the ground in Greece was virtually over. German air units were already based in Central Greece and Goering had switched some of his squadrons from attacks on ground targets in Greece to an air assault on British shipping in the Central Mediterranean.

On 18 April 1940, Winston Churchill signalled to General Wilson, his Middle East Commander, 'Crete's defenders should use bayonets against parachutist or airborne troops if necessary'. At the time, Hermann Goering was at the Air Ministry in Berlin, exchanging views with Generals Student, Loehr and Richthofen on the air resources needed for 'Operation Merkur', the code name given to the combined attack on Crete. The air resources committed to the operation consisted of just under 500 Ju 52 transport planes, some of these borrowed from Lufthansa civil airlines; the Eighth Air Corps was strengthened to a force of about 400 bombers, some 250 fighters and 40 reconnaissance planes.

Was the victory in Crete, in the ten days from 21 May to

31 May, 'Goering's prodigious air achievement' as Sir Winston Churchill dubbed it in his *Memoirs*? Surely not. The joint Hitler and Goering directive for Operation Merkur said the objective was 'to use Crete as an air base in the Eastern Mediterranean'. But in the event, Goering could only afford to base substantial air forces on Crete for very limited periods. Moreover the war diary of Student's Eleventh Air Corps, the operational field command for German airborne operations, summed up the Crete airborne operations as follows: 'There was a failure, owing to lack of information, to appreciate the enemy situation, which endangered the attack of the Eleventh Air Corps and resulted in exceptionally high and bloody losses'. Nearly 5,000 soldiers of the airborne Eleventh Air Corps were killed in the ten days from 21 May to 31 May 1970 of the 15,000 engaged. 52 transport planes were destroyed or heavily damaged.

Perhaps the worst effect of the Crete operations was the strain imposed on the overworked German Eighth Air Corps, particularly in view of its fairly imminent commitment to Operation Barbarossa. After seven weeks of intensive air operations over Jugoslavia, Greece, Crete and the Central Mediterranean, the squadrons needed much more than the three weeks available to rest, refit and transfer to new bases in preparation for the attack on the USSR. They had had notable anti-shipping successes in May, including the sinking of the British destroyer *Juno*, and the damaging of four British cruisers. They also hit the battleship *Warspite*.

In the period April to June 1941 Goering made no personal visits to any of his air units at their bases in the Balkans, Greece, Sicily or North Africa. He had become very worried about the prospect of German success in Operation Barbarossa. After much desperate thinking, he took his courage in both hands and went to see Hitler on 9 May 1941, at the Fuehrer's Chancellery in Berlin. He expressed grave doubts about the outcome of the planned attack on the Soviet Union. 'Germany will be taking a great risk in waging war on two fronts', said Goering, and added, '*Mein Kampf* has stressed this danger'. Hitler retorted with angry emphasis, 'There will be no war on two fronts. The Atlantic Wall will protect us in the west while we quickly conquer Russia.' Then the Fuehrer added trenchantly, 'The Luftwaffe will receive my instructions'.

It may well be that Hermann Goering's *démarche* of 9 May 1941 was rooted in a discussion he had had with Ernst Udet a month before in Paris. On 10 April 1941 Goering had visited the French capital, partly to see Herr Rosenberg about some new French art treasures, partly to discuss the air problems of the Western Front with Sperrle, Commander of the Third Air Fleet, and with Udet, his highly intelligent aircraft production chief. At this stage, the forthcoming war with Russia was, inevitably, a major topic of conversation at German Chiefs of Staff level. Goering encouraged his colleagues to express their views freely. He said to them, 'I cannot accept the Fuehrer's view that the USSR plans to attack Germany'. This had long been one of Hitler's strategic excuses for Barbarossa. Ernst Udet, who predicted disaster for Barbarossa, replied, 'You simply must prevent this war. Go and talk to the Fuehrer'. And so Goering did.

However, when Ernst Udet sent Goering a German air intelligence report dated 5 May 1941, showing major increases in Soviet aircraft production, the Reichsmarschall replied, 'I do not believe these figures'. In fact this report may have prompted him to see Hitler at his Berlin Chancellery four days later.

Goering's Jekyll and Hyde approach to Barbarossa was illustrated on the next day. He read a report by Colonel Wodag, his air intelligence chief, which dealt with the current strength of the Soviet Air Force. Based on extensive wireless listening data, it gave an estimated force of about 14,000 operational planes. Goering sent for Wodag and gave him a roasting. He tore the report in two and said angrily, 'Take this, Herr Oberst. The Soviet Air Force strength has been halved. The figure is now seven thousand planes'.

On 14 June 1941 Goering attended an important Chiefs of Staff meeting at Hitler's Berlin Chancellery. The air fleet and army commanders were also present. Barbarossa was of course the main subject of the discussion, which went on all day. Goering said very little. He summed up, 'The German Air Force will fulfil all its tasks'. The die of his future air leadership was now cast. It was too late to turn back.

The Wehrmacht attacked the Soviet Union on 22 June 1941. It made fantastically rapid advances of armour and infantry in the first three months of the campaign. But long before that three months was over the Luftwaffe showed that it was being

Preis **20** Pfg.

5. Dezember 1940

Nummer 49 / 15. Jahr

Druck und Verlag von J
DuMont Schauberg, K

Kölnis e

lustrierte Zeitung

XI.   Hitler and Goering at the French Capitulation, December 1940

XII. Last-minute Instructions to Aircrew, September 1940

XIII. Goering with Luftwaffe Aircrew on his Birthday

stretched well beyond its capacity. Hitler had established his
heaquarters at Rastenburg, in East Prussia. Goering set up an
eastern air headquarters close by, near his East Prussian hunting
lodge at Rominten. For the first week or so, Goering remained
quietly at Karinhall. For the most part he issued orders about
the support of the German armies and congratulated his air
units on their initial successes, which were considerable.

Goering had allocated four of his five air fleets to Operation
Barbarossa, including part of the weak Fifth Air Fleet based in
Norway. The combined Luftwaffe strength for Barbarossa in
June 1941 was about 3,200 planes. It broke down into about
1,000 twin-engined bombers, 300 dive-bombers, 800 single-
engined fighters, 500 reconnaissance planes, 500 transport aircraft and 120 twin-engined fighters. All the five tactical air
corps available were thrown into the battle. Only small air
forces were left to cope with the air problems of the Western
Front and the Mediterranean. The blitzes on Britain and on
Malta were virtually abandoned for the time being.

There is no evidence available to show that Goering and his
air staff appreciated in advance the radical differences between
the tactical support of German armies in the Western campaigns
of 1939 and 1940 and in the Russian war of 1941. In Flanders,
Poland and France the density of Luftwaffe air support was at
least six times as great as in the Barbarossa operations. Within
two or three months the flying was spread out along a front of
1,500 to 2,000 miles. The distance factor also affected the air
supply of bombs, fuel and ammunition and placed a very heavy
burden on Goering's air transport resources. But he still hoped
for a blitzkrieg air success. The initial reports from the Air Fleet
commanders were optimistic. Thousands of Soviet planes were
claimed destroyed on the ground or in the air. The information
may not have been accurate but it was cheerful. And the
advance of the German Army was remarkable. By the third week
in July, Hitler's ground forces had reached Pskov in the north,
Smolensk in the centre and the river Dniester in the south.

But already, in July, Goering's Air Force in the east was
beginning to feel the pinch. After due consultation with Hitler,
Goering ordered the first bombing raids on Moscow to begin on
21 July. To raise a force of 200 bombers for the air assault on
the Soviet capital, he had to pull out 100 Heinkel twin-engined

I

bombers from France. And, within a week, the Luftwaffe raiding
force had to be reduced to about fifty Junkers and Heinkel
bombers. Most of the squadrons had to be diverted to give
tactical support to the German armies now planning fresh drives
towards Moscow and Leningrad, named as the two great
strategic targets in the original Barbarossa plan.

Before the end of July, the Soviet Air Force was counter-
attacking on the Leningrad, Smolensk and Ukraine fronts. There
had been extensive reinforcements from Soviet air regiments in
the Far East. Goering was now getting signals from German
Army commanders asking for more fighter cover for their ground
forces. He was unable to help. He was already short of fighters
on other fronts, for example in North Africa, France and in
Sicily. And in that same month of July German Air Force
commanders on the Eastern Front were sending urgent signals
to Goering's air headquarters, at Rominten in East Prussia,
asking desperately for up-to-date estimates of Soviet Air Force
strength. They also signalled to other German air commanders
in the East asking for evidence of the movements of Soviet air
regiments along the Eastern Front.

Goering put his worried head in the sand and sent an ostrich
reply: 'The air strength of Soviet air units must not be exaggerated. The German Army must be given maximum support.
If necessary, close support units must fly up to six missions a
day.'

In August, Barbarossa air problems became more acute.
General von Loeb asked urgently for more air support for the
drive of his ground forces to Leningrad. Goering went to consult
with Hitler at his Rastenburg headquarters on 7 August. A week
later, he ordered his crack close-support Eighth Air Corps to pull
out of the Ukraine and switch to the Leningrad front. The move
left the German Air Force on the Ukraine front in a very weak
position. Von Loeb's attack on Leningrad fell short of victory.
Goering and Hitler conferred again at Rastenburg in September.
They decided to pull out the Eighth Air Corps in readiness for
the autumn assault on Moscow. This decision came into force
on 24 September 1941.

By then, Goering's past air leadership mistakes were beginning
to produce noticeable cracks in the battle effectiveness of the
German Air Force. Squadrons were below strength because of

a shortage of replacement aircraft, tired crews meant inaccurate attacks in many instances and it was difficult to get aircraft spares to maintain serviceability. Goering's air support for Barbarossa was becoming frayed. He was rapidly losing the air initiative in the East.

At another Rastenburg conference on 24 September, Hitler asked Goering to throw in fresh units of the Luftwaffe for what was intended to be the final autumn air assault on Moscow. Goering replied: 'I have no reserve units'. Hitler then asked: 'What forces have you for the Moscow attack?' Goering answered: '1,500 planes'.

By drawing heavily on the air units engaged on the Leningrad and Ukraine fronts, Goering was able to raise the promised force. But he had to rob Peter to pay Paul. While Goering remained the full-blooded personality that he was during the Moscow attacks, his Air Force in the East was becoming anaemic. German pilots gave of their skilful, heroic best. Their operational commitments were, however, much too great.

Goering had believed that Operation Barbarossa would be over in three or four months at the most. And so he and his Air Force were quite unprepared for the difficulties of winter flying which were soon to be encountered. But long before he had to deal with the difficulties of operations and maintenance in the severity of a Russian winter, Goering must have realised that he had a basic overall problem of aircraft supply on his hands.

On 27 August, Ernst Udet had gone to see Goering at Karinhall. He told his old friend and Commander-in-Chief: 'I wish to resign. We cannot meet the problems of supplying aircraft for Barbarossa'. Goering replied paternally to his aircraft production chief, 'You need a few weeks' rest'. When Udet got back to his Berlin office, at the end of September, the news about Barbarossa and aircraft supply on the Eastern Front was blacker. On 17 November 1941 Ernst Udet committed suicide. A few days later General Moelders, in charge of the Luftwaffe's fighter arm, was killed in an air crash. Goering chose Adolf Galland to succeed him. It was an excellent choice. Milch took over Udet's aircraft production responsibilities, this too a good move.

Goering's tribute to Ernst Udet at his Berlin funeral, three days after his suicide, was made with genuine sadness. He said: 'By your wartime operations you gave our brave young pilots confidence in their weapons, for what you conceived and flew they took for granted. You must have been very proud when I was able to say that our aircraft, which were the best, would always remain so, thanks to your work'. It was of course a funeral panegyric.

The day after Udet's funeral, Hermann Goering went to Paris and stayed for a week at the Ritz Hotel. Ostensibly he went to see Marshal Pétain, and to visit the Third Air Fleet headquarters. But he also did some extensive Christmas shopping and gave furious thought to the problems of the Luftwaffe. He told the aged French Marshal, 'You must be more energetic in defending your colonies against the British'. Pétain tried to hand Goering a memorandum asking for more forces and war material to do this. Goering refused to read it, but Pétain managed to stuff it into the Reichsmarschall's pocket as he left. To Field Marshal Hugo Sperrle, the Commander of the Third Air Fleet, Goering offered lavish hospitality but less lavish promises of air reinforcements for the moribund air assaults on Britain.

Perhaps Goering went to Paris in November 1941 to convince himself that he still had the nerve to travel west when the immediate crisis was in the east. On his return from Paris he went once more to see Hitler at Rastenburg on 30 November. They agreed that the Second Air Fleet, commanded by Field Marshal Kesselring should be transferred from the Eastern Front to the Mediterranean in order to resume the attack on Malta and to bolster Rommel's forces in North Africa.

With the departure of Kesselring's Air Fleet to the Mediterranean, Goering's Air Force on the 2,000-mile Eastern Front, stretching from Murmansk to the Crimea, totalled between 1,600 and 1,700 planes. This was less than a quarter of Soviet Air Force strength and many of the Russian air regiments now had more modern equipment, both fighters and bombers, than they had had back in June. Soviet resistance had imposed on Goering a patchwork policy of make do and mend by the end of 1941. In aeronautical terms, Goering was beginning to lead a hand-to-mouth existence as Commander-in-Chief of the Luftwaffe. His future was now being governed by other armies, navies and air forces. His power to exert his own strategic initiative was rapidly disappearing.

There were two further crises in December 1941. In the north,

on the Lake Ilmen front, Soviet armed forces had surrounded
the German Sixteenth Army. Goering again went to the Fuehrer's
headquarters at Rastenburg where this crisis was discussed on
8 December. Goering assured Hitler: 'The Sixteenth Army can
and will be supplied by air'. This time he was as good as his
word. Some four hundred Ju 52 transport planes were thrown
in. They played a major role in feeding and supplying the
German troops on this front in the winter of 1941-42; but they
came under heavy Soviet tank and artillery fire as they landed
at airfields near Lake Ilmen. Because of bad weather conditions,
the crash rate was high. Over 200 transport planes were lost.
This was within six months of the heavy air transport losses over
Crete. Goering's 1942 aircraft plans to operate over 1,000
transport planes were in fact whittled down to about 750, and
the mobility of German air squadrons and the serviceability of
units suffered accordingly. Spare parts could no longer be flown
to forward bases with the previous facility. And both Rommel's
air transport needs in North Africa and those of von Paulus at
Stalingrad suffered in consequence, later in 1942.

The second crisis of December 1941 was the Japanese attack
on Pearl Harbour. This brought the United States into the war
in Europe, when Adolf Hitler decided to declare war on America
on 9 December.

Goering seemed to have double vision when he looked at the
prospect of the development of United States air power. Back in
June 1940 he had urged Hitler to seize Iceland, the Canaries
and the Azores 'so that the United States could not use them
for naval and air operations'. And in conference with Hitler at
the Berlin Chancellery at the end of July he had agreed strongly
with his Fuehrer's note to the German Chiefs of Staff that 'when
the Soviet Union is defeated, then Germany must deal with the
United States'. But despite all the warning he had about US air
developments, Goering underestimated his new opponents for
the next two crucial years.

Goering's air leadership was now to be stretched by what
proved to be the heaviest addition to his air responsibilities. A
much more powerful daylight fighter defence force was needed
for Germany and Western Europe to meet the growth of United
States air power. But Goering put his head in the sand with, at
times, cynical indifference. During 1942, while the evidence of

the US Eighth Air Force build-up in Britain was apparent to all, he spoke almost sneeringly of US air potential. As late as 4 October 1942, he made this immoderate statement to a gathering of senior air force personnel and German officials in a speech at the Air Ministry in Berlin : 'Some astronomical figures are to be expected from the American war industry. Now I am the last to underrate this industry. Obviously the American do very well in some technical fields. We know they produce a colossal number of fast cars. The development of radio is one of their special achievements, and razor blades. But you must not forget that there is one word in their language that is used and written with a capital letter. That word is Bluff'. When President Roosevelt announced in December 1942 that US aircraft production was running at over 5,000 aircraft a month, it was. He was not bluffing.

When Goering surveyed the German aeronautical position in the early months of 1942, some of his inner confidence must surely have dwindled. He was still plagued by weight and glandular troubles. He still took mainly paracodeine tablets with some morphia. But outwardly he remained brash and buoyant. If he knew that his future as an air leader was inevitably bleak, he rarely showed signs of pessimism about the future at this stage.

One radical change in his approach to leadership might have been made at the beginning of 1942. Instead of a maverick attitude to air strategy and planning, he might usefully have asked himself two personal questions. The first was, 'Shall I give up the reins of some of my various offices and concentrate on the leadership of the German Air Force?' The second was, 'Shall I seek serious medical and psychiatric treatment to help me give up drugs?' American doctors were able to get him off drugs in his period of captivity after the war; but neither power nor drugs were easy for him to abandon after so many years.

When Albert Speer, who had great organising ability and intelligence, was made Reichsminister for Armaments on 8 February 1942, Goering had a great opportunity to hand over the future of German aircraft production to him, to Milch and their advisers. This would have left Goering much freer to deal with the day-to-day operational problems now piling up in his often unread in-tray. But Goering was proud and vain. His confidence remained myopic. His judgement was blinded by his temperament. His intelligence and determination, therefore, became negative assets.

On 27 January 1942 he left Berlin by train for Rome. Hitler had asked him to spend a week there discussing the war in general, and Mediterranean strategy in particular, with Mussolini, Count Ciano and the Italian Chiefs of Staff. Ciano's diary notes that Goering was 'a paunchy individual' and that he was very confident about the future. He assured the Italians: 'The USSR will be defeated in 1942 and Great Britain in 1943'. In an unguarded moment, Goering admitted to his Italian hosts, 'We are having hard times'. Perhaps he had in mind that about a fortnight before, on 12 January 1942, he had despatched Jeschonnek, his Chief of Air Staff, to Hitler at Rastenburg, to deliver a forbidding note to the Fuehrer. It said: 'It is impossible at the moment to strengthen the Luftwaffe in the West'. Hitler was keen on heavier reprisal bombing attacks on Britain. These were now at a low ebb.

What Goering had told Hitler about the Luftwaffe in the west was virtually true also of the Luftwaffe in the Mediterranean and the East. In the event, even the arrival of Kesselring's Second Air Fleet in Sicily did not break Malta's resistance and so help to solve the supply problems of Rommel's ground forces. Goering seemed to find cause for only occasional personal intervention in the 1942 air campaigns on the Russian front and in the Mediterranean. But on 2 and 3 February he paid a rare visit to the Ukrainian Front to talk to the leaders of his Fourth Air Fleet. But he seldom went to the daily briefing by Hitler and his staff on the Barbarossa situation. He would usually send Jeschonnek or his chief air aide, General Bodenschatz, to speak for him.

Goering was soon back in Rome with Adolf Galland, his General for Fighters, to discuss the coming attacks on Malta with Field Marshal Kesselring. This was in the first week of March 1942. He was entirely confident of the outcome and had planned a follow-up airborne troop assault with General Student, his airborne forces commander. About the attack on Malta, Goering said to his colleagues with great optimism, 'A new trial of absolute air warfare will be staged'. On some days in January and February 1942, Goering's bombers and fighters had carried out over 500 sorties against Malta.

On 25 April 1942 Goering was instrumental in setting up the
Central Planning Board, though Albert Speer drafted the text
of the decree. Its sane, but belated purpose was to allocate raw
materials to the three branches of the armed forces. Goering was
rarely present at the meetings which followed, despite his continuing overall responsibility for manpower and raw materials
in the German Four Year Economic Plan. At the Nuremberg
trials, Speer commented succinctly about Goering's absences.
'We would not have had any use for him. After all, we had to
carry out practical work'.

On 3 May 1942 Goering went to Rastenburg to see Hitler
about the prospects of the airborne troop assault on Malta. The
plan quickly took shape. The code name was to be 'Hercules'.
The proposed forces comprised one division of German and one
of Italian parachutists, plus three divisions of Italian airborne
infantry. Goering was very keen on the operation. Hitler, however, had second thoughts and told Goering that the air transport
resources were much more needed on the Eastern Front, though
the bombers and fighters available should be used to support
Rommel in North Africa. Goering dutifully agreed. It was by
now clear that Adolf Hitler, who had left nearly all major air
questions to Goering's judgement in 1940, was taking over some
of the main air leadership issues by 1942.

However, when a new air attack on Malta and its supply
sources was launched in August 1942, Goering's Second Air
Fleet had a temporary success in a four day and night attack on
a heavily-escorted British convoy trying to break through to
Malta. Two cruisers, seven merchants ships and the carrier
Eagle were sunk by Luftwaffe planes and two cruisers damaged.
But a new batch of Spitfires reached Malta and Goering's last
hope of securing even local air superiority in the Mediterranean
had gone.

He spent a few days in Sicily, in the first week of September,
visiting his Messerschmitt fighter squadrons at Catania and
Palermo. September had been a bad month for sinkings by
Allied forces of Axis tankers and supply ships plying for Rommel.
While he was in Sicily, Goering castigated the Me 109 units
for 'failing to protect the bomber formations in the attacks on
Malta'. Later in the month, on 20 September, he held a Luft-
waffe Chiefs of Staff meeting in Berlin at the Air Ministry. He

told his colleagues that 'he did not agree that without air superiority over the Central Mediterranean, Rommel's supply problem could not be solved'. The fact is that Goering had no reply to the impressive 1942 build-up of Air Chief Marshal Tedder's air forces in Egypt, Malta and North Africa. By the autumn of 1942 Goering's Mediterranean air policy was in tattered shreds. When, at the beginning of October 1942, he ordered Kesselring to use some of his Ju 88 bombers to fly fuel to North Africa to help Rommel, it was no more than a helpless gesture. He then switched other Ju 88 planes to provide air cover for the Axis convoys. But the sinking of Italian ships went on.

The Russian front also presented grave new problems to which Goering had no solution. The Soviet Air Force of 1942 was larger, more modern and more battle-experienced than in 1941. Moreover, Goering could no longer deploy two-thirds of his air resources in support of Operation Barbarossa, as he had in June 1941. To help the offensive of the German armies in the summer and autumn of 1942, Goering had about a thousand operational aircraft, fewer than in June 1941.

In addition, many Messerschmitt fighter units on the Eastern Front were well below average strength and serviceability. The reconnaissance units were also under strength and training standards were suffering. This meant ineffectual front-line operations in 1942 compared with the high standards of 1941.

For the main 1942 summer offensive, Goering was able to afford only 1,500 planes to support a front which stretched from Voronezh to the Crimea. In September, it looked as though Hitler might keep his public promise to take Stalingrad. But when the Stalingrad crisis came in November, Goering had little in hand. In October he had had to switch air squadrons from the south to the Leningrad front. On 24 November he went once more to the Fuehrer's headquarters at Rastenburg. It was agreed that von Paulus' Sixth German Army needed an air lift of 750 tons a day if the beleaguered troops were to survive. This was of course well beyond Goering's air lift resources. After intense discussion with the German Chiefs of Staff, a minimum figure of 300 tons a day was agreed on. Brushing aside the objections of Jeschonnek, his Chief of Staff, Goering said, 'The task is difficult but the Luftwaffe will carry it out. We shall need to use 200 planes'.

When the Stalingrad air lift began in the first week of December, Goering's Fourth Air Fleet had in fact nearly 400 transport planes. Half were genuine Junkers transports. The rest were mainly Heinkel bombers drawn from the Western Front, some He 177 four-engined bombers pressed into premature service, a few Focke-Wulf 200 four-engined bombers borrowed from Battle of the Atlantic duties and some obsolete Ju 86 planes. The Soviet Air Force had overwhelming local air superiority and shot down large numbers of German planes. An average of only about 100 tons a day was dropped. The minimum figure of 300 tons was not reached even on a single day. On 30 January 1943, Goering knew that his air lift had irrevocably failed. He signalled to von Paulus: 'The fight of the Sixth Army will go down in history'. Two days later Goering broadcast to the German people: 'A thousand years hence, Germans will speak of the battle with reverence and awe'. Like many leaders, he loved to indulge in rhetoric to mask unpleasant realities.

The Stalingrad bill was heavy for the Luftwaffe. They lost about 350 transport planes, 100 fighters and over 2,000 air crew members and ground staff. And on the North African front, when Rommel's forces retreated from Alamein to Tripolitania and beyond, Goering's air force fought a hopeless rearguard action in which his air leadership was totally ineffective. The Anglo-American landing in North Africa in November 1942 produced a new and more pressing air situation in the Central Mediterranean, to which Goering had no reply. The man who saw air warfare in 1940 in terms of lavish blitzkrieg, now found himself with inadequate air resources on all of his major air fronts.

It would be wrong to think that Goering had done no serious forward planning to meet the expanding air eventualities of 1942. German Air Ministry records show that he chaired a number of lengthy discussions with his colleagues on the future production and operational strength requirements of the German Air Force. These began in the autumn of 1941. It may be of interest to see the difference between the targets he set and the achievement of the industry. He saw the 1942 needs of the

Luftwaffe as a front-line strength of between 9,500 and 10,000 planes. For this an estimated production of 32,200 planes would be required for front-line expansion. The actual 1942 production figure, 15,556 aircraft, was thus less than half the target figure. The front-line strength was about 4,000 to 5,000 aircraft, short of the target of about 10,000 at various stages of 1942. If he had ordered a two-shift working system in factories, and put his production responsibilities on the capable shoulders of Milch and Speer, and given them both a free hand, if he had taken the US air threat more seriously in 1942, if he had done more to encourage the production of Heinkel and Messerschmitt jet planes in 1942—the list of ifs and buts in Goering's air leadership is a long one. At the end of 1942, he was becoming out of favour with Hitler and out of touch with the reality of the mounting problems of restoring the air initiative to his overworked and overstrained Luftwaffe.

CHAPTER SEVEN

The Air Defence of Germany

IN SOME respects, the air defence of Germany was not in Goering's hands. There were, for example, factors in German strategy which called for the extensive use of Luftwaffe anti-aircraft guns and fighters well outside the Third Reich or its adjacent territories. Goering had a very limited control over these strategic factors. Hitler was very much Goering's war lord.

Whenever the German Army moved to the attack, in Poland, France, the Balkans or in Russia, they drew heavily on Hermann Goering's air defence potential. The Commander-in-Chief of the German Air Force knew from the beginning that a high proportion of his air resources would be at the beck and call of Hitler's ground strategies. Indeed, the basic combat organisation of the Luftwaffe was, at first, the Air Division, and then the Air Corps, designed to give close tactical support, with fighters, bombers, dive-bombers and transport planes, to German armoured and infantry units.

Goering's air leadership, in terms of the air defence of the Third Reich, underwent many changes of both fortune and attitude. After initial indifference in 1939, he developed his night-fighter arm almost to its maximum potential. But his attitude to the problems of daylight air defence was erratic and, by 1943, almost schizophrenic. The first crisis stage in the daylight defence of the Third Reich began in 1942, with the arrival of the US Eighth Air Force in Great Britain. There followed a build-up of US four-engined Flying Fortresses and Liberator bombers which posed a new threat to the strategic air defences of Germany. Until it was almost too late, Goering turned a blind eye to the new situation. He formally forbade discussion of the growth of US air power in Britain, even at 1943 air staff meetings held at the German Air Ministry in Berlin. It must be accounted one of Goering's greatest failures that he was so insensitive to the growing American threat. How far this was due to his inability or unwillingness to oppose the amateur air strategy of Adolf Hitler is difficult to say. But the Fuehrer certainly pressed him constantly for bombers at the expense of fighters.

From 1942 onwards, the Fuehrer decided air policy matters on such important issues as the Messerschmitt 262 jet plane and other aspects of aircraft production. When Goering's senior advisers, for example Milch and Galland, asked for greater priority for fighter aircraft production, the Reichsmarschall allowed Hitler to decide against it. The basic fact of the situation was that by the end of 1942 the Fuehrer's confidence in Goering's air leadership had dwindled. Goering had been wrong about so many things.

Goering's basic air philosophy was opposed to setting up strong air defences for the Third Reich. Air forces, as he saw them, were intended to attack and not defend. In 1939, only about a third of the military aircraft built in Germany were fighter planes, and in 1940 only about a quarter. Like many other air leaders, Goering believed that the bomber would get through to its target. There is no evidence that he formally supported the views of the Italian theoretician, Douhet, who wrote and preached about the war-winning potential of the bomber; but he was by proxy a Douhet fan.

If bombers get through to their target, how then can one explain Goering's much publicised speeches made during his tour of the Rhineland in July 1939? His Ruhr audiences erupted into laughter and applause when he said: 'If an enemy bomber reaches the Ruhr, my name is not Hermann Goering. You can call me Meier'.

These Rhineland speeches produced new jokes about Goering. At first they were friendly, but from 1942 onwards there was a note of bitterness and hostility. The German people called him affectionately 'Our Meier', ironically 'Little Meier', realistically 'Thick Meier' and bitterly 'Stupid Meier'. But, in 1939, the Fuehrer still had great faith in Hermann Goering. Albert Speer, then Hitler's chief architect, recalls a conversation in that year with the Fuehrer, in which Hitler said with great simplicity,

'Goering has assured me that no enemy plane will penetrate Germany'.

It would seem that Goering believed the essence of his Rhineland speeches on the eve of the outbreak of the Second World War. There was no pressure from him to build up the radar early warning system of the Third Reich, or to create even an embryonic defensive Fighter Command. Ernst Udet, ex-fighter pilot, persuaded Goering to experiment with a force of 30-40 Arado 68 and Me 109 single-engined fighters, to do duty primarily as night-fighters. They did some primitive training operations, co-ordinating with searchlights in their attempts to intercept, but had no blind-landing or radar aids. When General Jeschonnek, the German Air Force Chief of Staff, raised the matter at a meeting at the German Air Ministry in Berlin on 5 September 1939, Goering told him, 'Night-fighting will never happen'!

The air operations in the first nine months of the Second World War were scarcely conducive to any re-thinking of Goering's views on the air defence of Germany. The French Air Force bombers were quiescent, the Royal Air Force bomber attacks on Germany had been slight. But in the winter of 1939-40 British bombers and reconnaissance planes had regularly penetrated the German air defences and dropped bombs and leaflets on Germany. Goering's view that his anti-aircraft guns and searchlights would be an adequate deterrent to night bombing was radically changed by June 1940. In the previous month, RAF Bomber Command had dropped bombs on the Ruhr without intolerable casualties, despite German anti-aircraft fire.

And so, on 18 June 1940, Hermann Goering sent for Josef Kammhuber. In the course of a long discussion at Karinhall, Goering asked him to set up a force of twin-engined night-fighters. It was initially a night-fighter division of less than 50 planes, which grew to over 150 planes by the end of 1940.

The appointment of Josef Kammhuber to the new night-fighter post was interesting. In the first place it was a reversal of Goering's views about the potential of night-fighters. It showed some flexibility of leadership and a willingness to see the threat of Bomber Command night raids on Germany in good time. It also showed tolerance in the choice of an air leader. Josef Kammhuber, a strong-minded, conscientious man who neither smoked nor drank, was not at all typical of Goering's immediate coterie of air generals. Moreover, Kammhuber was the man whom Goering had sacked in January 1940, when one of his pilots force-landed in bad weather in Belgium, carrying in his plane a copy of the German plans to attack France and the Low Countries. It was an interesting, but by no means isolated, example to show that Goering could forgive and forget. There was more than a touch of generosity in his make-up as an air leader. The man he made General of his Fighter Arm was Adolf Galland, who had been more than cheeky to him in the Battle of Britain when he asked for a squadron of Spitfires. This was when Goering had asked what he could do for Galland's fighter squadrons.

A further point of interest about General Kammhuber's new Night-Fighter Division was that it had to be equipped with twin-engined Me 110 planes flown in part by air crews previously used to give tactical air support to the German Army in the French and Flanders campaigns in May 1940. This was an interesting example which showed that, as early as the summer of 1940, Goering had no real depth of aircraft and crew reserves on which to draw, to develop the air defences of the Third Reich. If he had a plan to build up serious night-fighter defence in Holland and Western Germany in the summer and autumn of 1940, he would have to use mainly existing operational crews and aircraft and convert them to night-fighting. His force of about a quarter of a million men who manned well over a thousand light, medium and heavy anti-aircraft guns seemed to Goering adequate for the time being. But the new air defence emphasis was on the expansion and sophistication of the night-fighter arm.

Hermann Goering's attitude to the daylight defence of Germany in the autumn of 1940 was conditioned by the vague belief that enough fighters would be available to defend the Third Reich. Any diversionary air campaigns in the Mediterranean, and on the Russian Front, would last for a matter of six weeks or perhaps a few months. After that, the fighter squadrons, freed from their duty to support the army, would be available to return for the air defence of the Fatherland.

Even before the end of 1940, Adolf Hitler was bringing his untutored influence to bear on the policy and future of Germany's air defence forces. In his post-war evidence, General Josef Kammhuber, who was to become the first post-war Commander-in-Chief of the new Luftwaffe, declared 'Goering gave me much support in expanding and modernising German night-fighters. It was Hitler who was sometimes the fly in the ointment'.

Whereas in the first week of January 1941, and on a number of subsequent occasions, Goering had sent signals to Air Fleet and Air Corps commanders encouraging them 'to request the best bomber and reconnaissance air crews to volunteer for the night-fighter defence of the Reich', Hitler had already expressed doubt about the wisdom of this policy. The Fuehrer had also clamped down on the development of the offensive potential of General Kammhuber's night-fighter plans.

At the end of October 1940, Kammhuber went to see Goering at Karinhall and spoke enthusiastically about the use of 'intruders' as an aid to German night-fighter defences. These intruders were to be Do 17 and Ju 88 bombers, which were to attack British night bombers and their bases, at the time of take-off and landing, and so reduce the scale of bomber operations against Germany. Kammhuber asked for an initial force of about 40 intruder planes, to which Goering readily agreed. When Hitler got to hear of the new move he insisted on a reduction of intruder forces to about 20.

What is more important than the reduction in the number of planes—intruder operations on both sides proved to be a valuable irritant rather than a decisive weapon—is the fact that by the end of 1940 Adolf Hitler was already interfering in relatively secondary aspects of German Air Force policy. The air leadership of Germany was already passing from Goering's hands. Later, Hitler was to veto Kammhuber's intruder operations again. In December 1941, the Fuehrer persuaded Goering to switch some of the Ju 88 intruder planes to the Mediterranean to protect Italian convoys bearing supplies to North Africa. And in August 1943, when RAF Bomber Command had moved on to a peak night blitz on Hamburg, the Ruhr and Berlin, Hitler told Goering to disband General Kammhuber's intruder units at a time when their potential was more substantial. This may have been a contributory factor to Kammhuber's resignation a few months later.

In terms of general support from Goering for training, crew and aircraft priorities, General Kammhuber had little to complain about. The growth of the German night-fighter arm in the Second World War was greater than that of any other air arm of the German Air Force. Its combat strength increased from about 160 planes at the end of 1940 to over 400 at the end of 1941, more than 650 at the end of 1942, over 950 in December 1943, and over 1,300 at the end of 1944. Goering's night-fighter units then formed about a fifth of the strength of all units—bomber, fighter-bomber, dive-bomber, reconnaissance and transport planes. No other arm of the German Air Force expanded anything like as much as the night-fighters in the period 1940 to 1944.

To provide suitable aircraft was only part of the air leadership requirement. To operate at maximum efficiency, the Luftwaffe night-fighter organisation needed élite crews with a flair for bomber interception at night. Goering did all that could reasonably be expected of him. He continued to encourage German Air Force units to transfer their more experienced pilots to the night-fighter units. He sent signals exhorting them to do so. But, as the German documents show, the shortage of fully operational night-fighter crews was the Achilles heel. Above all there was a lack of night-fighter aces like Hermann and Schoenert. It was the general night-fighting experience of the Second World War that the ordinary run of night-fighter pilots and observers did not have the flair for hunting night bombers that brings a big run of success. The British night-fighter ace Group Captain Cunningham was called 'cat's-eyes' because he had that flair. We had few Cunninghams. The Luftwaffe had few Hermanns.

It was rather late in the day to set up a training organisation for night-fighters in 1941 and 1942, and to have to expand that organisation at the same time. Hermann Goering had made a late decision; but compared with some of his other air defence decisions, it was an outstanding example of long-term anticipation.

From 1941 onwards, the strain on Goering's training facilities increased. In 1942 trainer aircraft were being taken from flying training schools to be used in operational front-line units on the Eastern Front and in the case of the night-fighters, flying

K

instructors had to be used on operations to meet the increased air defence needs of the rising tide of the RAF offensive. Moreover, these raids disrupted night-fighter training by their mere presence over Holland and Germany.

The upshot of all this was that, in March 1942 for example, less than two-thirds of the night-fighter planes had crews trained to operational standard. The proportion dropped to less than a half in June 1942, and stayed at roughly that proportion until March 1944. The fact that a peak figure of well over two-thirds was reached in September 1944 was scarcely relevant. At that time, Goering had a night-fighter operational strength of over 1,000 planes with nearly 800 crews trained to operational standard. But by then there was an acute fuel shortage, the Allies had reached the Dutch border and had eliminated parts of the German early warning radar system, so that the prospect of a practical air defence of Germany either at night or in daylight had virtually gone.

There would be little justice in criticising Goering for not creating an adequate night-fighter training organisation in 1940, to meet the expanding needs of his night-fighter arm. He lived in an aviation age in which no contemporary air force had made really effective large-scale plans to train or operate night-fighters. Thus, for example, by 1940 neither the Soviet Air Force, the Japanese Air Force nor the defensively-minded Royal Air Force had made much progress in this field.

German night-fighter pilots shot down more than sixty bombers in a single night on a number of occasions in 1943 and 1944. It will surely be the verdict of aviation history that they had the best night-fighter record in the Second World War. But they neither deterred nor limited the night bombing of Germany to the extent required. The night-fighter success of Luftflotte Reich, as Germany's Air Defence Command was called, was outstanding but inadequate.

Goering's decision to expand his night-fighter arm had of course the negative effect of limiting the use of Messerschmitt and Junkers twin-engined fighters in their tactical support roles of ground attack and reconnaissance on behalf of the German Army. He also had to use a certain number of night-fighters for daylight defensive operations over Germany. The elements of dilution in tactical air support and the thin stretch of his daylight fighter cover of the Third Reich plagued his air leadership, particularly in 1943 and thereafter.

Goering was no long-term planner. He was a natural gambler who chanced his arm. He waited until the crisis was at hand. Even then he would bluster his way through the air staff debates using verbal anger as a substitute for sane decision. The evidence of Galland, Kammhuber, Udet, Jeschonnek and Albert Speer on this is supported by Kesselring, Milch and others. But they also say that Goering could be kind, gracious, charming and hospitable. This ebullient extravert was perceptive but confused. And he produced confusion and disarray in Luftwaffe senior circles from 1941 onwards. Goering had none of the quiet but trenchant leadership qualities of, for example, Air Chief Marshal Sir Charles Portal, the RAF Commander-in-Chief, or the kindly perception and willingness to listen of General Carl Spaatz, the Commander-in-Chief of the US Strategic Air Force in Europe. Goering would brush awkward evidence aside. Portal and Spaatz had the earnest willingness to listen and re-assess.

Goering was able to expand the use of anti-aircraft guns despite the heavy demand of the German Army for their use in the field. In terms of personnel, the anti-aircraft and search-light battery strength rose from about 255,000 in the first year of the war to about 350,000 at the end of 1941. In 1942, there was an increase of a further 100,000 and by the end of 1944 the high figure of 850,000 men was reached. The number of anti-aircraft guns increased correspondingly from about 1,000 at the end of 1940 to over 1,750 at the end of 1942. By the end of 1943 some 2,750 were deployed and nearly 3,500 at the end of 1944. As in the case of night-fighter crews, the quality of German anti-aircraft gunners declined in the last year or so of the war when inexperienced youths had to be pressed into service.

In his capacity as Commander-in-Chief of the Luftwaffe, Goering had nominal control of Germany's anti-aircraft gun resources. And so, despite the loud calls of Rommel, von Rundstedt and other army generals for more anti-aircraft guns in Africa and on the Russian and Western Fronts, Goering was nevertheless able to expand the Reich's domestic anti-aircraft defences. There is no really valid way of assessing their effectiveness. This is because fighter and anti-aircraft gun claims of enemy planes shot down at night are often difficult or impossible to disentangle. They were, however, only of secondary importance compared with the day and night-fighter units. Goering's main contribution to their tactical deployment was to suggest greater use of larger batteries of six, eight or even ten guns. But compared with his involvement in fighter policy in the defence of the Third Reich, his day-to-day commitment and interest in the tactical use of the guns was minimal.

1941 was the year which gave Goering a sense of false security in terms of the air defence of the Third Reich. RAF Bomber Command presented no daylight threat and at night their bombing techniques were still in an early formative stage. The weight of attack was moderate, partly because British bomber resources had to be diverted to Battle of the Atlantic operations and partly to the Middle East theatre. The British use of such navigational aids as Gee and Oboe was still to come, as was the radar aid, H2S, which indicated the target area at night. The later development of pathfinder techniques—the concentration of the raids into much shorter time and space was also to limit the future potential of Goering's night-fighters, who needed time to track and hunt their quarry, especially in conditions of poor visibility. The British switch in bomber tactics in 1942 was a grave handicap for German night-fighter crews. If larger numbers of bombers could pass, at the same time, through a Luftwaffe night-fighter ground controlled interception area, it would mean fewer potential German controlled interceptions.

The daylight fighter defences of Germany were in no condition to meet heavy bomber attacks throughout 1941. But they did not need to. At the end of July 1941, Luftflotte Reich had a combat strength of only 35-40 single-engined fighters and a twin-engined day-fighter strength of 40-45 planes, compared with over 250 twin-engined night-fighters. The need to increase fighter production was raised by General Moelders, then Head of the Fighter Arm, by Kammhuber and by Hans Jeschonnek, Goering's Chief of Staff, at at least two Air Staff meetings held in Berlin in August 1941. The Luftwaffe Commander-in-Chief assured his colleagues 'The Russians will soon be beaten. Once I get my fighters back to the West, the whole business will be different'.

Goering's optimism was at the time almost intact. His confidence was possibly bolstered by further morphia injections.

The big disasters in the Mediterranean, the East and in the air over Germany were still to come. But by the autumn of 1941 some of Goering's senior air colleagues were beginning to worry. On 9 and 10 October 1941, there was a two-day conference at Goering's castle at Veltenstein in Franconia. Generals Kammhuber, Moelders and Galland were present.

The three Luftwaffe air generals, all highly intelligent and experienced fighter specialists, urged Goering to examine the need to expand the day-fighters of Luftflotte Reich. They raised the alarm about the growing single and twin-engined fighter wastage on the Eastern Front. They pointed out that the increased use of fighter-bombers in the Luftwaffe was affecting the growth of the fighter arm. They asked for increased fighter production.

Goering was adamant in his reply. 'The Luftwaffe must attack and not defend. The reprisal raids on Britain ordered by the Fuehrer must be agreed to and carried out.' The German Air Force bomber attacks on Britain, in the autumn of 1941, were at a low and ineffective level. The blitz on Britain had subsided and was to remain no more than an intermittent pin-prick compared with the Allied raids on Germany.

Hermann Goering's cavalier approach to the potential threat of US air power is almost unbelievable. Long before the United States entered the war in Europe, Ernst Udet, Goering's aircraft production chief, had warned him about the growth of US aircraft production and, more important still, of its capacity to expand rapidly. Goering knew that Udet was a loyal friend and well-informed about air events in USA. Between the wars he had been Germany's leading test pilot. As such, he had demonstrated German Messerschmitt and Heinkel planes in competition with US aircraft in many parts of the world. In August 1941, when Udet was sick, he spent about two weeks at Karinhall and at Goering's hunting lodge at Rominten. He tried to warn the Reichsmarschall about the growth and modernisation of the US aircraft industry. Goering laughed and poured out some wine and produced his stock joke on the subject. 'It is bluff, my dear Ernst. They can make cars and refrigerators but not aircraft.'

When, at the end of 1941, Hitler declared war on the United States, Goering continued to maintain his ostrich approach to

US air potential. There was dissent from Goering's views in Hitler's entourage. In February 1942, Himmler's intelligence service, which liked to compete with Goering's own air intelligence staff, produced a report on US war production. A copy was sent to Goering. It predicted an annual US aircraft production of over 40,000 planes per annum in the next year or so. In addition there would be a major force of several hundred four-engined bombers available for operations against Germany. Goering at first made no comment on the report. And so, in the first week of February 1942 Himmler sent the head of his foreign intelligence service, Walter Schellenberg, to see Goering at Karinhall. After some initial courtesy and hospitality, Goering exploded. 'Everything you have written in this report is utter nonsense. You need a psychiatrist to examine your head.' Schellenberg left and reported the situation to Himmler, who relayed Goering's reaction to the Fuehrer.

And yet the impression of some of his colleagues in March 1942 was that the Luftwaffe Commander-in-Chief was in good shape. Thus the Goebbels diaries for that period record that 'Goering was in exceptionally good condition physically', the text going on to pay tribute to Goering's 'hard work, great successes and sound commonsense'. Goebbels, of course, knew little of Goering's problems as leader of the Luftwaffe. It was in March 1942, at Karinhall, that Goering told Karl Bodenschatz, his senior air aide, 'I am worried about the prospects of the spring and summer offensives against the Russians. Many of our single-engined fighters are committed to the Eastern Front. We have few reserve aircraft and crews to strengthen Germany's daylight defences'.

And so Goering said to Bodenschatz in March 1942 what he could not accept as being valid from Kammhuber, Galland and Moelders in October 1941. But he did not really see either the way or the need to strengthen Germany's daylight fighter defences in 1942. There were no US raids on Germany in that year. When 12 British Lancaster bombers attacked Augsburg in Southern Germany in April, it proved to be the only daylight bomber attack of the year on Germany. Seven of the twelve attacking four-engined bombers were shot down by German fighters and anti-aircraft guns—a prohibitive loss rate. Perhaps there was temporary substance in Goering's optimism.

But as to night raids, 1942 was a black year which discredited Goering's air leadership in the eyes of Hitler, the German Chiefs of Staff and the German public. In a broad sense, he was not to blame for the new situation. As Commander-in-Chief of the Luftwaffe he had done his best to strengthen the night-fighter and gun defences of Germany. Faced with more concentrated and heavier bomber attacks from 1942 onwards, by planes equipped with modern electronic navigational aids and using pathfinder techniques and radar bombing aids, no night air defence could hope to be a real deterrent.

RAF Bomber Command, in striking their massive bombing blows at Germany, also struck at the pride and prestige of Goering. In the attack on Luebeck in North Germany, on the night of 28/29 March 1942, civilian casualties reached four figures for the first time.

Despite his public assertion that no bombs would be dropped on Germany, Hermann Goering had, in 1935, created a civil defence organisation with a good training system for air-raid wardens and a closely integrated national fire service which could send help from town to town. The German police, together with the Gauleiter, were responsible for local policy. The Luebeck raid cast the first major doubts about the effectiveness of the civil defence system devised by Goering.

But the big shock for Goering's air leadership and for both German air and civil defence came in the thousand-bomber raid on Cologne, on the night of 30/31 May 1942. 1,455 tons of bombs were dropped; 1,047 British bomber planes operated; over 400 Germans were killed; over 400,000 were rendered homeless. 39 British bombers, less than four per cent, were shot down by German air defences.

Hitler was at his headquarters at Rastenburg in East Prussia when he heard the news of the Cologne raid on the morning of 31 May. Goering was relaxing at his castle at Veltenstein in Franconia. He was unaware of the storm that was about to break. On the morning after the raid, he was visited by Albert Speer and Erhard Milch, who were due to discuss aircraft production problems with him. When they arrived, Goering had just had the first report of the Cologne raid which he genuinely did not believe. Goering phoned the Gauleiter of Cologne and said shrewdly to him, 'How can you count incendiary bombs?

Your figures are just estimates. Send another report to the
Fuehrer and change the figures.' Goering at this stage was quite
calm and in command of the situation, or so he thought.

But at the Fuehrer's briefing conference at Rastenburg, Hans
Jeschonnek, Goering's Chief of Staff, was in some trouble. He
had begun his air briefing rather nervously on the morning of
31 May 1942. 'There was a fairly heavy enemy attack on
Cologne last night . . .' 'How heavy?' shouted Hitler. 'Preliminary reports suggest that 200 planes penetrated our defences.
The damage is heavy,' said Jeschonnek. Hitler rose to his feet
and screamed, 'Goering is not here . . . of course not. But if the
Luftwaffe deceives me, I can, thank God, rely on my Gauleiter.
There were a thousand or more English planes, do you hear, a
thousand, perhaps twelve hundred, perhaps more !'

Goering did not attend the Rastenburg daily conferences at
all regularly; but, sensing the crisis this time, he flew to the
Fuehrer's headquarters to join in the discussion on the Cologne
raid. Before leaving Veltenstein, Goering again telephoned the
Gauleiter of Cologne and told him, 'The report from your police
commissioner is a lie. I have already delivered my report to the
Fuehrer with the true figures.'

But the Fuehrer did not accept them. Hitler even refused to
shake hands with Goering when he arrived at Rastenburg. The
atmosphere was tense. It was decided that Goebbels and Hitler
would be responsible for energising German civil defence in
future, and that Goering would institute reprisal raids on British
cities. This was no new notion. But Goering did not have the
resources to produce more than pinprick reprisals in the
'Baedeker' raids on Bath, Canterbury, Exeter and other cities.
He urgently signalled the Third Air Fleet in France asking for
'a maximum effort including if possible double sorties'. He
promised 'reinforcement of bomber units when the victory in
the East has been secured'.

Hitler's anger with Goering, because he had attempted to
cover up the truth about the raid on Cologne, did not last long.
On 1 June 1942 the Fuehrer had a meeting at Rastenburg
with Goering and Speer on the general air situation. Nothing
tangible emerged but Speer says the atmosphere was 'friendly
and peaceful'. About a week later, Hitler appointed Goering
head of the Third Reich's Research Council, 'to emphasise its

importance', said the Fuehrer. Among the Council's briefs was the assessment of long-term defence projects. At the time, Goering was sensibly having a new air-raid shelter built at his Veltenstein castle.

Hermann Goering was a mixture of acute realism and self-delusion. As his problems increased, so did the proportion of self-delusion in his air leadership. Thus he hit upon a plan, following the raid on Cologne, of showing how effective German air defences were. There were two elements. First, the German claims of enemy planes shot down had to be accepted without question. Secondly, one had to under-estimate the enemy scale of attack on the target area or areas. By this means a greater percentage of kills could be claimed. Of course, juggling with pilots' claims was not a Goering speciality. It was a general feature of the Second World War and the wars which followed. It led Hanson Baldwin, the eminent US writer on military matters, to the conclusion that 'airmen are indifferent mathematicians'.

But there were some practical results. At last Goering personally approved an aircraft production programme for the period January to June 1942, in which the production of German fighter planes was to be nearly 400 a month compared with about 330 bombers. Of course this was inadequate for the future, in view of the potential day bombing of Germany by US air forces based in Britain. But it was the right trend, reversing the previous priority for bomber production.

Two meetings, held in September 1942 in Berlin at the Air Ministry, make it clear that Goering had, at least in part, a realistic approach to the aircraft needs of Germany at that time. The first was on 12 September 1942. Goering spoke to his senior air staff colleagues about the relative merits of German, English and American fighters. He said, 'In general, we have had a certain superiority with the Me 109 in all its developments and then the Focke-Wulf 190. However, to some extent, they have been caught up and overtaken by English and American fighters, particularly in the climb. To my annoyance, they seem to have a greater range and this is very unpleasant.' Goering then went on to talk of the Do 335, the Ta 152 Focke-Wulf fighter, and the Me 209 and 309 coming into squadrons. But since maximum fighter production was the great need, as Milch insisted, none of these new fighters ever came into serious combat use.

Goering seems to have forgotten his views on the greater range of American fighters when they began to operate over Germany. His capacious memory was fitted with special safety valves which did not admit too many unpleasant facts. It was however, remarkable that Goering had admitted that British fighters had overtaken German fighters in some respects. This may have been the salutary reporting of Colonel Wodag, Goering's new intelligence chief, as compared with that of his predecessor, Beppo Schmid, who was inclined to feed Goering with dubious reports about British planes, underestimating their capability.

On 13 September 1942 Goering held another meeting at the Air Ministry with senior officials of the German aircraft industry. He reminded them urgently of the orders he had given them in June 1942, for the dispersal of German aircraft factories eastwards. He urged the aircraft firms' representatives to increase output and went on, 'We have aircraft with great capabilities for which much has been promised. They have failed to live up to that promise. Will you let the interest of your firms take second place?'

Goering was referring to such planes as the He 177 heavy bomber, the Me 410 twin-engined machine and perhaps the Focke-Wulf Ta 152 and 154 of which much was originally hoped. But he did not on this occasion raise the subject of jet aircraft production. His plans for the development of the Arado 234 and Me 262 lacked urgency, although they were the best means of achieving technical superiority over British and American planes. On the other hand, the development and testing of the two jet planes was inevitably a slow business.

Although Goering had increased the strength of Germany's night-fighter units substantially in 1942, as has been seen, the process of modernisation was slow. There was a need for more suitable planes. The Me 110 was really a stopgap fighter, The Ju 88 was faster and sturdier. But during 1942, less than 10 per cent of the 3,000 which came from German factories were allocated to German night-fighter units. However, at the end of 1942, the new Do 217 began to reach Kammhuber's night-fighter squadrons, equipped with Lichtenstein airborne radar.

On 10 October 1942 Goering had obtained Hitler's agreement to 'priority for radar and communications equipment for Luftflotte Reich', the German Air Defence Command. Goering also discussed with the Fuehrer, at that time, the co-ordination of day and night-fighters, enabling some squadrons to operate both in daylight and darkness. It seemed, at the end of 1942, that Goering was alert to the new problems he had to face in the air defence of Germany. He must surely have foreseen the American raids on Germany. But he remained obstinate about their potential. In particular, he was unwilling throughout 1943, to envisage the threat of long-range US fighter escort.

Goering did, however, see the increased bombing threat to Germany's aircraft industry in fairly good time. Thus, he ordered a study to be made in April 1942 on dispersing the industry eastwards. This was at a two-day meeting held at the German Air Ministry in Berlin. On at least two occasions in June 1942 he urged Otto Staub, who was responsible to Hitler for organising the dispersal, to speed up the process. But it was the threat of the US Eighth Air Force bombing in the spring and summer of 1943 which hastened the business of evacuating a large part of the German aircraft industry to Eastern Germany, East Prussia, Poland and Czechoslovakia. The 27 main plants were eventually splintered into about 300 small factories, some of which were set up in railway tunnels, disused mines, salt mines and old quarries. This dispersal produced new problems of assembly and supply for the German aircraft industry; but it also produced problems for Anglo-American intelligence when new decisions were made to attack the German aircraft industry at the beginning of 1944.

Looking back at 1942, Goering may have had some temporary satisfaction about the state of the air defences of Germany. The new airborne radar was coming more and more into use at night. The new scheme for controlled night-fighter interception was working well. It was based on what German pilots called the four-poster bed (*Himmelbett*). The elements were a plotting table, the early warning Freya radar equipment and two Wurzburg radar sets, one for plotting and one for tracking. The plotter on the ground spoke to the tracker in the air.

There is a tribute to the 1942 air defences of Germany in the account of the air war against Germany written by Sir Charles

Webster and Dr Noble Frankland (HMSO 1961). It refers to the 'constantly increasing scale, ingenuity and efficiency of German air defences and in particular of the night-fighter force.' Goering would have been pleased with this critique.

1942 had not been a very good year for RAF Bomber Command, despite the untypical success of the 1,000 bomber raid on Cologne. They lost over 1,400 bombers in raids over Germany and a further 2,700 bombers were damaged. The Manchester night bomber had to be pulled out of operations, in June 1942, and some of the Halifax four-engined bombers were unsatisfactory. There was very little expansion of Bomber Command squadrons in 1942. Goering would have been cheered by a note sent to Winston Churchill by his Chief of Air Staff of 7 November 1942 : 'Fighter escort into Germany will prove impractical and the bombers must look after themselves.' In the event, the note was misleading.

The fact is that there was no previous experience in air warfare of the use of long-range escort fighters against strong fighter defences. And, at the end of 1942, there was no promise that a sufficient number of long-range escort Mustang P51s would be available to protect US bombers penetrating as far as Berlin. There was certainly no British long-range fighter in use, or on the stocks, which could attempt to do the job of long-range bomber protection in daylight.

When the Anglo-American Chiefs of Staff met at Casablanca, in January 1943, they served notice to Germany that an increased round-the-clock air assault was now a serious prospect. The new planned attack on Germany was given the code name 'Operation Point Blank'. The directive said to the British and American air commanders : 'Your primary objective will be the progressive destruction and dislocation of the German military, industrial and economic system and the undermining of the German people to the point where their capacity for armed resistance is fatally weakened'.

Goering did not need to read the text of the Casablanca directive to know what was afoot. The first daylight raid on Germany by US four-engined bombers took place on 27 January 1943, when the target was Wilhelmshaven. In the spring of 1943, the Ruhr was attacked at night more heavily than ever before by RAF bombers.

Goering seems now to have gone into a kind of mental retreat, from which he emerged only at intervals. From February 1943, his summer house at Obersalzburg in Southern Germany and his castle at Veltenstein were used as an escape from the stresses and strains of his air leadership and other commitments. Galland and others have said too that Goering 'was offended by Hitler's criticisms of his leadership of the air force'. At Veltenstein and Obersalzburg, Goering was to have many key meetings with Speer, Galland and Milch on the problems of Germany's air defences and on German aircraft production problems. Goering would sometimes receive his guests in a splendid purple dressing-gown and, as the conversation flowed, the Reichsmarschall would play with uncut diamonds. More than one of those present have stated that he used perfume and rouged his cheeks. There was a touch of the Roman emperor about Hermann Goering.

He certainly remained imperiously indifferent to the threat of escorted US bombers penetrating into the heart of Germany. His senior air advisers pointed to the menace in no uncertain terms. Milch went to see him on a number of occasions in 1943, urging Goering to put more emphasis on fighter production. Thus, on 25 August 1943, he said to the Reichsmarschall at Karinhall: 'I would tell the Fuehrer that the front is Germany itself, and that the mass of fighters must go to its defence.' Galland, the General of Fighters, told Goering that Germany's air defences 'needed three or four fighters for each raiding US bomber and a further fighter to deal with each escorting US fighter.'

It was simple enough for Milch to say that the mass of fighters must go to the defence of Germany; but it was a tough business to get the Fuehrer's assent to such a radical change in policy. In terms of twin-engined fighters about 80 per cent of all Luftwaffe resources were already engaged in the air defence of the Reich at the beginning of 1943. In the case of single-engined fighters it was just over a quarter. By February 1944, the total number of single-engined fighters protecting Germany had been roughly doubled and a new force of some 200 twin-engined day fighters emerged, equipped with the new 21 cm rocket used at long range against US Flying Fortresses and Liberators. All this amounted to some 1,200 fighters. A more precise estimate is difficult to give as fighters in France could intervene for some daylight operations over Germany.

In the view of General Galland and his fighter pilot colleagues, a force of 2,000 single and twin-engined fighters was needed to defend Germany. Of course, the matter was not as simple as statistics. The quality of US bomber and fighter pilots and air crews, the quality of German air crews, the US escort tactics, the absence or presence of German jet fighters were other important factors.

It is difficult to assess the varying quality of Goering's air leadership in all the various phases of the air war over Germany in 1943 and 1944. The initiative was no longer with him and in some senses the term leadership does not apply to the situation. The implementation of Anglo-American Chiefs of Staff planning, the skills of British and American air crews, the new British bomber tactics at night and their extended use of radio counter-measures and radar bombing aids, the changing escort fighter tactics in US raids—these and other things were more decisive factors in the air defence of Germany than Goering's leadership.

By the end of 1943, with the ability of RAF Bomber Command to sustain attacks using 800-900 bombers and the decision to build large numbers of Mustang long-range escort fighters, Goering's air leadership potential in the defence of Germany was reduced to very little. The moment to face the problem in all its seriousness had been when the United States entered the war at the end of 1941. Then the single-engined fighter strength in German Air Force units was about 1,250 as it had been in March 1940. A longish war with Russia was, by December 1941, at least a planning contingency. But at the end of 1941, German production of bombers still exceeded the production of fighters by nearly 100 planes a month. Since fighters could be also used for tactical short-range bombing and reconnaissance, a major switch to fighter production was then logical. But it came too slowly. In the first six months of 1942, the average production of fighters was about 390 but this exceeded the bomber production only by about 60 planes a month. Then came the intervention of the Fuehrer to check this trend.

Right up to the end of 1942, Goering had assured Hitler 'there is no need for big increases in day fighters for defensive purposes'. In one sense, the absence of United States Army Air

Force bombing operations over Germany justified this estimate. Even in 1943, the raids were not really intensive. After Wilhelmshaven in January came Bremen in April, Kassel in July. Regensburg and Ploesti in August and the Munster and Schweinfurt raids in October. The November raids were on Bremen, Kiel and Wilhelmshaven. Less than 100 American bombers were used in January against Wilhelmshaven, but by November the raiding bombers numbered some 500. There may be interest in comparing the official German and US reaction to the seesaw daylight air situation in 1943 over Germany.

After the Eighth Air Force raid on Bremen, Goering sent for Galland and told him desperately, 'German fighters are a miserable failure'. In fact they had shot down over 10 per cent of the raiding bombers and damaged over a third of them. As in the case of Luftwaffe raids on Malta and in the Battle of Britain, Goering indulged himself in outbursts of unjustified anger against Luftwaffe fighters. Bremen was a shallow penetration raid which made it impossible to bring all German fighter forces to bear fully. The inquest on the raid led to another aviation intervention by the Fuehrer, who insisted that 'raiding US bombers should be intercepted as near the German frontier as possible'. Goering agreed. But he must have known that, if German fighters committed themselves too soon, they could be more prone to outflanking or other deceptive tactics, particularly in the defence of oil and aircraft industry targets deep in Germany. They also needed time and space to assemble their maximum forces.

In October 1943, the crisis seemed to be in the United States Army Air Force camp. They lost nearly 150 four-engined bombers in a week over Germany in that month. In a speech delivered in public on 17 September 1943, President Roosevelt had said, when he spoke of Hitler's European Fortress, 'The Fuehrer forgot to put a roof over the fortress'. In less than a month after this statement, on 15 October, General Eaker, Commander-in-Chief of the US Eighth Air Force, reported to his chief, General Arnold, as follows, 'The Luftwaffe has turned in a performance unprecedented in its magnitude, in the cleverness with which it was planned and in the severity with which it was executed. The Eighth Air Force is in no position to make raids either to Schweinfurt or to any other objective deep in

German territory'. General Arnold wrote later, 'No such savage air battles had been seen since the war began'.

The October air battles over Germany produced a high-level row in German air circles between Goering and Galland. Galland reported that US Thunderbolt (P47) fighters had escorted the US bombers as far as Aachen. This posed new air problems for German air defence. Goering refused to believe him. Galland offered the evidence of a Thunderbolt shot down in the area. Goering replied : 'The pilot must have glided on to Aachen after being shot down' ! Galland laughed at the suggestion.

Goering of course had previously dismissed the possibility of US fighter escort over Germany. He continued in this vein even after the evidence of such escort was abundant and concrete. The October 1943 raid on Schweinfurt had worried him for a particular reason. The raiding US bombers had severely damaged the ball-bearing plant in the city. Goering called a meeting at the Air Ministry in Berlin on 15 October, the day after the raid. In discussing the effect of the bomb damage, Goering said, 'Plans for the dispersal of the ball-bearing industry were drawn up months ago. Why were they not put into effect? They must be carried out immediately.' German industry saw no joy in dispersal and accepted the need reluctantly.

The success of German fighters against Eighth Air Force raids in October 1943 was short-lived. The US daylight raids in November 1943, against Bremen, Kiel and Wilhelmshaven, were made in bad weather. Then the raiding bombers used radar and navigational bombing aids. The raiders' losses were light and the defending fighters had high casualties, mainly due to crashes. Like other fighter forces, Luftwaffe day fighters were not fully trained and equipped for bad weather interception.

It was perhaps a pity that Goering could not have had a copy of the memorandum sent on 25 September 1943 by the Deputy Chief of Staff of the Royal Air Force to his Chief of Staff. It said, 'We are not progressing rapidly with measures to overcome the German night air defences, especially measures against their night-fighters. The radio countermeasures may go a considerable way to defeating them, but the strength of the German night-fighters continues to increase'.

It was a pity too that this authoritative British view on Germany's night defences stayed in Britain at the time. For in the first nine months of 1943, Hermann Goering's air leadership had need of such official encouragement. In the period February-June 1943, RAF Bomber Command struck in strength with night raids on Wilhelmshaven, Hamburg, Berlin and Essen, and other Ruhr targets. The raids struck personally at Goering. They discredited him further in the eyes of the Fuehrer. They tarnished his already tarnished reputation as Germany's air leader. When Goebbels visited Essen after one of the March 1943 raids, he spoke loudly and publicly about 'the negligence of Goering'. And in his diary entry of 10 April 1943, he again overpainted his picture: 'The negligence of Goering and Udet, their sins of omission, are on a scale deserving to be commemorated by history'.

Whatever history does to Hermann Goering, it will surely not condemn him for neglecting the night defences of the Third Reich. He had in the first months of 1943 sponsored the introduction of single-engined night-fighters to stiffen the defences. The crews, specially trained for night and blind-flying, were guided by searchlights and ground control which could use the benefits of early warning and tracking radar. In addition, the bulk of all the Luftwaffe twin-engined fighter units were now part of the air defence of the Third Reich.

But the capacity to defend with fighters against night bomber attack was always below the deterrent level in the Second World War. With ground-to-air guided weapons things might have been different. Goering had such experimental weapons by the end of 1942, but they did not reach operational status before the end of the war.

The limitations of German night air defence were shown in the heavy raids on Hamburg in July 1943. Over a quarter of a million houses in the city were estimated to have been destroyed and over 180 factories. The docks were seriously damaged and some 180,000 tons of shipping sunk in the harbour.

Goering did not go to Hamburg after the raids as he might have been expected to do. He sent Milch and Jeschonnek to represent him and despatched a telegram of condolence to the Gauleiter of Hamburg. Goering remained at Karinhall preparing his brief for a very important policy conference to take place at the Fuehrer's headquarters in East Prussia in the last few days of July.

L

This Rastenburg conference illustrated the extent to which Hermann Goering had lost the power to implement German air policy. It lasted two days. Its main theme was the air defence of Germany. All Goering's senior air staff officers—not merely Galland and Milch who had long backed this policy line—but also Jeschonnek, Goering's Chief of Staff and a loyal Hitler man, and even General Pelz, who was in charge of the German bomber arm, agreed that the emphasis in production and operations must now be on fighters. At the end of the first day of the conference, Goering found it in him to say to his Chiefs of Staff, 'After its offensive phase, in which it has achieved outstanding success, the German Air Force must now change over to the defensive'. The process had of course already begun.

On the morning of the second day of the conference, Goering went to see the Fuehrer in his bunker. He came out about an hour later looking white and shaken. He rejoined his Luftwaffe colleagues but could scarcely speak at first. Hitler had reversed Goering's policy agreed by his senior colleagues. The Fuehrer had said, 'The Luftwaffe has disappointed me too often. A change from offensive to defensive in the West is out of the question. I am giving the Luftwaffe its last chance. The air offensive against England must be resumed on a large scale'.

And so the air leadership of Germany passed into the inept hands of Adolf Hitler to an even greater extent, with the influential Martin Bormann, at Hitler's elbow, seeking to diminish Goering's influence in all spheres.

In August 1943, Goering suffered the loss of another air leader when Hans Jeschonnek shot himself. The Luftwaffe Chief of Staff was worried by the Barbarossa failures and harassed by the problem of working for Goering who was unwilling to see him, or unable to, on many difficult occasions. Jeschonnek was succeeded by General Korten.

Milch and Speer continued to advise Goering to put the case to Hitler for stronger fighter defences. Thus, at a policy conference held at Rechlin, near Berlin, at the end of September 1943, they urged Goering to have a paper written on the growth of American and Soviet air power. Goering would not hear of it and said, 'The Fuehrer knows it is all propaganda. Don't let them fool you'.

It was Goering who was fooling himself. He had the instincts of a wild gambler who knew which cards he wanted to play and was not interested in anyone's hand apart from his own. German air intelligence had plenty of hard evidence, in September 1943, about the growth of Soviet and US air power. Goering believed that intelligence was something to be taken up or torn up as the mood suited. At times he seemed to live for the next throw of the dice or the turn of a card.

If one had to pick the greatest air defence blunder in Hermann Goering's leadership, it would be his failure to anticipate the long-range escort of US bombers in daylight over Germany. Next perhaps was his lack of support for the development of German jet fighters. Hitler was, of course, opposed to jet fighters, but Goering did have the chance to develop them while he was still in favour with the Fuehrer.

The Fuehrer's decree of October 1940 stopped all technical experiments not ready for front-line use within eighteen months. But with the need for fighter aircraft supremacy so clearly spelled out in the recent Battle of Britain, with his personal prestige largely intact, Goering could surely have huffed and bluffed his way past the Fuehrer decree by pleading for the prototype Heinkel 280 and Messerschmitt 262 jets. The Me 262 jet plane, encouraged in the bud, could perhaps have helped to transform the air defence situation over Germany. But Goering did almost nothing to press for its services as a fighter.

On the other hand, the design, development and flight testing of the Heinkel, Arado and Messerschmitt jets took time. One wonders to what extent such radically new planes could have gone into large-scale series production in Germany before 1944, whatever the attitude and decisions of Hitler and Goering. The Me 262, which could have been a key fighter in the air defence of Germany, first flew on 18 April 1941. It had inevitable troubles in development. There were problems of takeoff and broken compressor blades. On 17 August 1942, the German Air Ministry test pilot crashed the plane at an airfield near Berlin. When General Adolf Galland flew the Me 262 at Lechfeld in South Germany on 22 May 1943, he was flying a prototype model. Off went Galland to see Goering to report enthusiastically on its fighter potential. 'This plane is tremendous', he said to Goering, and proposed a switch of all Messerschmitt fighter production to Me 262 jets.

But Hitler was by now deciding German air policy issues to a much greater extent, in some way, than Goering. When Galland took up the question of a high priority for Me 262 fighter production with Milch in June 1943, he was told 'The Fuehrer feels that the risk is too great . . . As a soldier I have no choice but to obey orders. If the Fuehrer orders caution, then we must be cautious'.

By the autumn of 1943, Hermann Goering must have known that the prospects of using the Me 262 fighter in large numbers against US daylight bombing were fairly remote. On 2 November, as a result of Goering's intervention, a commission was at last set up to study the development and future of the Me 262 jet. This was the day that Goering went to Augsburg to discuss with Professor Willi Messerschmitt the potential bomb load of the Me 262. Goering must have known that the future of the Me 262 jet as a daylight interceptor over Germany was now compromised.

On 5 December 1943, when he was at Karinhall, Goering received a cable from Hitler's office which again illustrated how the leadership of the Luftwaffe was slipping from his hands. It dealt with the production of jet planes for use as fighter-bombers. It said, 'It is imperative that the Luftwaffe has a number of jet bombers ready for operations by the spring of 1944. The Fuehrer has asked for two-monthly reports on the Me 262 and Arado 234 programme.'

Later, in December 1943, Hitler at last gave the order for series production of the Me 262. What Galland had urged over six months before, and had been refused by Milch and Goering, now became policy, but to make bombers for the Fuehrer's aeronautical whim and not defensive fighters.

It is impossible to estimate how far the earlier introduction of the Me 262 fighter in large numbers could have checked the Anglo-American daylight raids on Germany. How much earlier could it have been produced? The first production models did not come off the line until June 1944, by which time the final air battles had almost been finally lost on all fronts. In the light of the development problems, the shortage of skilled aircraft workers, the shortage of nickel and chrome for the Jumo engines, one wonders how far resolute insistence by Goering on the development of Me 262 as a defensive fighter would have changed the balance in the 1944 daylight defences of Germany. To the problems of production must be added the shortage of skilled pilots needed in the changeover to flying jets. But an alternative view is feasible. Without interference from Hitler, it is conceivable that 50-100 Me 262 jets might have been flying in the air defence of Germany by the spring of 1944. But this is a hypothesis. The reality was two-fold. Goering failed to support the Messerschmitt jet as an interceptor fighter. But much more important, he refused to accept the reality of US long-range fighter escort in the early months of 1944.

When Goering returned from seeing Hitler at Rastenburg in East Prussia on 11 December 1943, he conferred at Karinhall with Milch and Galland. 'If we cannot protect our aircraft factories, we cannot make enough Messerschmitt jets, whether they are fighters or bombers,' said Milch. Goering nodded but said nothing in reply.

In 1944 the air defence situation of the Third Reich no longer hinged on aircraft production. It was in fact a record year for output, in which the German aircraft industry reached the figure of over 40,000 planes. This included highest-ever output figures for single and twin-engined fighters. The Luftwaffe reached the maximum ever total operational strength of over 3,000 single-engined and twin-engined fighters for some periods of 1944. Of these most were single-engined.

The real factors which caused the final collapse of the air defences of the Third Reich were the increased weight of Anglo-American bombing and the introduction of the Mustang for daylight escort, the dilution of German training facilities aggravated by fuel shortage, and the dilution of the quality of air defence personnel. While German Air Force men were drafted for ground duties on the Eastern Front, Goering impounded Poles, Russians, Czechs and Hungarians into anti-aircraft units. He commented grimly, 'My anti-aircraft batteries are like a League of Nations meeting.'

It was ironic that, at last, in February 1944, Erhard Milch and Albert Speer were allowed to step up fighter production. It was in January and February 1944 that the US Army Air Forces began their attacks on the German aircraft industry and other targets with the help of long-range escort fighters. When in March 1944 General Carl Spaatz agreed that Mustangs could be allowed to roam and engage in freelance operations as opposed to close escort, he was setting Germany a new and insoluble air defence problem.

When Galland asked Goering to change Luftwaffe air defence tactics, Goering replied. 'Only US bombers are to be attacked.' As in the Battle of Britain, Goering interfered at the tactical level and failed to see the advantages of giving his fighters a greater measure of freedom. And, belatedly, in the first week of March 1944, he held a meeting with Galland, Pelz and Korten, his Chief of Staff, and at last agreed to go for the target of 2,000 day and night-fighters for the air defence of Germany. The only major change in the daylight air defences of Germany, since the summer of 1943, had been the creation of a force of about 200 twin-engined fighters which fired 21cm mortars effectively at the raiding formations of US bombers. But now in 1944 these fighters were vulnerable to the roving US Mustang attacks. When Galland asked Goering's blessing to give the mortar-firing planes German fighter escort, the Reichsmarschall refused the request. He then re-issued an order that raiding US planes should be intercepted as early as possible over Germany, whatever the targets and tactical situation. It was not until a US raid on Brunswick on 21 February 1944 that Goering finally accepted the evidence of his own eyes. He was visiting Brunswick at the time. One of his aides drew his attention to the Mustang escort planes flying overhead. He muttered, 'My God, yes!'

In the period February to May 1944, there was some increase in the daylight fighter defences of Germany from something like 400 to about 500 single-engined fighters. Twin-engined day fighters increased to about 260 planes and twin-engined night fighters by over 100 planes from about 850 machines. But the concentration, greater weight and radar aids of Bomber Command operations at night and the growth of US fighter escort in daylight more than cancelled the effect of these Luftwaffe increases. In some of the night bomber 1944 raids, German night fighters may have shot down 80 or 90 of the raiders. But this was on isolated occasions. They were not a vital hindrance.

Goering persisted with his illusions about US fighter escort limitations. On 10 April 1944, at a conference at Obersalzburg, he said to his senior air colleagues, 'The range of the enemy fighter escort does not extend beyond the Elbe'. By then there had been hard reports of Mustang fighters well beyond the Elbe in the Berlin area. It was also at this meeting that he told Speer, Milch and Galland, now the air general for both day and night-fighters, that 'The heavy bomber is the heart of armament in the air. We need a minimum of 400 Heinkel 177s and 500 Junkers 88s a month'.

This was pure fantasy. Were the paracodeine tablets and morphia injections blinding Goering to Germany's aircraft production problems? The chances of producing 400 heavy He 177 bombers a month from a heavily-dispersed and battered industry, at that time, must have been very remote. But this was not the only fantasy of this period. In March 1944, Galland had sent Hitler a report on the increased range of US fighters. Goering angrily sent for Galland and said, 'Why tell the Fuehrer that US fighters can penetrate into Reich territory? What gives you such fantasies? It is bluff'. When Galland asked Goering to check the facts, the Reichsmarschall erupted, 'I officially claim that US fighter planes do not penetrate into the Reich'.

Such scenes can only have been promoted by a mixture of despair and drug-inspired euphoria. By then Goering had already lost some 200,000 ground staff and air crew members in training to meet the needs of the German ground forces on the Eastern Front. By then he must have realised that despite the best efforts of his highly-competent night air defence, and a resolute and skilled day fighter force, there was little he could do as an air leader to stop the blitz on Germany. By the spring of 1944, US bomber losses in daylight raids over Germany were at about the same low average level as Bomber Command's losses at night.

What gave perhaps a fatal blow to Goering's prestige and effectiveness as an air leader was the series of Anglo-American attacks on the German oil industry which were resumed in May. On 12 May 1944, 935 US bombers escorted by about 1,000 fighters attacked oil plants at Brux, Leuna, Merseburg and other areas, and night attacks by RAF Bomber Command were also made on petroleum plants. From June onwards there was a shortage of aviation fuel in the German Air Force. Further Anglo-American attacks carried out in the period June to September reduced the aviation fuel available to about a fifth of German Air Force needs.

The fact of the matter is that by May 1944 most of the

problems of air leadership confronting Goering were insoluble.
As the threat to German industry from Anglo-American bombing
waxed in the period March-May 1944, so did the threat to
Hitler's West Wall and to the French roads, bridges and railways
needed to reinforce and move men and supplies. What then
should Goering have done? How much fighter cover should be
taken from the Third Reich and sent to Northern France to
meet the pre-invasion air attacks by great Anglo-American
armadas? The three major air forces opposed to the Luftwaffe
in the summer of 1944, the United States Army Air Forces in
Europe, the Royal Air Force in Britain, and the Soviet Air Force
in the USSR, not only outnumbered the Luftwaffe by more
than five to one, but also held the strategic initiative. This meant
they were able to concentrate and get a local air advantage of
more than ten to one on many occasions.

While Anglo-American long-range bombers could be switched
from attacks on Germany to attacks on France and the Low
Countries without changing bases, Luftwaffe fighters had to
switch bag and baggage from Germany to France if needed
locally. Goering had an air force with a front-line strength of
about 7,000 aircraft of all types on all fronts. He had to spread
it over four major fronts: West European potential invasion
zones, Italy, the air defence of Germany and the Eastern Front,
where the Soviet Air Force now deployed over 20,000 planes
as the documents have shown.

Looking back at the many problems of the air defence of
Germany, it would seem that Goering's main mistake as an air
leader was that he did not heed the early advice of Galland,
Speer and others to step up the production of fighters. But would
he have had enough skilled pilots to do the job for him, if he
had had the planes? One can blame him for not opposing the
military concepts of Adolf Hitler. But this was exactly what the
German army and navy Chiefs of Staff had also failed to do.
Once Barbarossa had failed and the United States was in the
war in Europe, the air defence of Germany was perhaps bound
to fail. No one will ever knew how many competent pilots would
have flown the Me 262 jet fighter, if Messerschmitt and Galland
had had their way and not Hitler.

German day and night-fighter pilots made heroic efforts in
the air battle of Germany. They fought longer and harder than

the fighter pilot heroes of the Battle of Britain. They had a lost leader in Hermann Goering. Long before the summer of 1944 he had lost caste with Hitler, lost face in Germany as a whole, lost control of his air leadership problems and must have lost considerable belief in himself.

CHAPTER EIGHT

The Lost Leader

FROM THE autumn of 1943 until the end of the Second World War in Europe, Hermann Goering's air power was overwhelmed by the avalanche of air power ranged against the Luftwaffe. The front line strength of German air units in the last eighteen months of the war varied between 6,000 and 7,000 planes. During that period, the combined strength of the Soviet, British and American Air Forces aligned against the Luftwaffe rose from about 30,000 to 35,000 operational aircraft. And because Germany had lost the initiative on all fronts, all Goering could hope to do was to patch up a series of desperate air situations as best he could. His power of serious leadership was virtually nil.

Numerically the strongest air opposition was on the Eastern Front. In the period 1943 to 1945, as the documents have shown, Soviet air regiments increased in strength from about 15,000 to over 20,000 planes. At the same time, the combat qualities of Soviet pilots and air crews improved and the Soviet regiments were equipped with more modern Ilyushin and Tupolev tactical bombers and Lavochkin and Mig fighters. In contrast, Goering had to use many half-trained inexperienced air crews and obsolescent Arado and Gotha planes in a desperate attempt to keep a front-line strength on the Eastern Front of about 2,000 planes. He also had to convert some of his Heinkel bomber squadrons into air transport units.

But it was the air battles over Germany which brought home the full failure of Goering's air leadership to Hitler, to the German Chiefs of Staff and to the German people. The Anglo-American bombing of Germany placed in jeopardy Hitler's ability to make any kind of war. German industry and German communications looked as though they might no longer survive.

Goering's hopes of victory were fast ebbing away in the

autumn of 1943. He still had moments of optimism. Thus at an
Air Staff meeting, held at the Air Ministry in Berlin on 7 October
1943, he said energetically, 'Under the protection of the forces
concentrating on the air defence of Germany the Luftwaffe will
soon recover the power to attack once more'.

But this burst of confidence had soon evaporated. On
30 November 1943, he made his last broadcast to the German
people. It struck a sombre note and held out nothing but bleak
prospects; but it had a touch of that splendid eloquence which
recalled some of his earlier public speeches made in happier
days. He reminded his German listeners of the way the Spartans
defended the pass of Thermopylae against the Persian invaders,
and went on, 'If every German city is razed to the ground, the
German people will still survive . . . we may even have to live
in holes in the ground . . . if Berlin vanishes from the face of the
earth it would be dreadful but not fatal'. And he ended his
broadcast grimly, 'If the Russians reach Berlin, the German
people would have ceased to exist'.

Was the speech made in the kind of fit of depression to which
Goering was at times prone? Certainly he had reason enough to
be depressed. Three months previously Italy had opted out of
the war. And just before that, the main German summer offensive on the Eastern Front had come to a halt in less than a
fortnight. And whatever Goering may have said to Galland and
his other senior colleagues about US fighter escort covering the
daylight bombing attacks on Germany in 1943, he must have
realised that the 1944 build-up of Anglo-American bombing
would be beyond his air defence resources, even if he could not
say so in public, or to his colleagues.

Goering was not alone among high-ranking Germans in his
pessimism about the outcome of the war. General Halder, Hitler's
Chief of Staff, recalled in a post-war statement, 'Towards the
end of 1943 it had become unmistakably clear that the military
war was lost'. And Goebbels' diary entry for 10 September 1943
shows that he had discussed possible peace terms with Hitler,
who replied, 'No negotiations for the moment'. The Fuehrer
added that he was 'worried about the coming Anglo-American
landing in France'.

However, when Goering sounded out his Swedish contacts
about peace negotiations at the beginning of October 1943,

Hitler heard of the move through the Himmler grapevine, and sent for him. Goering went to see the Fuehrer at his Rastenburg headquarters on 10 October. Hitler screamed, 'I'll have you shot if you do this again'.

But Goering's loyalty to Hitler was unimpaired, despite the growing chaos in the German High Command, the Fuehrer's constant interference in Luftwaffe affairs and the plotting against Goering by Bormann and other Nazi leaders close to Hitler.

The fact is that, by the end of 1943, Goering was no longer the Commander-in-Chief of the Luftwaffe in the sense that he had been in the first two years of the war. Other people were now taking the kind of key decision about aircraft production and allocation of squadrons that Goering used to take in consultation with his Chiefs of Air Staff. Thus at the end of 1943 Albert Speer, the Minister of Armaments, had formulated his plans for fighter aircraft production without detailed reference to Goering. And on the Eastern Front, the Luftwaffe's First and Fourth Air Fleets were getting operational orders direct from Hitler's headquarters, with a copy duly sent to Goering for information.

It was not merely the Me 262 jet aircraft which was a bone of contention between Hitler and Goering's air chiefs. There was also a hiatus between the Fuehrer and Goering about the operational use of the new He 177 heavy bomber, which had been rushed into premature and disastrous use as a transport plane in the desperate attempt to supply the German Sixth Army at Stalingrad.

At two conferences at Rastenburg early in July 1943, Hitler had made it clear that he wanted the He 177 to be used as a strategic heavy bomber on the Eastern Front against Soviet industrial targets, such as power stations. Meanwhile Admiral Doenitz, Commander-in-Chief of the German Navy, was asking for it to be used mainly as an anti-shipping bomber. There was support for Hitler's view from Albert Speer and from a young Luftwaffe bomber leader, Colonel Baumbach. But Goering supported the Doenitz request, and their joint view prevailed on this occasion.

The He 177 did not, however, have a very distinguished record. Over 800 of them were produced in 1943 and 1944. But their attacks on convoys had very little success. Their crash rate

was high and their combat casualties too. There was a shortage
of crews for them by the spring of 1944 and a shortage of fuel
and replacement engines by the summer of 1944.

By the beginning of 1944 the development of Soviet, British
and American air power in Europe was so great that almost all
the decisions reached either by Hitler or Goering and his air
staff were without major operational effect. Hermann Goering
was now a lost leader. He had no way of escape. There were no
solutions to his problems. His blind, excessive loyalty to Hitler
and his utter disregard of reality, ever since the air defeat over
Dunkirk, had piled up a succession of air headaches which were
now incurable. The year to aim at a production of 40,000 planes
was 1941 and not, as was achieved, in 1944.

The 1943 decline in Goering's status is illustrated in both the
Galland and Speer post-war memoirs. Perhaps the most dramatic
example was a meeting on 1 August between General Jeschonnek, then Goering's Chief of Staff, and Hitler. Jeschonnek is reported to have said, 'Fuehrer, I suggest you take over command
of the Luftwaffe as you have of the army. You alone can restore
the prestige of our air force. The Reichsmarschall is never available for consultation'.

There was both substance and absurdity in Jeschonnek's
statement, made under great stress, for he committed suicide
soon after. General Koller, who later became Goering's Chief of
Air Staff, complained how difficult it was to get regular access
to the Reichsmarschall in 1944. Goering now tended to withdraw
more often to his homes at Veltenstein, Obersalzburg and Karinhall and to send for senior air colleagues when he wished to see
them. His attendance at the Fuehrer's daily briefing conferences
at Rastenburg in East Prussia or at the Berghof in Southern
Germany continued erratic. Perhaps he knew, by the end of
1943, that his leadership of the Luftwaffe had become largely
nominal, as Adolf Hitler was taking many of the major air
decisions. In any event, Germany's air inferiority was such that
any decision that Goering might make would have little effect
on the war. Despite his cavalcade of blunders, Hermann Goering
was a highly intelligent person. He realised that the time for
persistent bluster was now past.

On 30 July 1943, Goering had said to General Pelz at the
Luftwaffe's East Prussian headquarters, 'I appoint you assault

leader of the raids on England'. He was merely echoing a decision taken already by Hitler at a Rastenburg conference on the day before. The Fuehrer ordered the resumption of the blitz on Britain to begin in January 1944. Goering had the job of scratching together the bomber forces needed to carry out the Fuehrer's command.

At the time, the operational strength of Goering's entire front-line force of high-level bombers was about 1,600 planes. This figure was less than he had in the spring of 1940. Then, however, the luxury of a one-front war in Western Europe was the background to Goering's bomber responsibilities. At the beginning of 1944 he had to split his bomber force of 1,600 between four air fronts. There were the dispersed operations on the Eastern Front, the war in the Mediterranean, where new Anglo-American landings in Italy threatened, the resumption of the air attack on Britain ordered by Hitler, and, finally, the support of Admiral Doenitz's naval operations in the Battle of the Atlantic. To be really effective on all four fronts, a force of 1,600 bombers was probably needed for each one of them. Moreover, the bomber crew standards of the German Air Force at the beginning of 1944 were declining further.

When Hitler instructed Goering to resume the blitz on Britain at the beginning of 1944, a daylight attack was out of the question. British and American fighter squadrons based in England totalled over 4,000 planes. The German Third Air Fleet in France had only about 100 single-engined fighters available both for defence and for escorting German planes to attack Southern England. Goering went off to see the Commander of his Third Air Fleet in Paris in the first week of January and suggested a renewal of the daylight attack on Britain. Field Marshal Sperrle simply answered, 'Impossible'. Goering did not pursue the matter.

At the time of Goering's meeting with Sperrle, the Third Air Fleet had a force of about 350 twin-engined bombers for the new night blitz on Britain. Goering skimmed off a few bomber squadrons from the Russian and Italian Fronts and two air units engaged in the Battle of the Atlantic. This gave his bomber chief, General Pelz, an initial force of just over 500 bombers.

But the new wave of air raids on Britain were a failure. Thus, when London was attacked on the night of 21 January, only about ten per cent of the bomb-load fell in the London area. And during the whole of January and February 1944, the Pelz mini-blitz unloaded only about 1,700 tons of bombs on Britain, that is less than the total which was being dropped on Germany in one twenty-four hour period by British and American bombers.

Before the end of January 1944 Goering had to switch two squadrons of He 177 heavy bombers away from the air attack on Britain back to their base at Marseilles. This was because of the Allied landings at Anzio. It was just one of many examples which illustrate Goering's need to respond to the moves of his opponents. He was also desperately trying to plan to meet the forthcoming Anglo-American invasion of Northern France.

In January and February 1944 Goering held a number of conferences at the Air Ministry in Berlin and at his homes at Veltenstein and Karinhall. He told his colleagues, 'We must build up an anti-invasion reserve of 1,000 fighters and fighter-bombers'. This was merely air leadership on paper. The reserve of 1,000 planes was unlikely to be forthcoming, and if it had materialised, it would be no more than a gesture. At this stage of the war there was nothing more feasible that Goering could plan or propose. Across the Channel, Anglo-American air power was building up to a force of some 12,000 planes. The total strength of the Third Air Fleet in France in the spring of 1944 was just under 500 aircraft of all types. And so, even if Goering's anti-invasion reinforcement of 1,000 planes had taken effect, his air squadrons would still have been swamped by overwhelming Anglo-American air power. In the spring of 1944 the Luftwaffe could deploy about 6,750 planes on all air fronts. Germany's air opponents then had about 35,000 planes. The quality of Luftwaffe crews and air training was on the slide. From June onwards there were to be serious problems about supplies of fuel because of Anglo-American bombing of the German oil industry.

Clearly Goering must be blamed for much of this. But to blame him alone would be to ignore the remarkable development of British, American and Soviet air power. It was no fault of Goering's that his air force had to deal with three such major aeronautical giants. This was much more the fruit of Hitler's strategy.

At the time of 'Operation Overlord', code name for the Anglo-American landing in Normandy, German air power on the Western Front had reached a remarkably low level of strength and activity. On 6 June 1944, the day of the Overlord landings, the Third Air Fleet under Field Marshal Sperrle had a strength of only 481 planes, of which 319 were ready for operations. The force included a mere 100 single-engined fighters, 64 reconnaissance planes and 317 twin-engined bombers.

Analysis of this Air Fleet and of its anti-invasion commitments illustrates the state of ineffectiveness to which Goering's leadership had now come. In terms of the spring and summer air commitments of 1944, it was entirely impotent. It is true that German production of single-engined aircraft was increasing strongly and that this had caused concern at Anglo-American Chiefs of Staff level. But the necessary trained crews with experienced squadron commanders were not available to give substance to the expansion in the output of Messerschmitt and Focke Wulf fighters.

There were only about 50 serviceable reconnaissances planes in the Third Air Fleet in the spring and summer of 1944. There were a mere 75-80 serviceable single-engined fighters. There were two vital jobs to do in preparation for Operation Overlord. The first was to reconnoitre and take photographs of invasion harbours and troop concentrations in Southern England. The second was to defend the French communications and rail system from Anglo-American air attacks, so that the railways needs of the German Army could be met, that is, the bringing up of weapons and equipment and of materials to strengthen the Atlantic wall.

Goering was confronted by a first-class dilemma. If he used his limited force of fighters to cover the reconnaissance planes, he would leave the German Army in France unprotected from enemy daylight air attack. If he gave the reconnaissance planes no fighter cover, they would be shot down and would provide little or no information on the timing and direction of the Anglo-American landing.

In the event, Goering's Air Force disposed on the invasion front failed miserably in all its roles. Given the great numerical inferiority and the lack of initiative, no air leader could have retrieved the situation. Goering's personal valet, Robert, who stayed with his master almost till the end, recalls that, in the spring and summer of 1944, the Reichsmarschall would often come home at night in a state of nervous exhaustion and slump into an armchair. As the mounting operational problems crowded in on him, Goering became more irascible, more desperate and more confused. When he again ordered his fighter squadrons to 'shoot down the bombers and ignore the escort fighters', after the new crop of American raids in May 1944, he must have known that the US escort fighters were the real menace that had to be overcome before a satisfactory toll of US bombers could be exacted. But the Fuehrer had ordered, 'Shoot down the bombers'. By May 1944, Goering was acquiring some of his Fuehrer's unrivalled capacity for self-delusion. Not that he had lacked such tendencies hitherto; but they were now more pronounced. The morphine drugs may, once again, have brought the potential euphoria to the surface and made it manifest.

One of the most superb examples of Goering's optimistic ability to deceive himself was the memorandum he circulated to the German Chiefs of Staff at the end of March 1944. The subject was the use of the Me 262 jet bomber as a means of repelling the June 1944 invasion of Normandy. The Me 262, called *Blitzbomber* in Luftwaffe slang, was one of the great anti-invasion hopes of the Fuehrer. This is what Goering wrote about the way the aircraft was to be used: 'The action can be carried out at once over the English coast by raiding the embarkation points and then the beaches, then during the landing by dropping bombs on landing craft and tanks. I visualise the operation in this way. The aircraft fly along the beach and blast the landing parties which, at first, will not be co-ordinated. This is how the Fuehrer sees the action and it is to be prepared in this way.'

Incredible as it may seem, at the time Goering circulated this memorandum, the first experimental squadron of 15 Me 262 planes had not yet been formed. The prospects of mounting a force of even 50 Blitzbombers to oppose the invasion were very remote indeed. In fact, the first Me 262 bombing operations were not carried out until the end of July 1944. By then, Anglo-American forces were fully established in France.

Contrasting with the success fantasy in Goering's mind was the modest reality of the Third Air Fleet's operational reports, most of which he actually read in the pre-invasion period. In February and March only nine bomber raids were made on

M

London, averaging less than a hundred planes per attack. And in April and May this modest scale of attacks was barely maintained, when operations were switched to the ports and shipping lanes of Southern England. The emphasis was now on mine-laying rather than bombing.

When Goering signalled Sperrle in the first week of May ordering the Third Air Fleet 'to carry out intensive reconnaissance of the harbours of Southern England', Sperrle replied, 'The air superiority of the enemy prevents reconnaissance over the Channel and the invasion ports'. Field Marshal Rommel, now a senior commander of German anti-invasion forces in France, added to Goering's discomfort by reporting quite accurately to the Army Chiefs of Staff that 'the Luftwaffe was failing to provide the necessary information on the build-up of the invasion forces'. At the end of May, the German High Command appreciated vaguely that 'the invasion would take place somewhere between Dieppe and Dunkirk'. So much for the combined efforts of Goering's air reconnaissance and other German intelligence sources.

Thus Goering's air reconnaissance failed German intelligence badly on the subject of where the landing of 6 June 1944 was to be; he was also unable to protect the Wehrmacht's vital transport system in France against the Anglo-American air attacks in the period March to May. The German armies in France needed a minimum of a hundred trains a day to bring in supplies and equipment and to stock up the key anti-invasion areas with petrol and ammunition. But by April Anglo-American bombing had reduced the daily average to 60, and in May to about 30.

To sum up, both in attack and defence, Goering's air leadership was utterly ineffective on the Western Front in the months before Operation Overlord. But the roots of Goering's failure went back to the years even before the war, when he had been unable to think seriously ahead in terms of a four or five year war, even though he himself had predicted such a war.

On the eve of the Anglo-American invasion of France, relations between Goering and Hitler were cool. It must have been already clear to the Fuehrer that the German Air Force could not play a serious role in repelling the invading armies. He said, reportedly, to Goebbels and Bormann on 1 June 1944, at his Rastenburg bunker, 'Goering lives a life of idle luxury while the German people suffer. He no longer cares for Germany'. Goering certainly lived in luxury. But he was never an idle man for long and he cared about Germany with his own brand of patriotism. But his status in the Fuehrer's entourage was now much lower, and his control of the Luftwaffe was greatly reduced. He was now barely hanging on to his authority as Commander-in-Chief of the German Air Force.

How can one fairly measure Goering's level of air generalship on the eve of the Anglo-American landings in France? On all the war fronts, German military leadership was just the flotsam and jetsam of hastily improvised policies, conceived desperately while the enemy pushed ahead with their own substantial plans.

On the day of Operation Overlord, 6 June 1944, Goering and the other German Chiefs of Staff were taken by surprise. Goering was staying at his castle at Veltenstein on the night of 5-6 June. As the German High Command intelligence had decided that the initial Anglo-American landing was only a sideshow, there was no great haste to react. There had been so many invasion scares and alarms in April and May, that neither Goering nor the other Chiefs of Staff were inclined to take them seriously. But at midday on June 6 Hitler called a Chiefs of Staff meeting at Kleissheim, near Salzburg, which Goering attended. Himmler and Ribbentrop were also present. Hitler called for maximum reinforcement of the Third Air Fleet on the anti-invasion front. Goering promised immediate but inadequate reinforcement by 600 planes, of which 300 would be fighter-bombers to support the army and 300 fighters to escort and patrol.

On 6 June, the German Third Air Fleet carried out some 340 sorties; many of them were ineffective. While nearly 100 twin-engined bombers laid mines at night in the shipping departure and arrival areas, only two of the fighter-bomber sorties reached the invasion beaches to make a quick pass. The other Luftwaffe fighter sorties were swamped by some 12,000 British and American planes attacking airfields, troop concentrations, transport and communications in Northern France. The Luftwaffe was outnumbered by more than twenty to one. On the evening of 6 June, Sperrle signalled to Goering, 'The position is grave'. The next day Goering returned to Karinhall and said, reportedly, to his wife Emmy, 'If things go wrong I shall take my life'.

Things were certainly going very wrong for Goering in the first days of Operation Overlord. Because of communications difficulties there was a fatal delay of twenty-four hours in sending the 600-plane reinforcement to Northern France. And when the aircraft did attempt to move to their new bases, they suffered heavy casualties in transit. There was also confusion because they flew to the wrong bases. Then, under the great pressure of Anglo-American air power, there were further casualties because the Luftwaffe bases were often not camouflaged and so were more effectively strafed by British and US planes.

Talking of this period of the Anglo-American invasion, Erhard Milch, Goering's deputy, commented after the war, 'There was great confusion and even disintegration from this time onwards in the German High Command'.

Despite the reinforcement of the Third Air Fleet in the second week of June, by 600 fighters and fighter bombers from Germany, the size and scope of German Air Force operations in France remained unaffected. On most days in June and July they put out an effort of between 250 and 500 sorties against more than twenty times that number by British and American air squadrons. When Rommel reported to Hitler on 6 July, 'Today there were 45 German planes in the air. They simply could not get through,' he was underlining the general impotence of the Luftwaffe from Goering downwards. On the same day, the German Seventh Army in France recorded, 'The enemy controls the air to such an extent that movement on the road is impossible'. And in mid-June the Second Panzer Division had reported, 'The Allies have total air supremacy. They bomb and shoot at anything which moves. Our territory is under constant observation. We have a feeling of being powerless against enemy aircraft'.

Goering must have come near to despair at this stage. On 10 June 1944 Hitler had issued the following wild, irrelevant order: 'Half of all fighter units in Germany must be kept in readiness to support the army with low-level attacks; and in an emergency all fighter units.' Goering had already agreed with Galland and other senior air leaders to build up a force of over 500 planes to meet the continuous threat to German industries, particularly the fuel industry, from Anglo-American bombing. This was to be achieved partly by converting twin-engined day fighter units into single-engined fighter squadrons, because the former had proved vulnerable against the increased numbers of US Mustang escort fighters.

And so the aviation gap between Hitler and Goering grew wider. The Fuehrer had already assumed direction of the V weapon policies and the jet aircraft planning. Now he was taking a firmer grip on decisions to move air units on all fronts. And, as he did so, Hermann Goering's status as an air-leader declined more steeply. Views on when the decline began vary. General Galland thought that Goering's prestige and influence began to suffer after the Battle of Britain. General Karl Bodenschatz, Goering's great friend and senior air aide, puts the failure of the Luftwaffe at Stalingrad, early in 1943, as the chief turning point.

By the summer of 1944, persistent aeronautical failures on all fronts had reduced Goering's air leadership to a handful of unimportant gestures. But at least Goering remained partly realistic. He read the German Army leaders' reports on Allied air supremacy and began to accept them. On 14 July von Runstedt's signal had spoken of 'the most effective and most impressive use of air power ever witnessed'. On 28 July von Kluge had stressed 'the psychological effect on the fighting troops, especially the infantry, caused by a cascade of falling bombs'. But the Fuehrer believed that the German air situation could still be reprieved. He could believe almost anything.

He asked Goering to come to see him at Rastenburg. The Reichsmarschall went there on 31 July 1944 and listened while his leader ranted on. 'One must realise that, in France, a turn of the tide can only come about if we manage to re-establish air superiority, if only for a certain period. I am therefore of the opinion that we ought to do everything possible, however hard it may be at the moment, to hold the air force units now being formed as a last reserve for an extreme urgency.'

Goering listened to the Fuehrer's views and nodded sombre agreement. He thought, perhaps desperately, that the re-establishment of limited local air superiority might have been just feasible with the large-scale use of Messerschmitt jet fighters. But at the end of July this was out of the question. By now, too, the Vi flying bomb, which had promised much, was soon to be relegated to the catalogue of interesting technical failures in Goering's air career.

This is no snub to Goering, to his scientists or to his technical advisers. Under Goering's air leadership, the German Air Force developed the widest range of modern air weapons of any air force in the world. Perhaps the V1 flying bomb—the buzz-bomb as it was called—was the least important of the technical innovations. Its launching sites in Northern France certainly absorbed thousands of tons of British and American bombs in the months before the June 1944 invasion of Normandy. These bombs would otherwise have damaged, even more, the German Army communications in France.

The first flying bomb fell on London on 13 June. By the end of September over 3,500 Londoners were killed and over 10,000 seriously injured through these attacks. But both the morale of Londoners and the invasion plans remained largely unaffected by the V1 attacks.

Why therefore did Goering persist in the V1 attacks from aircraft after September 1944, when the launching sites in France had been overrun? Back in July, both he and the Fuehrer had realised that V1 and V2 ground-launchings might be overtaken by the Anglo-American advance towards the German frontier. All that would be left to continue the rump of Hitler's V weapons campaign, was a small force of Heinkel bombers which could launch V1 flying bombs at a range of over 500 miles. And so, from July to November 1944, the Heinkel V1 launchers were built up in strength by Goering at the expense of Luftwaffe Heinkel units on the Russian front. They fired some 300 V1 buzz-bombs per month in the period July-November, mainly at London, but also at Southampton and Antwerp. They had no real military effect on the Allied invasion build-up. The V1 operations were a classic example of Goering's technical initiative being almost utterly irrelevant.

The same is broadly true of the radio-guided bombs, the Henschel 293 and the FX 1400, which Goering had pressed his scientists to develop as far back as 1941. These guided weapons first became operational in the early autumn of 1943. When Italy surrendered to the Allies, Luftwaffe bombers, using the guided bombs, sank an Italian battleship and a destroyer. But in the major air assaults on Atlantic convoys, in September 1943, the new weapons turned out to be failures, and the losses in the Dornier and Heinkel bombers which carried them were heavy

There were minor guided bomb successes against US and British shipping at Anzio and Salerno in 1944, which made one wonder what their potential would be against the Anglo-American landings in France in June and August 1944. But, because of technical troubles, the guided bombs were not used again until the early spring of 1945. Then, in the last desperate phase of the war, they were used in attempts to destroy the bridges over the Elbe and scored some hits.

Other irrelevant technical air developments achieved under Goering's leadership were the Me 163 rocket-fighter, a four-engined jet Junkers bomber and ground-to-air guided missiles such as the *Rheintochter* (Rhine maiden). They were irrelevant because they never came into serious operational use during Goering's air stewardship. They were highly important, however, because, together with the Messerschmitt and Arado jets and German radar equipment, they provided the USSR at the end of the war with a great haul, a remarkable technological legacy, which contributed vastly to Soviet progress in the new jet, super-sonic and space age. Because so much of Germany's sophisticated aero-space industry had been moved eastward, to avoid the full threat of Anglo-American bombing, to Poland, Czechoslovakia, Hungary, East Prussia and Rumania, German technicians and aero-space products fell into Soviet hands much sooner and in larger numbers. There is no doubt that many of the weapons which Goering sponsored became important landmarks in Soviet aero-space development in the ten years which followed the end of the Second World War.

The air front which probably caused Goering the greatest disappointment and frustration was the Mediterranean theatre. His personal links with Mussolini were strong and long. Goering's first official visit to Rome on behalf of the Fuehrer went back to April 1933. He had planned the early strategy with Admiral Raeder in some detail. In the first year or so of Mediter-ranean air operations there had been major successes against British shipping and a real prospect of bringing Malta to its knees, or so Goering thought. But in 1942 the problem of Rommel's supplies to North Africa by sea and air had developed into an acute Axis headache which Goering had done little to cure. When Rommel met Goering in Rome in the first week of August 1942, and urged on him the importance of more air transport, Goering replied with a few absent-minded remarks about his private art collection.

Was Goering really indifferent to Rommel's supply problems? He could scarcely have been. Rommel was at that time one of Hitler's favourite generals, and the Fuehrer had raised the issue of Rommel's supply problems on many occasions at German Chiefs of Staff meetings.

Goering had already taken such limited steps as he could to remedy the situation. The move of the Second Air Fleet from Russia early in 1942 had weakened his air forces in the East, but had strengthened his air forces in Sicily. Rommel's supplies did not, however, benefit from this very much. The use of German night-fighters to escort Italian convoys plying to North Africa and of Ju 88 bombers to fly fuel to Rommel were both measures born of Goering's desperation in the Mediterranean theatre. The lack of major German air opposition at the Battle of Alamein in October 1942 underlined further the severe limitations of Goering's air potential. For him Alamein had to be a sideshow whether it marked a turning point in the war or not. Serious air leadership at strategic level was no longer feasible in the Mediterranean.

And in the first week of November 1942 Goering's uncertainty about Torch, the new Anglo-American landing in North Africa, was illustrated by a telephone conversation he had with Field Marshal Kesselring, then in Sicily. Goering had no luck at all in trying to guess the destination of the approaching convoys, as the following exchange of views shows:

Goering: The convoy will be in range of our Air Force in the next forty to fifty hours, and therefore everything must be held in readiness.

Kesselring: Herr Reichsmarschall, suppose a convoy attempts a landing in Africa?

Goering: To my mind a landing will be attempted in Corsica, in Sardinia, or at Derna or Tripoli.

Kesselring: It is more probably at a North African port.

Goering: Yes, but not a French port.

The landings of 9 November were in Algiers and Tunisia. The next day, at the Fuehrer's Chiefs of Staff meeting at Rastenburg, Goering said to Hitler, 'In my view, the occupation of North Africa represents the first point scored by the Allies since the beginning of the war'. The Reichsmarschall was absurdly frugal in his award of points. The defence of Malta, the Battle of Britain and the bombing of Germany should surely have rated something on Goering's scoreboard of the Second World War. It was Winston Churchill who summed up the North African situation realistically at a Cabinet meeting of 5 November 1942 : 'The German Air Force has given up the hopeless task of combating our air superiority.'

Hitler now recognised the crisis in his Mediterranean affairs. He sent Goering to Rome to parley with Rommel, Kesselring, Count Ciano, Mussolini and the Italian Chiefs of Staff. Goering arrived on 30 November 1942 and a week of discussions on the Mediterranean situation followed. Goering was instructed to promise a reinforcement for North Africa of three German armoured divisions. But no one seriously expected all of them to arrive in Tunisia or Tripolitania in time, because Italian sea and air power and German air power were inadequate to transport them safely. Goering made a series of easy and optimistic comments to Mussolini about the outcome of the 1943 offensive on the Russian front, and he promised air reinforcements for North Africa.

Italian reaction to Goering's performance as Hitler's envoy in Rome was not appreciative. Members of the Italian General Staff 'expressed surprise at the amount of nonsense the Reichsmarschall could talk', and found his 'arrogance and hectoring manner' unpleasant. Ciano commented at the time, 'Is Goering really thinking of becoming Reichsprotektor of Italy?'

Goering returned to Karinhall from Rome in the second week of December 1942, and asked Galland to go to Sicily to see what could be done to repair the North African situation. Neither the Luftwaffe nor the Italian Navy could begin to cope with the problems of supplying the ground forces of Rommel and von Arnim. On 22 January 1943 Goering received a copy of von Arnim's signal to Kesselring, Commander-in-Chief of the Luftwaffe in the Mediterranean. It said, 'The supply situation is catastrophic. The army cannot fight with shells which are at the bottom of the Mediterranean.'

Goering did the little that he could. He transferred a few

fighter and fighter-bomber units to bases in Tunisia. And although the Fuehrer had just told him that air transport for the Eastern Front must have priority, Goering despatched nearly 150 Junkers and Messerschmitt transport planes to Sicily. But he had insufficient fighter cover for them and so they suffered heavy casualties in the spring of 1943 in a hopeless attempt to help supply von Arnim's forces. In his despatches to Berlin, von Arnim referred more than once to the 'inadequate support of the Luftwaffe'. There was justice in the comment. With an average number of fighter sorties of about 100 a day, Goering's air force could not cover the minimum duties of close support for von Arnim's ground forces, the protection of port facilities and the escort of transport planes.

When von Arnim surrendered in May 1943, Goering knew, of course, that an Anglo-American attack on Sicily would follow very soon. He despatched two new fighter-bomber units of about 75 planes to Sicily and ordered intensive reconnaissance of Malta and the Tunisian ports. The concentration of Spitfires on Malta and of British and US squadrons on Tunisian air bases was duly reported to him.

Back in the days of 1940-1941, one would have expected a directive to blitz the air bases of Malta and Tunisia. But now Goering was no blitzer; he was the recipient of blitz. The Anglo-American assault of June and early July on the Luftwaffe bases in Sicily, Sardinia and Corsica reduced the German air potential in the Central Mediterranean to a low ebb.

While his Anglo-American opponents could throw more than a thousand planes into a local air battle on any one of the main air fronts, Goering could no longer reply even with the minimum forces required to do serious battle. He had no time to pause, draw breath and reflect since the defeat in Tunisia. And if he had had more time, he would not have had the resources for successful air planning.

Goering did, however, manage to strengthen the leadership of his air squadrons in Sicily and Italy at the time of the Anglo-American invasion. Field Marshal von Richthofen, one of the ablest of the Luftwaffe field commanders, was moved to Sicily from the Eastern Front. He had two major problems. First, the great numerical inferiority of his squadrons and, secondly, the liaison problems with the Italian Air Force.

Remembering Goering's long affection for Mussolini, one might have expected Germano-Italian air force relations to have gradually improved. They had now fought together in the Mediterranean for over two years. But co-operation in many fields such as tactics, telephone systems and signalling had been poor, and the relations between air and ground crews had often been prickly. Goering was no Eisenhower. He did almost nothing to cement the rapport between the German and Italian Air Forces. However, by the summer of 1943, further co-operation with the Italian Air Force was to be short-lived.

By 10 July 1943, that is less than a week after the invasion of Sicily, the activities of the Luftwaffe in the Central Mediterranean had become almost negligible. Under the most difficult operational conditions, German Air Force pilots of transport planes flew spare parts and ammunition to German ground forces in Sicily.

On 25 July the Fascist Grand Council deposed Mussolini. On 9 September 1943 an Anglo-American landing at Salerno took place. Only one of the 700 ships mounting the assault was sunk by Luftwaffe action. A force of less than 50 fighters and fighter-bombers was all the Luftwaffe could operate against the invading forces.

Apart from the campaigns in Greece, Crete and Jugoslavia in 1941, the story of Goering's air leadership in the Mediterranean is one of persistent failure. There was very little he or his Luftwaffe could do to block the Anglo-American advance to the north of Italy. It was the tenacity of German ground forces in 1944, commanded by Goering's one-time Chief of Air Staff, Field Marshal Kesselring, which slowed up the Allied rate of progress. A further element was the bad weather. By 1944 adverse weather was in general a more serious battle factor than the Luftwaffe. In 1940 they had called the fine weather 'Goering's weather'. In 1944 the Reichsmarschall must have hoped for the protection of foul weather to ground British, American and Soviet air squadrons.

On the Eastern Front, too, Goering's potential since the Stalingrad disaster had become very slight indeed. Many times in 1943 and 1944 Hitler had said at his daily briefings that the Russian Front must have priority. By then the persistent evidence of German Air Force signals intelligence had at last convinced

Goering that the strength of Soviet air regiments was something like ten times the strength of Luftwaffe units.. The Fuehrer's insistence on special priority could therefore in practice amount to very little.

Scraping the very bottom of the aeronautical barrel was the only option open to Goering in the final phases of the war on the Eastern Front. The Ju 87 dive-bomber units, which had spearheaded the first air attacks of June 1941, had to be disbanded and replaced by the more modern but less feared Focke Wulf 190 fighter-bomber units. Many of the Heinkel bomber units had to be converted to air transport work. Large numbers of Gotha gliders were thrown in perilously to lift supplies to the sorely-pressed German Army. Over 400 of the new He 219 defensive anti-tank planes were lost in 1943 and 1944. What use was it that Goering concentrated 175 Junkers transport planes in March and April 1944 to supply the German First Panzer Army in the Kamensk Podolsk area or later on to help German ground forces encircled near Breslau?

By the summer of 1944 Anglo-American attacks on oil had caused a fuel crisis in the Luftwaffe on all fronts. Even the mobility through air transport, which Goering had sponsored as a major plank of his air leadership, was now threatened by the lack of petrol. From a strength of over 700 transport planes in May 1944, the German Air Force was reduced to about 200 at the end of that year.

Goering paid only one or two visits to the Eastern and Mediterranean air fronts in the last year of the war. He preferred to stay in Germany for the political battles with Hitler's senior cronies, for the disputes with his own air colleagues and with Hitler about the final Luftwaffe futilities in the air war in the West. It was a period in which individual German pilots' heroism was quite remarkable, particularly during the air battles over Germany. It was also a period in which Goering's lapses of leadership and foresight made in the previous years came home to roost and left him utterly confused and impotent.

August 1944 was certainly not a happy month. Goering's health again suffered and he took to his bed. His air force had failed to support the German Army retreating to Holland, Belgium and Eastern France. So successful were the Anglo-American attacks on German fuel plants that, in September,

Goering's air force had only 30,000 tons of fuel instead of the monthly 160,000 tons needed. The Fuehrer was again angry about the poor performance of Goering's fighter units, which were now endeavouring to build up a reserve of squadrons so as to inflict one great devastating blow on the American raiders.

Goering left his sick bed on 20 August to discuss in Berlin, with his Chiefs of Staff, ways and means of building up to a strength of over 2,000 fighters for the air defence of Germany. Goering said to them, 'The Luftwaffe must be ready for the great gamble by the middle of September at the latest. The most experienced pilots, including flying instructors, are to be used. It will be the beginning of a new air force, or the end of the Luftwaffe'. This was Goering the grim and desperate.

In the first week of September 1944, Hitler held a special two-day conference at his Rastenburg headquarters, to which he also invited Speer and Galland, to discuss current air policy. When they spoke of the need for jet fighter production and the creation of a fighter reserve for the air defence of Germany, the Fuehrer's frenzy rose. He shouted, 'I will dissolve the fighter arm, apart from a few units equipped with modern aircraft. I will continue the air defence with anti-aircraft guns. Speer, I order you to furnish me with a new programme. Production has to be switched from fighters to anti-aircraft guns'. Goering was told about this Hitler outburst by the Luftwaffe Chief of Staff General Koller, who says that Goering was still not well at this time and taking a large number of pills. Albert Speer typically ignored the Fuehrer's neurotic outburst and continued to encourage the production of fighters. In September 1944 over 3,000 of the total aircraft output of 4,103 planes were in fact fighters.

And so, by the autumn of 1944, German air power and policy were entirely without co-ordinated leadership. Goering, Hitler, Galland, Speer and Koller, the Luftwaffe Chief of Staff, each had their separate views. But there was no central guiding hand. While Hitler planned air support for the German Army in some wishful counter-offensive, Speer and Galland concentrated on planning greater forces for the air defence of Germany. Goering vacillated between blind loyalty to the Fuehrer and bursts of bad temper in opposing Koller and Galland. 'You are trying to sabotage the Luftwaffe, you are a traitor,' was a fairly typical current Goering comment. Then it might be followed by an abject apology.

Goering was by now utterly confused. Having opposed Galland in 1943, in the latter's support of the Me 262 as a jet fighter plane, and having at the time supported Hitler's view that it should be used as a bomber, Goering became a Galland convert in September 1944. But he asked Himmler to intercede with Hitler to get the position changed, for he felt that his own influence with the Fuehrer was now in a state of rapid decline. The first Me 262 jet fighter unit was eventually formed at Osnabrueck in North-West Germany in October 1944. That Goering signed the order for its formation was no more than a formality. His signature was as unimportant as were most of the 564 Me 262 planes built in 1944. The majority of them were destroyed at air bases or in transit from assembly plants or were crashed on flying conversion courses.

Goering's inadequate grasp of the realities of developing German jet fighters is even better illustrated by the Heinkel 162 jet fighter affair. This was, in part, the brainchild of Albert Speer and his chief of fighter aircraft production, Otto Sauer. Galland opposed the scheme. He wanted more Me 262 jet fighters. Goering called a staff meeting at his Rominten air headquarters in East Prussia on 23 September and spoke for the He 162 jet. Galland opposed his views and Goering shouted at him, 'The industry promises you thousands of jets in a few months and you say no'.

There is no evidence that the He 162 jets ever went into serious air action. Perhaps this was a good thing for German pilots. Goering's scheme was to take members of the Hitler Youth and give them glider training, then ask them to convert on to the new jet planes. He called the He 162 units the People's Fighters (Volksjaeger). It was a kind of desperate aeronautical Home Guard. Goering was now clearly out of contact with aviation realities. He could not have seriously hoped to train jet fighter pilots to combat standards in a few months. But by now he was desperate and prepared to consider almost any remedy, however absurd.

By October 1944 Hermann Goering was merely a witness of German air policy, if such a thing as German air policy could

still claim to seriously exist. In August 1944 Goering had
appointed a new and energetic Chief of Air Staff, General
Werner Kreipe, knowing that Kreipe particularly wanted to
fight the issue of the Me 262 fighter against the Fuehrer's views
and decisions. On 19 September Kreipe resigned in disgust. But
at the time, the new Me 262 fighter unit was in fact being
formed. Indeed, by early October, the Me 262 jet fighter unit
at Osnabrueck had a strength of 40 planes. And on 4 November
1944 Hitler belatedly gave his official blessing to the Me 262
as a front-line fighter aircraft.

About six months before, on 29 May 1944, Goering had held
a Luftwaffe Chiefs of Staff meeting at Obersalzburg. Galland,
Bodenschatz and Korten, then Chief of Staff, had pressed the
Reichsmarschall to give the Me 262 priority as a jet fighter.
Goering had then answered, 'The commands of the Fuehrer
must be obeyed. The Me 262 is to be a bomber'.

In the autumn of 1944 and thereafter it probably did not
much matter whether the Me 262 jet was used as a bomber or
a fighter. Thus, for example, 60 of them were destroyed on
10 October in a USAF raid on their airfield at Lechfeld in
Southern Germany. And if, in 1944, Goering submitted weakly
to Hitler's wild dictation, it was no more or less than other
leading German military leaders had felt bound to do—Model
and von Runstedt for example.

There was still one last desperate Luftwaffe air plan to come.
It was conceived by Goering and Galland in October 1944. The
two German air leaders had been at loggerheads on many
subjects since 1940, notably over fighter tactics and the future of
Germany's jet planes; but now they joined forces in joint and
desperate planning. It was desperate and bound to fail because
the heavily-escorted US bombers had the complete initiative. US
Air Forces decided when and how to strike. Goering's response
was inevitably that of a puppet air commander, at this juncture,
who danced to the American tune. And he had even heavier
operational problems in the autumn of 1944 to save fuel and
find fresh pilots to train in fighter squadrons. These were to be
hoarded carefully. Then, at the right moment, they were to
launch one massive and devastating attack on United States
raiding bombers and fighters. By November it was hoped to
assemble 2,500 German fighters who would shoot down perhaps

400-500 US bombers on one day, for the loss of perhaps 400-500 German fighters. It was planned to strike a great single air blow which would destroy USAF morale and so stop the attacks on German oil refineries.

At an Air Ministry meeting in Berlin on 10 October, Goering said that the attacks on the German fuel plants had 'all the signs and portents of a major catastrophe'. But his impotence to oppose the attacks was increased in October 1944, when RAF Bomber Command began a series of daylight attacks on these targets and sometimes encountered only token German fighter opposition.

The Goering-Galland plan came to an unhappy end on 2 November 1944. On that day 600 US bombers escorted by over 750 fighters attacked the Leuna oil plant. The German air operations in defence of the plant were an unpremeditated and disastrous rehearsal for the devastating air blow to be struck later. The Luftwaffe claimed to have shot down 50 US bombers but lost 200 fighters. Goering's last hope of swamping the American or British raiders by mass fighter attack was now finally gone.

Hitler demanded a full report of the day's operations and sent for Goering, who went once more to Rastenburg to listen to another Fuehrer tirade against the Luftwaffe. 'You have no hope of decimating the enemy with a mass attack,' said the Fuehrer with some justice. 'I will not let the Luftwaffe play about like this. It is madness.' Goering muttered in shame, 'Yes, Fuehrer. It was a disaster.'

By November 1944 it did not matter very much what Goering or Hitler thought or said about German air affairs. And Goering was fast becoming no more than a nominal Commander-in-Chief of the Luftwaffe. Thus when Hitler and Speer met on 4 November at Rastenburg and decided to give top priority to the production of anti-aircraft guns, there was no detailed consultation with Goering. And when Hitler decided in that month to use his fighter arm to support the German Army in the Ardennes counter-offensive, Goering passively agreed to the Fuehrer's demand. What else could he do? He was no longer first favourite at Hitler's Court. And it was, after all, the fashion for all German leaders to submit to Hitler's wildest follies.

In the event, Hitler's Ardennes offensive went off in mid-

December 1944, in bad weather and without any Luftwaffe air support or any air intervention by British or American squadrons. But when the weather cleared at Christmas time, Anglo-American squadrons put up 15,000 sorties in four days with very little reply from the Luftwaffe. The German Air Force was totally unable to protect its own airfields in Western Germany or to guard General Model's road transport against Anglo-American air attack.

Strangely enough, almost the last major air operation in the West ordered by Goering was neither in support of the German Army nor in defence of Germany. It was a snap attack of about 1,000 sorties on Allied air bases in Holland and Belgium, carried out on 1 January 1945. Goering's Air Force certainly achieved tactical surprise and inflicted heavy casualties; but the 350-400 planes lost by the British and American Air Forces were easily replaceable. The 300 German fighter pilots lost on this operation were irreplaceable. The Luftwaffe attack on the Allied airfields was perhaps a last desperate attempt by Goering to regain the confidence of his Fuehrer. It was futile.

By January 1945 the number of Luftwaffe pilot training schools had been reduced to fifteen, less than a fifth of the number required to maintain the flow of air crews. The advance of the Soviet Army on the Eastern Front was overrunning important sections of the German aircraft industry in Poland, Roumania, Hungary and East Prussia. Luftwaffe transport and bomber units were being disbanded, because of the chronic fuel shortage and lack of pilots. The Luftwaffe was shrinking fast and many of its ground and air crews had been transferred to the German ground forces.

Goering was now utterly bewildered. There was no practical air plan or policy he could hope to execute. He had to observe impotently the aeronautical moves of his enemies and make such local unimportant reply as he could. The new Me 262 fighter units had a few local successes in the first few months of 1945, and Goering sent them Hitler's irrelevant congratulations. 'The Fuehrer is delighted with the success of the Messerschmitt 262 against Allied bombers. This aircraft is making a decisive contribution to the whole course of the war.'

That Hitler could formulate such a thought in March 1945, and that Goering could communicate it is a measure of how far

N

from the track of reality the two German leaders had strayed. But Goering still had plans and hopes for the Me 262 as a fighter and as a bomber. Five major bomber units were intended to be re-equipped with the Me 262 and, in January 1945, a new crack jet fighter Me 262 unit, commanded by Adolf Galland, had been formed with senior ace fighter pilots as humble rank and file members. Goering had quarrelled with Galland in January 1945 and dismissed him from the key post of General of the Fighter Arm. At that stage perhaps it did not matter very much.

By March 1945 ground power was taking over from air power. In the West the crossing of the Rhine, in the East the Soviet Army's approach to the Oder in East Germany, signalled the closing phases of the war in Europe. Goering's leadership was now of no consequence in any air context. What remained was the evacuation to the south of Germany, the final fall from Hitler's favour and the loss of all Goering's positions, including that of head of the Luftwaffe. Then came Goering's arrest by SS officials and his capture by a US division from Texas. After that there was imprisonment, interrogation, the Nuremberg Trials and finally suicide.

To select incidents from the chaos of the period January to May 1945 could be misleading. But since Goering was a creature of so many moods, and so many faces, he is probably bound to elude the most careful analysis of his actions. On 12 January he had thrown a large birthday party at Karinhall, to mark his 52nd birthday. Hundreds of guests, including many Luftwaffe officers, were there to drink his health. Goering was cheerful to his guests, but suddenly he drew his wife Emmy aside and said, 'We have lost the war. If I take my life will you come with me?' Then just over a fortnight later, on 27 January, Goering was telling the Fuehrer at a Chiefs of Staff conference in Berlin that he thought the threat of the Soviet advance might lead to the conclusion of a separate peace with the British and the Americans. Hitler disagreed however.

For the next two or three months, Hermann Goering left much of the day-to-day business of Luftwaffe decisions, such as they were, to his Chief of Staff, General Koller. In the meantime, Goering was more concerned with the evacuation of Karinhall and his plans to blow it up, and with the establishment of new air force headquarters in Southern Germany. He attended some of the Fuehrer's conferences in Berlin in February and March as a matter of personal politics rather than to discuss serious air policy. He knew that Bormann was plotting against him, as was common knowledge in the Fuehrer's immediate circle. Speer had warned Goering about this. After the Fuehrer conference of 10 February, Goering returned to his headquarters at Obersalzburg and said to Robert, his valet, 'I wish I were younger and not so heavy. I'd like to fly again'. It was aviation nostalgia caused by impending final defeat.

Goering's last meeting with Hitler was on 20 April 1945, at the Fuehrer's bunker in Berlin. The Russians were then within a few miles of the German capital. It was Hitler's birthday. Ribbentrop, Himmler, Goebbels and the German Chiefs of Staff were all there to congratulate the Fuehrer. Goering urged Hitler to go south with him and abandon the German capital, to fight on in the mountains of Bavaria. Hitler refused to budge. But he told Goering to go, and to leave his Chief of Staff, General Koller, behind in Berlin.

Goering's journey southwards by car was full of incident. He was no doubt aware that the Luftwaffe was by now almost entirely without supplies of petrol. On the way south, he had to take refuge in air-raid shelters. He managed to joke despite everything. 'Let me introduce myself,' he would say. 'My name is Meier.' The occupants of the shelters laughed and clapped.

Back at the Fuehrer's headquarters, Hitler was ranting at Koller: 'The Luftwaffe is useless. Its leaders should be hanged. Let Goering take over the leadership down there in the south. But no one will fight for the Reichsmarschall.'

On 23 April, General Koller flew south to Berchtesgaden to see Goering, who had now come to feel he must take some action to bring the war to a close. He said reportedly to Koller, 'If I act now, they will call me a traitor. If I don't act, I will be reproached for having failed Germany in the decisive hour.' And so, on that day, Koller and Goering carefully drafted a message for Hitler which was to have violent repercussions. It was a logical thing for Goering to do. He was trying to be tactful in his text. It ran as follows: 'My Fuehrer, as you are determined to remain at your post in Fortress Berlin, do you agree that I, as your deputy, in accordance with your decree of 29 June 1941, assume at once the full leadership of the Reich with complete freedom of action at home and abroad. If by 2200 hours I receive no answer, I shall assume you have been deprived of your freedom of action. I will then assume the terms of your decree to be in force and will act accordingly for the good of the people and the Fatherland. You must realise what I feel for you in these most difficult hours of my life. I am quite unable to find words to express it. God bless you and grant that you may come here after all as soon as possible. Your most loyal Hermann Goering.'

Adolf Hitler, closely advised by Bormann, reacted violently. He cancelled the decree of 29 June 1941, forbad Goering to take any action, deprived him of all his offices including the position of Commander-in-Chief of the Luftwaffe, despatched two senior SS officers to arrest him for high treason, and invited General von Greim, a senior Luftwaffe staff officer, to take over the command of the German Air Force.

On 25 April, Goering persuaded his SS guards to shift him from Obersalzburg to his castle home at Mauterndorf. On 30 April Hitler committed suicide. On 4 May, Goering was released from his SS guards by a Luftwaffe signals unit which happened to be passing through Mauterndorf. The next day, a US detachment of troops passed through the village and Goering was a much fêted prisoner-of-war. He asked to see General Eisenhower as soon as possible.

His request was ignored. On 9 May he left Mauterndorf for the headquarters of the US Army 37th Division at Zell am See, and then on to the American 7th Army headquarters at Kitzbuehl. He drank champagne with his captors. His rather handsome reception was not well received in higher US quarters. He was then flown to Augsburg prison on 10 May and was again well treated. The next day he was giving interviews to the press and drinking in the local officers' mess.

But once again higher US authority clamped down on American hospitality. On 21 May, Hermann Goering was flown from Augsburg in Southern Germany to Mondorf, near the borders of Luxembourg. Mondorf was the chief prisoner-of-war centre in the American zone of Germany. From now on he received no favoured treatment, but he was allowed to have one officer to attend him. Instead he preferred to take his valet and faithful servant, Robert Kropp. Hermann Goering could be tough and ruthless. He could also be sentimental and warm-hearted.

CHAPTER NINE

Some Other Opinions

MANY VIEWS on Hermann Goering have been expressed by his Luftwaffe colleagues, by diplomats, journalists and biographers. It seemed logical to offer a selection of these views if only to broaden the basis of both criticism and appreciation and so contribute to a more balanced assessment of Goering.

To begin with, some views on Goering from Albert Speer, Minister of War Production in the Third Reich from early 1942 onwards. Speer must have met Goering on at least a hundred occasions to discuss aircraft production and manpower problems. Apart from his intelligence and organising ability he was one of the most objective of the German leaders of the Second World War. His views on Goering are to be found mainly in the post-war interrogations of Speer and in his memoirs (*Inside the Third Reich*—Weidenfeld and Nicolson).

Speer recalls Goering when he attended a Hitler conference at Rastenburg in December 1942. He wrote, 'Goering gave the impression of a worn-out man at the end of 1942, when I sat with him in the pavilion, which had been built for his brief stays at headquarters . . . Depressed, the Reichsmarschall said, "We will have reason to be glad if Germany can keep the boundaries of 1933 after the war".' Speer continued, 'Goering quickly tried to cover up the remark by adding a few confident banalities.' However, Speer's impression was that 'despite the bluffness he put on, Goering saw defeat coming closer.'

In the context of the general German situation at the beginning of 1943, Speer makes this interesting comment: 'The present-day reader may well wonder why, when we were making a last effort to rally all our forces, our choice should have fallen on this man, who had done nothing but loll about in apathetic luxury for years. Goering had not always been this way, and his reputation as a violent, but also energetic and intelligent person, still lingered on from the days when he had built up the Air Force and the Four Year Plan. There seemed a chance that, if a task appealed to him, he might recover some of his old daring and energy.'

Several accounts have been given of Goering's reaction to the Stalingrad air-lift crisis. Speer's version is worth citing because it is based on authoritative on-the-spot knowledge. He recalls that at the Fuehrer's Rastenburg conference on 19 November 1942 'Goering appeared in the briefing room, brisk and beaming like an operetta tenor who is supposed to portray a victorious Reichsmarschall. Depressed and with an appealing note in his voice, Hitler asked Goering, "What about supplying Stalingrad by air?" Goering snapped to attention and declared solemnly, "My Fuehrer, I personally guarantee the supplying of Stalingrad by air." '

In the next few days, the Fuehrer received a daily statement of the tonnage of rations and munitions dropped by air. The figures were only a fraction of the amount promised by Goering.

At Hitler's briefing conference, on 24 November 1942, held again at Rastenburg, the Fuehrer asked Goering to account for his failure. Speer recalls the Reichsmarschall's embarrassment and his excuses such as 'the bad fog and snow storms'. Goering said, 'As soon as the weather clears, I will be able to deliver the promised tonnage.' Speer adds that he later discovered from Milch that Goering's staff had already told him that the air supply of the Sixth Army at Stalingrad was impossible.

Speer recalls one of his early meetings with Goering soon after Speer had become Armaments Minister. It was on 12 February 1942, at the Air Ministry in Berlin. Goering spoke cordially about harmony between the two men and said he hoped it would continue. Speer comments, 'When Goering wanted to, he could display a good deal of charm. He was hard to resist, if somewhat condescending.' Speer added, 'If I had agreed to Goering's proposals, I would have had my hands completely tied.'

Speer remembers another meeting with Goering about a year after this. It was on 28 February 1943, at Goering's summer house at Obersalzburg. Speer says that Goering had withdrawn to Obersalzburg 'because he was offended by Hitler's criticisms of his leadership of the Air Force'. Speer added that his conversation with Goering was friendly and lasted some hours. He expressed surprise at Goering's lacquered finger-nails and rouged face. Speer went on, 'The oversize ruby brooch on his green velvet dressing-gown was already a familiar sight to me.' As Goering listened to Speer's account of a recent Berlin conference, 'he scooped a handful of gems from his pocket and playfully let them glide through his fingers'. Others have, of course, witnessed to Goering's habit of playing with jewels. It seemed to provide relaxation.

One of Albert Speer's most trenchant comments on Goering refers to a visit to Veltenstein, Goering's castle home in Franconia. It was made on 31 May 1942, the day after the RAF 1,000 bomber raid on Cologne. The atmosphere was tense and Goering was in a bad mood, snarling and shouting about the British air attack. But he cooled down and showed his visitors over the castle and also his blue-print plans for expansions and extensions. Speer, summing up this Veltenstein visit, wrote, 'Hermann Goering did not allow war to interfere with his private pursuits'.

Albert Speer also confirms Goering's indifference to the air intelligence reports on the enemy offered by Luftwaffe specialists. At a conference held at Rechlin in September 1943, Milch told Speer that 'he had been trying for months to have experts on enemy armaments deliver a report to Goering. But he refused to hear anything about it.' And, when Hitler was shown the figures of enemy aircraft production, he commented to Goering, 'Don't let them fool you. It is all planted information. These defeatists in the Air Ministry fall for it.'

Speer summed up Goering succinctly as 'a mathematical romantic who often refrained from doing his air sums'. Goering's admiration for Speer was reflected at a July 1941 meeting when the Reichsmarschall said to him, 'I have told the Fuehrer that, after him, I consider you to be the greatest man Germany possesses'.

In terms of operational policies on the deployment and use of fighter aircraft, General Adolf Galland's memoirs (*The First and the Last*—Methuen) offer some of the most authoritative comments on Goering's air leadership. Galland's operational experience, at either combat or command level, covers the entire decade of German Air Force development from 1935 to 1945.

His memoirs, combined with his assessments given to Allied interrogators, provide rich material on Goering and the development of the Luftwaffe fighter arm. Galland writes and speaks as a great fighter specialist. His views on Goering are based on many official and private meetings. Galland was General of Goering's Fighter Arm. He was a man of great courage in combat, and keen intelligence in his staff work. He was enthusiastic and critical.

Galland first saw Goering in Berlin, in the spring of 1933. He recalls, 'I was amazed at his girth and displacement. But the first impression was soon dispelled by the conviction that an enthusiastic airman was speaking to us.'

Galland made critical comments on Goering's choice of leaders in the period between the two world wars. Thus, he wrote, 'The old fighter pilots of the First World War, who were now sitting at the Supreme Command of the Luftwaffe with Goering at their head, had a compulsory gap of fifteen years behind them, during which they had probably lost contact with the rapid development of aviation.'

Galland's recollections of Goering during the Battle of Britain have a special authority. Galland was then an ace fighter pilot, who also met his Commander-in-Chief from time to time. He wrote: 'Goering had nothing but reproaches for the fighter squadrons and he expressed his dissatisfaction in the harshest terms. The theme of fighter escort was discussed again and again. Goering clearly represented the point of view of the bombers and demanded close and rigid cover. Bomber protection, said Goering, was more important than record figures for enemy planes shot down.' But Galland recalls that Goering's attitude altered as the meeting, held in August 1940, came to an end. 'As his time ran short, he grew more amiable and asked about the needs of our fighter squadrons.'

Galland has also recorded Goering's reaction to the high German Air Force losses sustained in the daylight raids on London in September 1940. He wrote in his memoirs, 'Goering was shattered. He simply could not explain how the increasing loss of bombers came about. I assured him that in spite of the heavy losses we were inflicting on enemy fighters, no decisive decrease in their numbers or in their fighting efficiency was noticeable.'

One of the most fascinating of Galland's sidelights on Goering's technique of leadership is given in an account of a meeting of Luftwaffe commanders in France. It took place in the third week of May 1941, that is about a month before the German attack on the USSR. Goering was giving his air commanders a rundown on Hitler's strategy in the West. 'The Battle of Britain,' said Goering, 'has been only an air overture to the final attack on Britain. Intensification of U-boat warfare and the expansion of the Luftwaffe are the next major moves.'

A serious discussion of this Fuehrer strategy followed. But after the meeting, Goering took Galland and his fighter pilot friend Moelders aside and, rubbing his hands with glee, said to them, 'There's not a word of truth in that'.

From time to time, Adolf Galland makes interesting comments on German strategy which have a direct bearing on Goering's air problems. Thus he wrote, 'It was the fault of the overall strategy concept in our conduct of the war which made the task of the Luftwaffe, and particularly that of our fighters, so difficult and so exhausting. In the summer of 1940 we had quickly and unexpectedly come into possession of the West European Atlantic coast, a position which imperatively made England the strategic target. In the summer of 1942 we stood equally unexpectedly on the Egyptian border. In both cases we hoped to achieve our goal with insufficient forces and quick improvisation.'

Galland reinforces the view that Goering was unwilling to face reality. He wrote, 'The Luftwaffe High Command closed its eyes to undeniable facts and developing signs in aerial warfare.' Dealing more specifically with United States Air Force developments in Europe in 1942, Galland recorded this view: 'Goering not only denied these facts and figures publicly, but simply closed his eyes to them. This was not only propaganda but an irresponsibility of such magnitude that it can only be measured by the consequences it had for the Reich and all the people entrusted to its care and protection. Goering forbad the Luftwaffe to count on the alleged US production figures. He forbad even a mention of them.'

Galland's indictment of Goering's aircraft production policy was succinct: 'The fighter production figures of 1944 could have been reached in 1940 or 1941, and the Luftwaffe would never have lost air supremacy. Neither technical reasons nor shortage of raw materials prevented it.'

Galland probably had as many man-to-man debates with Goering as any other senior Luftwaffe officer. He recalls some of them in his memoirs. There was, for example, the meeting at Veltenstein in the autumn of 1943. The two men discussed Luftwaffe matters as they walked up and down the courtyard. As he had done during previous meetings, Goering criticised Luftwaffe fighter squadrons for what he called their short-comings in the air defence of Germany. Galland defended his fighter pilots vigorously and retorted, 'The fighter squadrons cannot be responsible for all their faults'. Galland then asked Goering for better training facilities and better aircraft which he said was what Luftwaffe flying and technical personnel had asked for.

Goering then became irritated and agitated and said to Galland, 'You do not conform to my idea of a general. I need someone who can execute my orders by any means available. I have not made you General of Fighters so that you can protect the fighter arm and sabotage the orders I have given, after deep and careful deliberation.' Goering, recalls Galland, was now shouting loudly and had great difficulty in keeping calm.

In this tense situation, Galland said to Goering, 'I cannot reconcile my conscience with the activities of the sort of general you have in mind. I wish to be relieved of my command and sent back to the air front.' After a pause, Goering said, 'Your request is granted.' But a week later, at another meeting at Veltenstein, Goering apologised to Galland who stayed on as General of Fighters until late in 1944.

It was the United States' daylight bombing raids on Germany which probably formed the chief topic of conversation between Goering and Galland in 1944. Galland recalls how the Reichs-marschall used to discuss the raids with individual German pilots and then with his General of Fighters. 'I had to agree with Goering on many points,' wrote Galland. But on key tactical issues there was a direct clash of viewpoint. Thus Goering wanted the intercepting Luftwaffe fighters to be massed close to Germany's borders. Galland knew this was difficult to achieve at times. He preferred to concentrate his fighter forces over Central Germany.

Another major difference between Goering and Galland arose on the question of combat fatigue and scale of effort. Goering wanted Luftwaffe fighters to carry out two or three combat sorties a day. Galland warned against this, saying it would overtax pilots and produce heavy losses on second and third sorties.

A rapid change of mood was typical of Hermann Goering, as Koller, Milch and other Luftwaffe leaders have said. Galland recalls a colourful instance of this. At one meeting, Goering produced a burst of bad temper and accused German fighter pilots of 'lack of spirit, being unworthy of decorations and faking combat reports to get them'. When Galland in great fury threw his Knight's Cross to the Iron Cross down on the table, Goering quickly calmed down and the incident was soon forgotten. Galland shows Goering to have been irascible, but approachable.

One of the most critical series of comments on Goering has been made by Hannah Reitsch, a woman of great spirit who was a Luftwaffe test pilot and an aeronautical research specialist. She was present in Hitler's Berlin bunker on 26 April 1945 when the Fuehrer said to von Greim, 'I hereby declare you to be Goering's successor as Commander-in-Chief of the Luftwaffe'.

Here are some of the main points of the Hannah Reitsch indictment of Hermann Goering given to US interrogators in November 1945. Her views are not as well founded as those of Speer and Galland, who had much more day-to-day knowledge of the Goering background.

Hannah Reitsch described Goering as 'grossly incompetent' and 'the man who allowed the decisive weapon (of air power) to be destroyed through his own mistakes. His personal example, attitude and character betrayed his own people.'

After railing against Goering's 'stupidities and failings', she went on to say, 'Much of the conduct and manner of Goering is, in my opinion, governed by his abnormal physical condition. Functional disturbances would easily be the fundamental cause for his Caesar complex. No doubt these disturbances are also the cause of his feminine manner, which was in stark contrast to his apparently iron commands. Goering's manner of dress, his use of cosmetics, his perfumed person and clothing, all created a decadent impression.'

Hannah Reitsch's views on the effect of Goering's drug-taking have little or no medical status, but may be of interest. She said, 'His constant use of morphine drove him to ecstasy, to overrate and to fail to distinguish fact from wishful thinking. He over-estimated the strength and potential of the Luftwaffe, he deceived Hitler and so prolonged the war.' She went on, 'Whenever Goering was confronted with aircraft production figures that were lower than those he imagined or hoped, he would rant and fume and deluge the individual with accusations of sabotage.'

Hannah Reitsch recalled a lunch she had had in August 1943 with Goering and his wife Emmy, at their Obersalzburg home. This was shortly after she had test-flown the new Me 163 rocket-propelled fighter. She recalls Goering saying, 'The 163 is our latest rocket plane. Thousands are now ready to sweep the heavens clean and shoot down bomber formations wherever we can find them.' Hannah Reitsch replied, 'That would be fine if it were true.' Goering then pounded the table and said angrily, 'What do you mean by that statement?'

Whatever Goering may have said on this occasion, documents show that he realised in August 1943 that no Me 163 units would be operational for a very long time. So it may have been just table talk.

Hannah Reitsch found some sympathetic things to say about Goering. She referred to his 'charm and sense of humour, his appreciation of tradition and culture and his kind and congenial manner with servants'. On the other side of the medal, she referred to Goering's 'abnormal vanity, gross incompetence and pitiful inefficiency'. She declared that Goering 'chose air leaders to fill the positions around him who mirrored his own personality and had no air knowledge or technical understanding. They were just friendly, congenial and hero-worshippers of Goering'.

Among other interesting assessments of Hermann Goering are those formulated by leading European diplomats of his time. Thus the British Ambassador in Berlin, Sir Neville Henderson, wrote: 'Of all the big Nazi leaders, Hermann Goering was, for me, by far the most sympathetic . . . in any crisis, as in war, he would be quite ruthless . . . He was a typical and brutal buccaneer, but he had certain attractive qualities and I must say frankly that I had a real personal liking for him.' The British Ambassador also referred to Goering's Falstaffian sense of

humour and his love of children and animals. He concluded,
'My recollections of Goering will be of a man who intervened
decisively in favour of peace in 1938, and would have done so
again in 1939 if he had been as brave morally as he was
physically.'

Count Ciano, Mussolini's Minister of Foreign Affairs, was no
admirer of Goering, whom he met professionally many times.
Ciano's Diary (Heinemann) has been described by Mr Sumner
Welles, President Roosevelt's envoy, in these terms: 'I believe it
to be one of the most valuable historical documents of our times.'
Here are nine extracts from the diary which show that Goering
was not Ciano's favourite character.

20 *February* 1940. 'Goering, in talking with our military
attaché in Berlin, spoke clearly about the position of Italy,
pronouncing judgements which reveal that he is disappointed
and very angry. We must keep them in mind. He is the most
human of the German chiefs, but he is emotional and violent
and might become dangerous.'

20 *July* 1940. 'In the afternoon, a visit to Goering (at
Karinhall). He looked feverish, but as he dangled the collar
of the Annunziata decoration from his neck, he was somewhat
rude and haughty towards me. I was more interested in the
luxurious decoration of his home than in him and his variable
humours. It is an ever increasing show of luxury. It is truly
incomprehensible how, in a country which is socialistic or
almost so, people can tolerate the extraordinary pomp dis-
played by this Western satrap.'

13 *May* 1941. 'The Germans are depressed. Von Ribbentrop
repeats his slogans against Britain with a monotony that made
Goering dub him Germany's No. 1 parrot.'

1 *June* 1941. 'I had a long conversation with Prince Otto
von Bismarck. According to him, Goering has lost a great
deal of his influence with Hitler because he admonishes the
Fuehrer too much and dictators do not like that.'

24 *November* 1941. 'Goering was impressive when he spoke
of the Russians who are eating each other and have also eaten
a German sentry in a prison camp. He recounted the incident
with the utmost indifference. And yet he is kind-hearted and
when he spoke of Udet and Moelders, who have lately lost
their lives, tears came into his eyes.'

29 *January* 1942. 'The Duce talked to Goering for about

three hours yesterday . . . Goering is bitter about things in Russia and takes it out of the German generals, who have little or no sympathy for the Nazis. He thinks that difficulties will last throughout the year, but is just as convinced that Russia will be defeated in 1942, and that Great Britain will lay down her arms in 1943.'

4 *February* 1942. 'Goering leaves Rome. We had dinner at the Excelsior Hotel. During dinner, Goering talked of little else but the jewels he owned. In fact he had some beautiful rings on his fingers. He explained that he had bought them for a relatively small sum in Holland . . . I am told that he plays with his gems like a little boy with his marbles. During the journey he was nervous. So his aides brought him a small vase filled with diamonds. One of his high officers said last evening, "He has two loves, beautiful objects and making war." '

2 *December* 1942. 'All Goering's promises are bound to be left up in the clouds . . . Goering's principal aim is to create confusion and give documentary proof that the blame for everything rests on our poor organisation of transport (i.e. of supplies for North Africa). The military technicians at the Embassy are surprised at the amount of nonsense which the Reichsmarschall is capable of talking.'

6 *December* 1942. 'The Duce has dictated to me a brief summary of his conferences with Goering which I have preserved elsewhere. No conclusion has been reached in the political field, but the Reichsmarschall has observed that our military efforts will have to be redoubled if we wish to avoid further grief in Africa. We too had come to this conclusion without the need of his precious insight.'

One of the ablest commentators on Goering as an air leader is Professor Brigadier Telford Taylor. In his book *The Breaking Wave* (Weidenfeld and Nicolson) he has provided much telling and succinct material on Goering. Taylor was one of the outstanding US intelligence officers in the war in Europe. He had the advantage of studying Goering's air leadership potential as it emerged, in the new intelligence during the war. He later observed the personality of Goering during the 1945-46 period of the Nuremberg Trials, where he was chief of the US Council. He is currently Professor of Law at Columbia University. He has studied many of the post-war documents on Goering and the Luftwaffe. I would rate his views on Goering very highly indeed. This is what he wrote in *The Breaking Wave*:

'Hermann Goering's credentials as a promoter were far more impressive than as a Commander-in-Chief. Make it possible for others to build on an air force he could; but he was quite unqualified to shape or lead it. As a flyer in the First World War, he had shown bravery and leadership capacity and he continued to fly professionally in the lean years that followed. But he was hopelessly passé on technical and tactical matters and he lacked the character and judgement for effective delegation of his air powers. He set a very bad example for his staff and often frustrated their efforts to lay the groundwork for considered decisions. Lacking time and patience for detailed operation analysis or intelligence estimates, he hated to be contradicted, especially with unwelcome information. His frequent preoccupation with political matters, aggravated by irresponsible and self-indulgent personal habits, destroyed the sequence and logic of Luftwaffe policy, which, all too often, was determined by impulse, emotion or wishful thinking.'

Other Telford Taylor comments are these: 'Unlike the RAF with its air staff of career officers, the Luftwaffe was a one-man show. Whatever his faults, and they were many and grave, it was Hermann Goering's ambition, energy and prestige and unquestioned, if spasmodically used, ability that accounted for the establishment of the Luftwaffe as an independent branch of the Wehrmacht and attracted to its service the men that helped to shape it. He was often indolent or occupied with other matters, but his decisions, when made, were not subject to challenge within the Luftwaffe. In administrative or tactical affairs, Hitler never interfered and, except on matters of major strategic or diplomatic significance, he left Goering free to handle his branch of the Armed Forces as he saw fit.' (Telford Taylor is referring to the situation up to the summer of 1940.)

Many interesting observations on the personality and air leadership of Goering have been made by a younger generation of British writers on aviation, who were not concerned with the Reichsmarschall during the Second World War. Their more detached view may serve to balance the contemporary assessments of those closely concerned with German air affairs. One of the most knowledgeable is William Green whose *War Planes*

XIV. Goering with Galland

GOERING

XV. A Russian Wartime Cartoon by 'Kukrinsky'

of the Third Reich (Macdonald) is a major source-book for any student of Goering and the Luftwaffe.

Here is Green's appreciation of the Commander-in-Chief of the German Air Force: 'He was a political revolutionary and an ambitious, forceful and flamboyant personality, whose egoism and arrogance were perhaps exceeded only by his lack of the most elementary technical knowledge. Widely considered something of a buffoon outside Germany, Goering was nevertheless the principal architect of the Luftwaffe, displaying ruthless energy, during its formative years, when his avowed intention was the creation of the largest and most modern air arm in the world. Goering possessed an innate common-sense which was perhaps his sole saving grace, although with the passage of years its application waned and his effectiveness was eroded by a steadily increasing lassitude which, at times, manifested itself as complete indifference towards the Luftwaffe over protracted periods. He was intoxicated by his authority to command, regardless of the necessity or logicality of the commands he issued; and motivated by self-agrandisement, he tended to abrogate everything to himself.

'He was unable to view problems objectively or take the most elementary precautions against any danger that he personally found distasteful to contemplate. He intervened in matters that he did not have the technical competence to understand and he was prone to vacillation, frequently withdrawing his support from development plans for programmes that he had encouraged in the first place.

'It was Goering's over-confidence, derived from the initial successes of the Luftwaffe against poorly trained and poorly equipped air forces, coupled with markedly lower combat attrition during his early campaigns, than the most sanguine of estimates had forecast, that was primarily responsible for pushing combat aircraft development and the expansion of aircraft production well down the list of war-time priorities.'

Two other young British writers, Derek Wood and Derek Dempster, have commented on Goering's air leadership in their well documented *Narrow Margin* (Hutchinson), which is mainly about the Battle of Britain, but also covers the preceding years. They wrote: 'The direction of air warfare he (Hitler) left to Goering, who, as a commander and a strategist, had few

o

qualifications. His flying knowledge was out-of-date and his understanding of technical subjects non-existent. The correct application of the air force which Milch built up was more than he could grasp.'

'The Luftwaffe lacked any long-term directive on economic warfare or any real guidance from above. After Wever's death in 1936, battle planning became a hand-to-mouth affair. The whole organisation was bedevilled with petty jealousies and intrigues arising from the haphazard way in which officials acquired senior jobs.'

Commenting on the Reichsmarschall during the Battle of Britain, Wood and Dempster wrote: 'Goering endeavoured to attribute failures to the operational units instead of to the manifest shortcomings of Luftwaffe command planning. In order, as he thought, to boost morale among fighter pilots, he promoted Moelders and Galland, two of his star pilots, to the command of a fighter Gruppe (unit of 30-40 planes). This was part of a belated policy of promoting younger operational officers to senior rank in place of those who were too old and lacked proper experience.'

Looking back on the Battle of Britain they wrote: 'There is no doubt that Goering and his commanders overrated the effectiveness of their own fighters in relation to the British. This may be deduced from the number of Messerschmitts assembled for the battle. A total of nearly 1,000 against a defending force of little more than 600 gave a degree of superiority, particularly as less than two-thirds of Dowding's aircraft were at any time within range of the battle area. But it was not a degree of superiority which a cautious commander would have accepted as sufficient for the job in hand, unless he thought the defending fighters were much inferior. In this uneven proportion of fighters and bombers may be found the fundamental reason for Goering's failure to achieve his objectives.'

One of the best biographies of Hermann Goering was written by Roger Manvell and Heinrich Fraenkel (Heinemann, 1962). This book is not a particular account of Goering as an air leader, though it does cover much aeronautical ground. But it is a very complete and well-compiled study on Goering's personality, which of course affected his aviation decisions. In particular, the material on Goering's drug-taking is of special value.

The authors recall how Goering had to be confined to a mental home in 1925 at the age of 32. They write: 'Goering, in fact, was finally certified as a dangerous drug addict, and police sanction was obtained to confine him to the Langbro (near Stockholm) lunatic asylum, on 1 September 1925, after he had violently attacked a nurse who had refused to supply him with morphine.' They record that Goering left Langbro after three months as an in-patient, but he had to return 'when he found he could not maintain abstinence from the drug.'

The authors record that when Goering returned to Germany he became a patient of Professor Hubert Kahle, who had devised a special method for a quick withdrawal from the use of narcotics. Goering underwent treatment from Kahle, but, unfortunately, the cure did not last. And so, 'every so often, about once a year, Goering would either attend the professor's clinic near Cologne or Kahle himself would come to Karinhall where Goering would shut himself away for treatment in one of the chalets on the estate. This intensive treatment began with drinking a brandy glass full of the preparation by Kahle, which sent Goering into a deep sleep which lasted some twenty-four hours, during which he sweated continuously. In order to control the revival of the rumours about his addiction, Goering actually attended the performance of an opera immediately after one of these drastic treatments, because he had heard there was gossip that he was attending the professor's clinic. Kropp (Goering's valet), who went with him to the theatre, had to hold him up from behind when he rose to acknowledge the cheers of the audience.'

There are many sources to confirm Goering's morphine practices. They range from François-Poncet, French Ambassador in Berlin in the late 1930's, who knew Goering well, the Swedish psychiatrist who treated him at Langbro in 1925, and the American psychiatrists who helped wean him off drugs in 1945, both at the Mondorf and Nuremberg prisons. They included Major Douglas M. Kelley and Major Leon N. Goldensohn. The evidence shows that Goering took morphine or paracodeine, or both, on and off for more than twenty years. What precise effect it had on individual air leadership decisions is almost impossible to say. That it probably made him at times more confident, more indifferent to problems on some occasions, seems to be a reasonable conclusion.

I would like to add the views of two people who have no great status in the aviation hierarchy, but whom I knew well and respected. William Blake, a keen mind and an expert on Germany, dealt personally with Goering in the early 1920s when they were both engaged in buying and selling parachutes and other aircraft equipment. Bill's informal views on Hermann Goering were decanted over a period of years in bits and pieces. 'Goering was bright but a bit of a bloody fool! He thought he could take on anybody . . . He was awfully good at deceiving himself . . . He used a visiting card as large as a postcard. That was typical of the man. He liked blowing things up, making them seem bigger than they were. An awful boaster. I suppose he thought people would believe him. He was fond of wine. Shouldn't think he was a womaniser. Inclined to make a lot of fuss about damn all. Not a bad salesman. Not someone you could trust. But he was intelligent, plenty of grey matter.'

And now the views of Heinz Loechner, who served in the Luftwaffe as a signals officer during the whole of the Second World War. After that he became head of the DIVO Market Research Institute in Frankfurt, where I met him on a number of occasions. Heinz was intelligent, gentle and fair-minded. He saw Goering from the junior officer viewpoint. He thought the Reichsmarschall remained fairly popular in the Luftwaffe right to the end, and despite all his mistakes. He said that Goering had far too much to do throughout the war, and particularly in the last two years. (This was a point also stressed by General Josef Kammhuber when I spoke to him.) Heinz said that Goering had an intelligent mind, but he should have used it to be just Air Minister and nothing else. As it was, Goering could not find time to ready many important signals, to attend many important meetings and talk to key Luftwaffe personnel. Heinz referred in particular to his own Luftwaffe boss, General Martini, complaining that he could not talk to Goering about vital electronic and avionic matters.

In the above selection of comment on Hermann Goering, I have blatantly omitted sources which perhaps offer important Goering data. Thus his wife, Emmy, has written a charming, sympathetic book about her husband which may be the most reliable source available on Goering as a domestic animal, or for that matter on the visit of the Duke and Duchess of Windsor to Karinhall.

She records her husband's love of opera, especially Wagner, and his paternal affection for their daughter, Edda. She confirms that Goering set up the first concentration camps, but says they were intended merely as places for the detention and re-education of Communists. We learn from her that Goering became a temporary vegetarian in the summer of 1933. More important for the historian, she reveals that when she visited her husband in the Nuremberg gaol in 1946, they were always separated by a glass partition and bars. If so, this would dispose of the repeatedly published view that she slipped a phial of cyanide to her husband during an affectionate kiss, in the course of these visits.

Naturally enough, perhaps, there is relatively little on Goering's air leadership in her biography of her late husband published in 1963. But she recalls Goebbels' interesting description of Goering as 'a soldier with the heart of a child' and she adds with affection and some naivety 'the thought never occurred to me that my husband could be inhuman or hateful.'

Then there is the official biography of Goering published by Erich Gritzbach in 1938, which recalls Goering's pilot days in the First World War, but says almost nothing about the revival of the Luftwaffe or the war in Spain.

CHAPTER TEN

At Nuremberg

'HANDLE WITH CARE.' The phrase quickly came to mind when one began to process the lavish quantities of captured information on the career of Hermann Goering which became available shortly after May 1945, particularly when the Nuremberg trials began in November of that year. Much of the evidence was published at the time for all the world to see, hear or read. It was a mixture of damning documentary material from authentic Third Reich files, albeit sometimes hastily translated or imperfectly understood. With this went an array of witnesses for the defence of Goering. Their memory of things past was naturally erratic and perhaps deliberately so at times. And then, providing background material, but working outside the court, were the US psychiatrists who treated and supervised Goering and the other Germans on trial. And, finally, came the military interrogators to add their quota of intelligence after quizzing Goering about his various professional careers.

A man on trial for his life may not do himself justice when justice is being done to him. But Hermann Goering rose to the occasion. Although in prison and under close and continuous guard, he was in a sense freer than at any time in his various Nazi careers. His US psychiatrists had cured him of his habit of taking drugs. The strain of responsibility and decision-taking, which he must have often felt, despite all his bravado, was now a thing of the past. Goering was ready to die if he had to. Now he could concentrate on the trial and hope to give a star performance, displaying the best facets of his personality. Nuremberg was trying a new man.

Before being moved to the Nuremberg gaol in September 1945, Goering had spent some five months at the Mondorf prison, where he was in the hands of US psychiatrists, Dr Kelley and Dr Miller. They helped to achieve two things: To reduce his weight from about 280 to 220 pounds, and to stop him taking the large quantities of paracodeine tablets and the morphia injections he had absorbed throughout the war. Thus Goering was better prepared, both mentally and physically, to face the ordeal of the Nuremburg trial. Spiritually he avoided the comforts of the Lutheran Church. But he enjoyed the attention of his US psychiatrists.

At the prison at Mondorf he had been extensively interrogated, mainly by US intelligence officers. He answered the questions with great volubility, but with varying accuracy. Perhaps he felt that he was merely limbering up for Nuremberg. Certainly his philosophy of air power, as told to Major Evans, one of his interrogators, was surprisingly reasonable. Goering said, 'An air force cannot occupy. It can disorganise, destroy and prepare the way for final battle. On the outbreak of war, the immediate objective must be the annihilation of enemy air forces. All must be subordinated to this task.'

This was not quite the Goering of Dunkirk and the Battle of Britain, when he had told the Fuehrer that the Luftwaffe victory would make a seaborne invasion unnecessary. Perhaps in the monastic atmosphere of the Mondorf gaol, and with improved physical and mental health, Goering was becoming a more logical, more sober, person. Perhaps the prospect of death was concentrating his mind.

The man who probably got to know Goering best during the Mondorf sojourn was Dr Douglas Kelley. This US psychiatrist described him as 'brilliant, brave, ruthless, grasping and a shrewd executive'. Dr Kelley also said that Goering had 'a tremendous drive and capacity for work, but no sense whatsoever of the value of human life, or of moral obligation, when they conflicted with his own egocentric views'. He thought that Goering had developed a morphine addiction, but he found no evidence of insane behaviour. It was some twenty years since Goering had been in the Langbro mental home in Sweden.

After various interrogations, Major Evans summed up the post-war Goering of the summer of 1945 as 'crafty, deliberately deceitful, amusing, pleasant in some respects and something of an actor'. He said that Goering's *tour de force* was the series of stories he liked to tell about Hitler. He particularly enjoyed mimicking the Fuehrer's fury, above all his foaming at the mouth.

When Goering was transferred to Nuremberg in September, he knew of course that death was close. Back in June, he had told his valet, Robert Kropp, that he had a capsule of poison so he could take his own life if and when he so decided. On parting, Robert said to his master, 'I hope you will be all right. They will never find out.' No one, except Goering, seems to know how he hid the capsule from his captors. Some say it was inside a main molar. Others think it was hidden under the large scar of his thigh wound, sustained in the Munich putsch of 1923. Various other personal cavities have been suggested. After taking advice from doctors and detectors of gold and diamond smugglers, I think it was the thigh scar which provided the hiding place.

The war trials at Nuremberg lasted from November 1945 to October 1946. They provided a unique opportunity for a fresh assessment of Hermann Goering, both as an aviation and political leader and even more so as a human being. At Nuremberg there was little scope for a show of the ruthless, brutal or slapdash strains which had punctuated Goering's various careers in the previous ten years. Now trenchant, high-ranking lawyers from the United States, Britain, France and the USSR were about to sit in judgement upon him, backed by an array of incriminating documents which were too massive to handle with maximum efficiency in the few months available.

The Nuremberg judges took their seats in court on 20 November 1945. Goering was one of twenty-three German leaders to be indicted. Now that Hitler was dead and Bormann presumed to be, the ex-Reichsmarschall was clearly the most important German in the dock. For most of the next few months he acted as though fully aware of this. But he was not only the senior defendant, he was the subject of world-wide curiosity and frequently in the news headlines of the Nuremberg trials.

More than any of the others, Hermann Goering was now on show. The documentary films of the Nuremberg proceedings abound in his gestures. They show him squirming in his seat, shrugging his vast shoulders with great vigour, scribbling notes with manifest energy, adjusting his earphones for the German translations, turning with contempt or indignation to other

German defendants in the dock, and then scribbling more notes with great emphasis.

For the first two months, Goering was bursting with impatience, for the case against him was not presented until 8 January 1946. Then Mr Ralph Albrecht, a US lawyer, read the charges against Goering on four counts, 'The Common Plan or Conspiracy', 'Crimes against Peace', 'War Crimes', and 'Crimes against Humanity'. When Goering was asked that evening, when he was back in his cell, what he thought in general of the indictments, his reply to a US psychiatrist was instant: 'The victor will always be the judge and the vanquished the accused.'

8 January 1946 must have been a particularly trying day for Hermann Goering. It was difficult for a man of his temperament to have to listen to the case against him and to know that he must wait two months attending each day in court before he could reply.

The charges raised in court were many and varied. They included his pursuit of German re-armament, his role in the Austrian Anschluss in 1938, in the rape of Czechoslovakia, in what was called his ruthless exploitation of occupied territory in the USSR, his slave-labour programme for Europe and his seizure of raw materials, works of art and other properties. Under the indictment 'Crimes against Humanity' came Goering's sponsorship of some of the anti-Jewish campaigns and his part responsibility for some of the concentration camps.

However grave the charges and the guilt, when Goering had to go into the witness-box to face his judges, in March 1946, he redeemed something from his past. Sir David Maxwell-Fyfe, who led the British prosecution of Goering, said to me after the trial, 'Goering is one of the most intelligent men I have ever encountered in court. His memory was excellent and he was courageous'. Others have commented with praise on the way he conducted himself at Nuremberg. A reporter of the trial, Mr R. W. Cooper, has said, 'Goering was one of the shrewdest men in the dock and always looked the bravest. His bearing throughout the trial was not without courage and sometimes defiance'. Dr Gilbert, the US psychiatrist, who watched over Goering at Nuremberg, said that he was more ready than the others in the dock to take responsibility for Nazi atrocities.

Mr Justice Birkett, who presided over the Nuremberg court at times, has also expressed admiration for the way Goering conducted himself. He declared, 'Goering held the stage for two days with cleverly constructed statements which were not strictly answers to the questions at all.' He also recalled that he himself was worried about the threat Goering presented to the dignity of the trial, and to its validity as a show of justice, rather than vengeance. He said, 'The first factor creating this situation was the extraordinary personality of Goering himself . . . Goering is the man who has really dominated the proceedings and that, remarkably enough, without ever uttering a word in public before he went into the witness-box . . . Nobody appears to have been quite prepared for this immense ability and knowledge, and his thorough mastery and understanding of the detail of the captured documents . . . Suave, shrewd, adroit, capable, resourceful, he quickly saw the elements of the situation, and as his self-confidence grew, his mastery became more apparent.' From a senior English judge this was praise indeed for Hermann Goering.

The Nuremberg Trial proceedings produced little fresh material in terms of the air leadership qualities and defects of Hermann Goering. In a sense this was not surprising. The former Commander-in-Chief of the Luftwaffe was mainly engaged in parrying questions on such topics as his relationship with Hitler, his responsibility for concentration camps, for German re-armament, his work for the Four Year Plan for German economics, the Reichstag fire, the SS organisation and the background to the German attack on the USSR.

And so Goering had relatively little opportunity to expand the principles and practice of his air strategy and operational planning. When the prosecuting counsels did raise topics of aviation moment, they were hampered, at times, by a too-hasty selection from the relevant documents.

As the day for his trial approached, Goering became more realistic and perhaps more cynical. He told a US psychiatrist in his cell : 'As far as the trial is concerned, it is just a cut-and-dried political affair and I am prepared for the consequences. I have no doubt that the press will play a bigger part in the decision than the judges.'

Goering's defence began on 8 March 1946, and was virtually

concluded on 22 March. During the thirteen days of hearing he rarely lost his temper and often contrived to sound plausible and reasonable. His defence lawyer was Dr Otto Stahmer, of Kiel. Although seventy years of age, he proved to be a good pleader and a helpful aide in the preparation of Goering's defence material.

They both knew there was no hope of successful defence. But they carefully studied the copy of the indictment handed to them thirty days before the trial began. It was a lengthy document of over 20,000 words. It summarised the record of the Nazi régime under the four headings of the Nuremberg indictment: Conspiracy, Crimes against Peace, War Crimes and Crimes against Humanity. Against such a broad frontal attack, Goering's limited defence capabilities were bound to be highly vulnerable.

Among the first witnesses to appear for Goering were three Luftwaffe colleagues. The first to testify was General Karl Bodenschatz, Goering's friend since the First World War and his chief aviation link with Adolf Hitler in the Second World War. The next was Field Marshal Erhard Milch, who had been virtually Goering's deputy for air affairs since the official creation of the new German Air Force in 1935. After Milch came Colonel von Brauchitsch, who was Goering's Air Adjutant, and then Field Marshal Albert Kesselring, a former Chief of Staff of the Luftwaffe and also a very experienced Air Fleet commander.

Nearly all the aviation points made by these German Air Force witnesses can be broadly confirmed by original documents. If they were at times evasive, it was because of their loyalty to Goering. The evidence of Karl Bodenschatz, on the relationship between Hitler and Goering was based on a fund of intimate knowledge. Bodenschatz was not entirely well at Nuremberg, for he had been badly wounded in the bomb plot attempt to assassinate Hitler at the Fuehrer's Rastenburg headquarters during a conference in July 1944.

Bodenschatz told the Nuremberg court that it was the large-scale RAF night raids, particularly the raid on Cologne at the end of May 1942, which first resulted in Goering losing influence with Hitler. He testified, 'From that moment, there were differences of opinion between Hitler and Goering which became more serious as time went on. The outward symptoms of this waning influence were as follows: first, the Fuehrer criticised

Goering most severely; secondly, the endless conversations between Adolf Hitler and Hermann Goering became shorter, less frequent and finally ceased altogether.'

The loyalty of Karl Bodenschatz to Goering at the Nuremberg trial led him, at times, to an almost absurd form of testimony. Thus he said, 'Hermann Goering was always of the opinion that the policy of the Reich must be directed in such a way as to avoid war if possible.' He also declared that Goering 'had no prior knowledge of the Nazi anti-Semitic actions in Germany in November 1938'. And when Dr Stahmer, Goering's defence counsel, asked, 'What was Goering's general attitude to human society?' Bodenschatz replied with a touch of saccharine: 'He was a benefactor to all in need'.

Goering's attitude to Operation Barbarossa was raised on more than half a dozen occasions in the Nuremberg trial. But in some ways Karl Bodenschatz's comments on the war against the USSR were more interesting. He alone mentioned both Hitler and Goering's reaction to the first Soviet military successes. 'Towards the end of 1941, after the first reverses in the Russian campaign, Hermann Goering talked with me about the fighting in the East. He said to me, "Adolf Hitler foresaw a very hard battle in the East, but he did not count on such reverses. Before the beginning of this campaign, I tried in vain to dissuade Adolf Hitler from the plan of attacking Russia. I reminded him that he himself, in his book *Mein Kampf,* was opposed to a war on two fronts and, in addition, I pointed out that the main forces of the German Luftwaffe would be occupied in the East, and England, whose air industry was hit, would breathe again and be able to recover." '

Mr Justice Jackson, the chief US prosecutor, cross-examined Bodenschatz on a number of points he had made in defence of Goering. Referring to 1943, he asked Bodenschatz if the air defences of Germany were inadequate. The reply was of considerable interest: 'The air defence of Germany was very difficult, as the entire defence did not depend on the air crews alone, but it was also a radio technical war, and in this radio technical war, it must be admitted frankly, the enemy was eventually better than we were.' This was a tribute to the British electronic boffins, who excelled in radar, navigational and bombing aids and radio counter-measures.

One cannot avoid the impression that in the rush to scurry through the great pile of documents, some of the leading prosecutors had little time to study the pertinent data. Thus, for example, when Mr Justice Jackson said to Bodenschatz, 'You know that the Air Force was greatly enlarged after Munich,' he could not have found evidence of any substantial increase. Bodenschatz replied, convincingly, but without offering any details. 'I can say for certain that the German Air Force at the beginning of the Polish campaign, as regards leadership, planning or equipment, was not equal to its task.' It was an odd aeronautical exchange. Unwittingly, Bodenschatz had produced an indictment of his own Commander-in-Chief's leadership of the German Air Force.

When Mr Justice Jackson observed that Goering 'had more confidence in air power as a weapon of war than most men of his time', Bodenschatz again answered with an unwitting criticism of Goering's air leadership. He said of the 1939 situation: 'I repeat that at that time the Air Force was, as far as leadership, training and equipment were concerned, not ready for war . . .' If Bodenschatz was referring to a long war or a war against a powerful air force, then he was testifying with accuracy.

Mr Justice Jackson also raised the question of Goering's promise in 1939 to the German public that the Luftwaffe would be able to keep enemy bombers away from Germany. Bodenschatz must have had a lapse of memory when he told the court, 'I cannot remember that he gave an official assurance to the German people in the form of a decree or a big speech.' In fact the Rhineland 'Call me Meier' speeches had very wide radio and press coverage in Germany. Speer's evidence was that Hitler himself believed that the Goering guarantee of immunity from enemy bombing would be achieved. Bodenschatz rephrased the speeches somewhat when he told the Nuremberg court: 'Goering said to the German people that the Air Force would do its job and do everything to spare the country from heavy raids. At the time that was justified. It was not clearly foreseen then that matters would develop differently.' This last sentence of Bodenschatz testimony contains the heart of Goering's air failure. He did not clearly foresee.

Perhaps the most charmingly inaccurate comment in all the Bodenschatz testimony was this: 'Discussions between Adolf

Hitler and the Reichsmarschall were, in spite of all the tension, always very moderate'. And then came this gem: 'The reports which the Air Force made to the Fuehrer were always correct.' Fortunately Mr Justice Jackson did not press for chapter and verse.

After Bodenschatz, Erhard Milch came to the witness-stand to testify. He was knowledgeable, intelligent, shrewd and tough. Like Bodenschatz, he bore witness to Goering's opposition to the German attack on the USSR in June 1941. He recalled in particular a meeting with Goering about a month before the attack, on 22 May. On that occasion, Milch reportedly said to Goering, 'We should not voluntarily burden ourselves with a two-front war'. Milch went on, 'The Reichsmarschall told me that he had also brought forward all these arguments, but that it was absolutely impossible to dissuade Hitler from this war.'

Milch, one of the most competent of German air leaders, produced this interesting blanket apologia covering the problems of Goering's air leadership in the pre-war period: 'During the few years 1935-1939, it would have been impossible for any soldier, in any country, to build an air force equal to the tasks with which we were faced from 1939 onwards, that is, impossible to create the units or to establish the schools and furnish them with adequate training staff. Nor is it possible to develop the planes which are necessary and then to build them by mass production.'

This was not a new Milch viewpoint concocted for the Nuremberg Trial. He had warned Goering in 1935-1939 about the problems of German Air Force expansion. Thus, at the time of Munich, he had told the Reichsmarschall that the Luftwaffe could not be made ready to go to war before 1942.

Milch was the only Nuremberg witness to refer in detail to Goering's long-term advanced air planning. He said, 'It was intended to create a large air force later. As far as I can remember, the plans envisaged were scheduled for completion in six to eight years, that is 1944-1946'. However, given Hitler's wild strategy, the plan never evolved beyond the paper stage.

Milch was interesting when giving his testimony on US war production. He said: 'When the question of American armament figures came up, the Reichsmarschall said to me, "Now you are going to turn defeatist and believe these large figures." '

Milch added later, 'The American figures were undoubtedly submitted to Hitler, but Hitler did not believe them.'

When Mr Justice Jackson asked Milch, 'Goering had no time to receive you?', the loyal reply was, 'Goering at the time had many other matters.' This was one of the several occasions on which the Nuremberg Trial underscored the substantial diversions from air leadership which Goering's other duties produced, in particular the German Four Year Economic Plan, with its responsibilities for manpower, food and raw materials. The view that he should have stuck to one job, that of Air Minister, and given up his other posts, was expressed by a number of Luftwaffe pilots to whom I spoke after the war. The Nuremberg Trials, concerned chiefly with the prosecution and defence of Goering, nevertheless provided unpremeditated evidence in support of these Luftwaffe pilots' views.

With so much better documentary evidence available, it was perhaps strange that Goering's pre-war speeches were cited in evidence at Nuremberg. Thus, Mr Roberts, a British prosecuting counsel, reminded Milch of a Goering speech of May 1934, which threatened, 'I intend to create a Luftwaffe which, if the hour should strike, will burst upon the foe like an avenging host. The enemy must feel he has lost, even before he has started fighting.' Later, Mr Roberts read to the court an extract from a Goering speech of October 1938, made less than a month after the Munich agreement. It said, 'Hitler has ordered me to organise a gigantic armament programme, which would make all previous achievements appear insignificant. I have ordered them to build me an air force five times as large as the present one.'

Erhard Milch commented aptly on these extracts: 'One has to distinguish between words and deeds . . . such an air force would have taken many years to build.' In October 1938, the front-line operational strength of the German Air Force was about 3,300 planes. It was never to be increased anything like five-fold.' Goering's speeches illustrated in part his self-delusion, but also his gift for strategic deception and the planting of false information. Both US and Soviet intelligence believed there was real substance in his threat to expand five-fold.

General Rudenko, the chief Soviet prosecutor at Nuremberg, naturally asked Milch a number of questions about the German plan to attack the USSR. In the cut and thrust of cross-examination, Milch must have surprised the court by saying of Goering 'He personally was opposed to any war.' Rudenko retorted rather tartly, 'That is strange!' He then asked Milch, 'You mean that Goering did not want a war against the Soviet Union?' Milch replied, 'On 22 May 1941, when I spoke to Goering about this matter, and urgently requested him to do everything to prevent a war with Russia, he told me he had used the same argument with Hitler, but that it was impossible to get Hitler to change his mind.'

When Milch stood down, Colonel von Brauchitsch took the stand. His testimony contained little of major importance. Asked by Goering's counsel, Dr Stahmer, about the treatment of enemy air crews who baled out over Germany—a point on which Goering was ultra-sensitive—von Brauchitz recalled an incident in March 1945. The observer of a US bomber crew was civilly received by the Reichsmarschall himself on the day after the raid. One would have imagined that Hermann Goering had more urgent things to do in March 1945. But he did enjoy talking to individual pilots, friendly or enemy. Perhaps it gave him a rejuvenated feeling, for flying was deep in his blood.

Von Brauchitsch told the Nuremberg court about Goering's popularity with the people even in the last months of the war. He testified, 'In a public air-raid shelter, the Reichsmarschall had no guards or escort and chatted with the people who greeted him with the old cry, "Hermann, keep your chin up!"' Then he cited another incident which occurred on a journey he made with Goering from Berlin to Berchtesgaden during the night of 20/21 April 1945: 'The Reichsmarschall arrived at a town in Sudetengau . . . the market place became so crowded with people asking for his autograph . . . here, too, he was greeted by the old cry, "Hermann!"'

When Dr Koerner came into the witness-box after von Brauchitsch, matters of graver substance than Goering's public relations were dealt with. Koerner had been Goering's State Secretary in Prussia. He told the Nuremberg court, 'The Reichsmarschall was in charge of the Gestapo in the concentration camps until the spring of 1934.' Then Heinrich Himmler became responsible for them.

Koerner also gave evidence of Goering's diversions from his

XVI. At the Nuremberg Trials, 1945

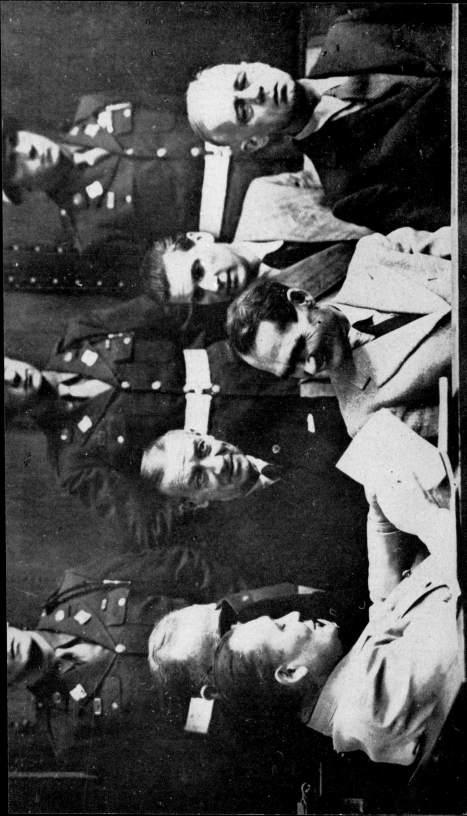

XVII. Goering at Nuremberg

air duties. He told the court: 'In the autumn of 1935, the Reichsmarschall received the order from the Fuehrer to make the food for the German people secure, as the food situation was serious, because of the bad harvests of 1934 and 1935.' This foreshadowed Goering's new responsibility for the Four Year Plan in 1936. But Koerner's most notable contribution to the Nuremberg story was his memorable description of Goering as 'the last big man of the Renaissance . . . the last great example of a man from the Renaissance period'. When Dr Koerner stood down, after those splendid remarks, Field Marshal Kesselring replaced him in the Nuremberg witness-box.

The highlights of Kesselring's evidence were the replies he gave on the subject of the bombing of Warsaw, Amsterdam and Coventry. He had been the Commander of the relevant German Air Fleet for all these three bombardments. Kesselring trod warily, as Dr Stahmer's questions guided him gently along the difficult path of Goering's Nuremberg defence. On Warsaw, Kesselring testified, 'The stipulations of the Hague Convention for land warfare, which can be applied by analogy to air warfare, were fulfilled.' He made a more revealing comment about the bombing of Amsterdam. 'Particularly on the third day, the Reichsmarschall, in his outspoken manner, intervened more than usual in the direction of the Air Fleet.' This was indeed a feature of Goering's air leadership. Thus in the bombing of Britain and the air defence of Germany, he oscillated between pre-occupation with the minutiae of individual air operations and spells of indifference to the whole air scene.

Perhaps Kesselring's best contribution to the Nuremberg Trials was this piece of aviation sanity: 'With an air force there is the further peculiarity that, if strong formations (of bombers) are employed, not the individual target but only the target area as a whole can be aimed it.'

This was surely a simple truism swamped at Nuremberg by the political illegalisms of bombing civilians. In the hectic disarray of some of the bombing evidence produced at Nuremberg, it passed almost unnoticed. The record of American, British, Japanese, Soviet or other military bombing makes it clear that, unfortunately, civilians must suffer when formations of bombers attack their targets. And in spite of the emphasis given to Coventry, Rotterdam, and Belgrade at Nuremberg, historians will surely refer to the much greater damage and loss of civilian life in cities like Hamburg, Berlin and Tokyo, not to mention Hiroshima and Nagasaki.

Like previous witnesses appearing in defence of Goering, Kesselring introduced the whitewash touch in his testimony. He said, 'We had complete confidence in our Reichsmarschall and we knew he was the only person who had a decisive influence on Adolf Hitler.' When one recalls the many heated exchanges between Goering and Kesselring on Mediterranean and Russian Front air affairs, the phrase, 'We had complete confidence in our Reichsmarschall' is a totally inadequate reflection of Kesselring's views on his Commander-in-Chief.

In answer to questions from Mr Justice Jackson, Kesselring agreed that Goering was responsible for the failure to develop four-engined bombers before the war and that this had been a mistake. But he did not expand on his thesis. Kesselring himself had done little to lobby for four-engined bombers.

Early in the afternoon of 13 March 1946, Hermann Goering himself took the stand. For the next ten days, he fought in the witness-box to justify his leadership of men. Despite the in-humanities to man of which he was justly accused, he emerged as an individual with a better reputation than before. He was a new man at Nuremberg. At the time, one reflected that, if he could have sustained the high level of intelligence, determination and even realism that he showed in those ten days in the Nuremberg dock, if only he could have encouraged his air chiefs to speak to him as freely as he himself spoke to the prosecuting Nuremberg counsels, then the whole trend of European history might have taken a different turn.

There was a touch of social pride—or was it snobbery—when Goering began to testify. He gave his full name, Hermann Wilhelm Goering, and then said, 'My father, the first Governor of South-West Africa, had connections at the time, particularly with the two British statesmen Cecil Rhodes and the elder Chamberlain.' It was in this vein that he had told Hitler in 1923 of his splendid connections with the Ruhr barons and members of the German Royal Family that was.

Goering went on, at first in moderate voice, to tell the Nuremberg court about his early career. He recalled his studies in history and political science at Munich University in 1922, and then how he married his Swedish wife Karin. Then came the Munich putsch in which he was wounded in the thigh. Of course he did not mention the morphia problem which ensued and resulted in a spell in the Langbro mental asylum in Sweden. This was a troublesome bit of autobiography for a man using all his skills in last-ditch defence.

In Goering's early evidence there were one or two light-hearted touches. Dealing with the first years of the Nazi rule in Germany, he told the court: 'Following the example of the United States, we combined the position of the Head of State with the Head of Government.' When he listed his 1933 responsibilities as Reichs Commissioner for Aviation, Minister of the Interior for Prussia and then Prime Minister for Prussia, Goering added almost carelessly, 'Then there were also several not very important offices, President of the State Council and so on.'

Goering had no difficulty in admitting that he had set up the Gestapo and the first concentration camps. He commented with a touch of almost callous indifference, 'Of course, in the beginning there were excesses, of course the innocent were also hurt here and there.' He added that he had taken a personal interest in the concentration camps up to the spring of 1934, when there were only two or three camps in Prussia. After that Himmler was in charge.

Goering's pride in his various high offices was a feature of the Nuremberg trial. Then came an unexpected touch almost of coyness. 'Constitutionally, as Prussian Minister, I was, to be sure, in a certain sense, the highest dignitary of the Prussian Church. But I did not concern myself with these matters very much . . . I myself am not what you might call a church-goer, but I have gone now and then.' Then, loyal always to his Fuehrer, Goering said of Hitler, 'His attitude to the Church was positive and generous.'

Goering had no difficulty in telling the court that he was in part responsible for the anti-Jewish Nuremberg Laws of 1935. He said, 'They were intended to produce a clear separation of races.' Nor did he contest his responsibility for imposing a fine of a billion marks on Jews and driving them out of German business and the professions.

But great as his crimes were against humanity, it is the Nuremberg elements of military air strategy and planning which provided relevant grist for air leadership assessment. Of course, the aviation testimony given at Nuremberg was not always historically helpful. Thus Goering stated, 'In 1933, when I founded the Air Ministry, we had not yet gone into the question of re-armament.' One would not think from Goering's statement that the early Luftwaffe Heinkel fighter planes were being developed in the late 1920's, that a Dornier bomber was flying in Germany in 1931, and a Junkers bomber in 1932. But perhaps Goering's gem of an attempt at misinformation was this: 'Originally it was my belief that a defensive, that is a fighter, air force might suffice. But on reflection I realised that one would be lost with simply a fighter force.' In fact Goering was much too eager to develop bombers at the expense of fighters from the very beginning.

Goering also gave a somewhat misleading picture of his early attitude to German aircraft production. He summarised his views in the mid-1930's as follows: 'Since nothing had existed before, I should be able to catch up quickly only if aircraft production, on the one hand, were made to work with as many shifts as possible.'

Goering misled his Nuremberg audience. He did virtually nothing to develop multi-shift aircraft factory work in the pre-war or early-war periods.

Goering probably gave his most accurate aviation evidence in his statement on German intervention in the Spanish Civil War in the period 1936-1939. He testified, 'Franco sent a call for help to Germany and asked for support particularly in the air. One should not forget that Franco and his troops were stationed in Africa and that he could not get the troops across, as the fleet was in the hands of the Communists . . . The Fuehrer thought the matter over. I urged him to give support in all circumstances. Firstly, in order to prevent the further spread of Communism in that area, and secondly, to test my young Luftwaffe.' Goering then told the court, 'With the permission of the Fuehrer, I sent a large part of my transport fleet and a number of experimental fighter units, bombers and anti-aircraft guns.' This was a piece of accurate testimony which contrasted with some of Goering's evasions at Nuremberg.

Goering's comments on German Air Force four-engined bomber development in the pre-war period included a burst of scarcely-veiled contempt for the more accurate evidence which Milch and Kesselring had given the Nuremberg tribunal. Goering declared : 'Much has been said here in cross-examination about four-engine bombers, two-engine bombers and so on. The witnesses made statements to the best of their knowledge and ability, but they were familiar with only part of the story and they gave their opinions from that point of view. I alone was responsible and am responsible, for I was Commander-in-Chief of the Luftwaffe and Minister for Air. I was responsible for the re-armament, the training and the morale of the Luftwaffe.'

Goering showed a splendid Atlas complex at Nuremberg. He bore all German air responsibilities on his broad shoulders. But in some instances he was loth to accept responsibility, especially when Sir David Maxwell-Fyfe cross-questioned him on the murder of RAF officers when they were trying to escape in March 1944 from the Stalag Luft III prisoner-of-war camp. And how could Goering assume responsibility for the morale of the Luftwaffe, which was inevitably affected, for example, by the rising tides of British, American and Soviet air power, against which the Reichsmarschall had been virtually impotent.

Goering continued his evidence on long-range bombers: 'If, at the beginning, I did not build any four-engine bombers, it was not because I had qualms that they might be construed as an aggressive force. That would not have disturbed me for one moment. My only reason was that the necessary technical and production facilities did not exist. That kind of bomber simply had not yet been developed by my industry, at any rate so that I could use it. Secondly, I was still short of aluminium, and anyone, only half an expert, knows how much aluminium a four-engine bomber swallows up, and how many fighters or two-engine bombers one can build with the same amount.'

Of the two reasons given for not developing four-engine bombers in the pre-war period, the shortage of aluminium was more likely to have been Goering's real reason. In terms of four-engine bomber development in 1936-37, the German Air Force was evolving Dornier, Junkers and Focke Wulf prototypes and was, at this stage, as advanced as either the Royal Air Force or the United States Army Air Force, the two greatest users of four-engined bombers in the Second World War.

One of Goering's more interesting comments on the subject

of long-range bombing showed that he had given thought to a possible air attack on the United States: 'In a speech to the aircraft industrialists, I let it be known clearly that I desired most urgently to have a bomber which could fly to America and back, so that if America entered the war, I could also reach the American armament industry.' Goering went on: 'The technical knowledge of that time led us to believe that after five years of war technical advances would be made.'

This was interesting confirmation that Goering foresaw the possibility of a five-year war which would, perhaps, involve Germany in air combat against the United States. He made no practical plans to attack the American armaments industry because he had no planes with the required range of action. But a German air attack on USA was a passionate subject of debate in Washington, as I found during my first visit to the White House in July 1943. The threat was never taken very seriously, especially when the limited nature of German four-engined bomber production became apparent to everybody concerned.

While some of Goering's testimony at Nuremberg was the stuff of accurate history, he had notable lapses. On his meeting with President Hacha of Czechoslovakia in March 1939, he told the court, 'I made the statement that I should be sorry to bomb beautiful Prague. The intention of bombing Prague did not exist . . . But a point like that might, I thought, serve as an argument and accelerate the whole matter.'

The secret German minutes of the meetings between Goering and Ribbentrop and the Czech president are, however, available. Dr Hacha and the Czech Foreign Minister, Mr Chvalkovsky, were hounded by bursts of Teutonic terror threats from Goering in the early hours of the morning. They were told that if they did not accept the German terms 'half of Prague would lie in ruins from bombing within two hours and this would only be the beginning. Hundreds of bombers were waiting the order to take off and they will receive that order at six in the morning.'

Throughout the Nuremberg trial, Goering gave no indication that the many diversions from his air force commitments had any serious effect on Luftwaffe affairs. Thus he said nonchalantly about the Fuehrer, 'Of course he informed me of all political and military problems. He initiated me into these

problems for the most part in many long discussions which
would take place for many hours, day after day.' And on the
same day Goering spoke about his responsibilities to the German
Four Year Economic Plan. 'I devoted a great deal of time and
work to this task.' Then came a favourite topic, 'The Research
Office of the Air Force'. This, said Goering, combined phone-
tapping and the interception and decoding of wireless messages:
'This machinery served to exert controls, above all over foreign
missions and important persons.' But it also served, at times, to
keep Goering's mind away from the more important funda-
mentals of planning ahead more meticulously for German Air
Force needs.

Goering also told the court: 'These secret reports were submitted only to the heads of departments.' This illustrated
Goering's amateur approach to the needs of sound intelligence
machinery. Most bits of information, however secret, have to
be filed and built up gradually into a firm picture. To restrict a
whole category of information to heads of department is to waste
most of its value. Goering desperately needed a posse of high-
grade intelligence officers he could trust, rather than batches of
often disconnected information, however secret.

In his long Nuremberg statement on the Nazi occupation of
Austria in 1938, Goering emphasised his heavy involvement in
the foreign policy of the Third Reich. There was also a typical
touch of romance: 'I personally felt a great affinity for Austria.
I had spent the greater part of my youth in an Austrian castle.'
For greater part, read small part.

The Nuremberg Trial helped to clarify the relationship
between Goering and Hitler at the time of the campaign in
Norway, in the spring and early summer of 1940. Clearly there
had been trouble between the Fuehrer and his deputy, but the
German documents on the subject are conflicting. Goering told
the court: 'The Norwegian project surprised me rather . . . But
since the most important part of the undertaking fell to the Air
Force, I expressed my views in an unmistakable and unfriendly
way. From a military point of view, I was definitely against this
undertaking. My objections were that, firstly, I had been
informed too late and, secondly, the plans did not seem quite
correct.' Goering was, of course, skating round the real situation
in his testimony. He was worried about the Norwegian war

spreading to Sweden where he had relatives. And he was piqued at being left out of some of the early planning for the invasion of Denmark and Norway.

Goering was not particularly impressive when he defended himself against the charge of attacking civilian objectives with his bomber forces. To cite, as he did, the views of the French Air Attaché to prove that the German Air Force had only attacked military targets in the Polish campaign was rather unconvincing. One wondered how a single Attaché, presumably based in a Warsaw office, could provide credible and comprehensive target intelligence. And when Goering described the Okecie airfield near Warsaw as the base, 'where the main enemy Polish Air Force was concentrated,' he was obviously claiming an excessive degree of concentration of Polish air power.

Goering was better on the subject of the bombing of Rotterdam in May 1940. He showed a firm grasp of details and gave a genuine impression that there had been a failure in German radio communication. But his statement on the 1940 bombing of London would not stand the test of cross-examination by an aviation specialist. On this occasion Goering seemed to be confused about the dates of this joint Hitler-Goering decision. Perhaps that is why he threw in a burst of flattery to impress the British judge. Goering testified: 'After the period 6-7 September, after repeated warnings to the English Government, and after the Fuehrer had reserved for himself the right to give the order for reprisal raids on London, and had long hesitated to give the order, and after German cities, which were not military objectives, had been bombed again and again, then London was declared a target for attack . . . The people of London can take a great deal . . . we could not break their resistance in this manner.'

In fact the bombing of London began on 7 September and not after. And since a modest RAF Bomber Command was then much concerned to attack the German invasion barges in August and September they had few resources to bomb German cities 'again and again'.

Nor was Goering impressive in justifying the German attack on the USSR, no doubt in part because he had been opposed to it. Referring to the autumn of 1940, he said, 'The Fuehrer thought that Churchill had already come to an understanding with Russia'. Goering then went on to say, 'Officers of ours, that is Germans, were suddenly shown the tremendous Russian armaments works of the aviation and tank industry. These reports strengthened the Fuehrer's conviction of the USSR attack on Germany'. But this could not have impressed Nuremberg. Apart from the Fuehrer's intuition, no evidence was produced of any planned Soviet attack on Germany. The reverse attack on the USSR had been planned in Nazi Germany as early as August 1940, at the height of the Battle of Britain.

But Goering was, in part, sincere in expounding the views he held in the autumn of 1940 about the proposed German attack on the USSR. 'I urged him (Hitler) most particularly not to start a war against Russia at that moment or a short time after. Not that I was moved by consideration of international law or similar reasons . . . I now told the Feuhrer that I always feared the danger from Russia.' Goering also testified that, at about that time, he also told the Fuehrer, 'I am definitely of the opinion that, sooner or later, the second great world power, the United States, will march against us.' And a little later Goering reinforced this view with these words, 'I unfortunately feared from the very beginning that America would, in any case, intervene in the war.'

But the possibility that the Luftwaffe might have to deal with two new major air powers in 1941 or later did not seem to register as important factors in the forward air planning of Goering and his senior air staff, although Milch certainly urged Goering to expand air training and aircraft production in 1941 and so did Udet, who committed suicide in that year. Both before and after Pearl Harbour, when the United States entered the war in Europe, Goering simply refused to give US air potential the serious attention it deserved. Goering's underestimate of both Soviet and US air potential was a major factor in the defeat of Germany.

Despite Goering's sanction of inhuman cruelty in the treatment of Jews, the exploitation of the USSR and the use of European slave labour, Nuremberg also provide touches of the more human side of Goering's personality. Thus he recalled, in evidence, one of the talks he gave to Luftwaffe flying personnel in May 1936: 'I demand nothing impossible of you. I do not ask that you should be model lads. I like to be generous. I understand that youth must have its follies.' Certainly Goering was glad that his airmen had good brothel facilities and drank a wide range of European wines culled from the vineyards of Italy, France, Germany, Austria, Hungary and Jugoslavia.

On the subject of the German siege of Leningrad in 1941-1942, Goering made a fairly factual confession to the Nuremberg court about the limitations of the Luftwaffe: 'The air force at Leningrad was very weak'. Then his pride flared up and he added, 'As long as my air force is willing to fly into the hell of London it will be equally prepared to attack the much less defended city of Leningrad. However, I lacked the necessary resources'. He had indeed told Hitler, at the end of 1941, that he had no fresh air squadrons to strengthen the air attack on Leningrad. He told the Fuehrer, 'You must not give so many tasks to my air force on the northern front.'

On the difficult subject of the bombing of civilians, Goering did his best. He switched the subject to the Anglo-German bombing of Germany and spoke to the Nuremberg court about the 'heavy and continual attacks on German cities in the course of which the population saw, to a certain extent, that the really important individual targets were less frequently hit than the houses and non-military targets.' This may have been an accurate summary of most long-range bombing both during the Second World War and perhaps since.

There was a touch of the imp when Goering told the court, in the context of bombing: 'In Germany, men of the rank of musician and composer, Tschaikovsky and the poets Pushkin and Tolstoy are too highly revered for the deliberate destruction of the graves of these great and creative men of culture.' And then when Goering was struggling to justify his use of labour from concentration camps for the German aircraft industry, he produced a Winston Churchill quotation which I cannot trace. It was a colourful touch, however. Goering said, 'I would like to use the same words which one of our greatest, most important and toughest opponents, the British Prime Minister, Winston Churchill, used—"In the struggle for life and death there is in the end no legality." '

Goering confirmed at Nuremberg his hope that the flying bomb and rocket weapons might somehow restore the balance of air power in 1944. 'I can only regret that we did not have enough of those V1 and V2 weapons; for an easing of the attacks on Germany could be brought about only if we could inflict equally heavy losses on the enemy.'

January 1945 was the month in which Goering believed the war was lost, because the Russians had reached the Oder and the German offensive in the Ardennes had failed. 'After January 1945 there were no more attacks on England, except perhaps a few single planes, because, at that time, I needed all my petrol for the fighter planes for defence.' Certainly the Luftwaffe bomber arm was disintegrating by January 1945.

It was the British prosecutng counsel, Sir David Maxwell-Fyfe, who really punctured Goering's flimsy but well conducted defence at Nuremberg. The former Commander-in-Chief of the Luftwaffe seemed to be much happier when Mr Justice Jackson was conducting the cross-examination. When the US prosecutor asked Goering if, in 1936, the German plans to reoccupy the Rhineland had to be kept entirely secret from foreign powers, Goering replied, impudently, 'I do not think I can recall reading beforehand the publication of the mobilisation plans of the United States.'

Mr Justice Jackson seemed to be rattled. He said to the President of the court, 'I respectfully submit that this witness is not being responsive.' And on the next day, 20 March 1946, the US prosecutor complained that 'propaganda is one of the purposes of the defendant . . . it does seem to me that that is the beginning of the trial getting out of hand.'

When he was cross-examined by Sir David Maxwell-Fyfe, something of Goering's ebullience began to fade away. Sir David had mastered the documents and led Goering gently but firmly along the path chosen by the prosecution. One major issue on which Goering was especially sensitive was the shooting of a large number of RAF officers who had escaped from Stalag Luft III prisoner-of-war camp in March 1944. Goering had previously told the court that he was on leave at the time and added, 'As I can prove'. But under the pressure of Sir David's mild but relentless queries, it was soon clear that Goering could prove nothing. He confessed lamely 'I cannot say exactly now whether I had heard about the shooting from the Chiefs of Staff or from other sources.' Sir David persisted, 'You said the other day you could prove when you were on leave. Am I to take it that you have not taken the trouble to look up what your leave dates were?' And he later admitted to Sir David, 'Of course I cannot establish the date with certainty.'

The duel between Sir David and Goering on the German treatment of escaped prisoners-of-wars was one of the highlights of the Nuremberg trials. Goering insisted that he did not know that escaped prisoners other than British and American were handed over to the police, taken to a concentration camp and shot. He protested to the court, 'No, I did not know that,' and 'No, I never gave such an order.'

On the morning of Thursday, 21 March, Sir David returned to the charge. Goering defended grimly on the subject of a Commander-in-Chief's responsibilities. He said, 'If they acted according to my directives and my instructions, yes, if they acted against my instruction and directives, no.' Of course, the real trouble was that Goering did not always read many of the documents he signed, not even the large print.

Sir David continued to pin Goering's ears back on the subject of escaping prisoners-of-war. 'In any other service in the world, an attempt to escape is regarded as the duty of an officer when he is a prisoner-of-war, is that not so?' 'Yes, that is so,' Goering replied, and added on the subject of the March 1944 Stalag Luft III shootings, 'I myself considered it the most serious incident of the whole war.'

Sir David concluded on this incident: 'I suggest that you did nothing to prevent these men from being shot but co-operated in this foul series of murders.'

Nor was Goering happier about other points raised by Sir David Maxwell-Fyfe. He agreed with Sir David's description of his harsh methods of dealing with partisans for example, burning their villages. And when Sir David read out to the court Hitler's order to Goering 'to destroy the capital city of Belgrade in attacks by waves of bombers,' Goering rather lamely told the court, 'Belgrade was far more a centre of military installations than any other capital in the world.'

Then General Rudenko, the Soviet prosecutor, began to cross-examine Goering. Goering was as defiant as he had been with the British and US prosecutors. 'Can you reply briefly?' said General Rudenko at one stage. 'Yes,' replied Goering, 'but not in the sense in which you are presenting the case.' But on the subject of German plans to seize Soviet territories revealed in a July 1941 document, Goering had to admit to the court, 'The Fuehrer wanted the Crimea.' But he was unabashed and added, 'Had we been victorious, we would in any case have decided how far annexation would have served our purpose.'

On the subject of the bad treatment of Soviet people by members of the German armed forces, Goering said to General Rudenko, 'If every order and every instruction which came through in the shape of an order, but which did not require my intervention, had had to be reported to me, I should have been drowned in a sea of papers.' That was a fair comment. In fact, Goering was so drowned during the Second World War in a sea of papers that he failed to read or sign many key Luftwaffe documents.

When Goering stood down from the witness-box on 22 March 1946, he must have known that, despite all his determination and mental agility, he would be condemned to death. But he was pleased with his performance and said that evening to a US psychiatrist, 'Rudenko was more nervous than I was.'

In the first week of July, Dr Stahmer made his final speech in defence of Goering. He told the court, 'Until the end of the war Reichsmarschall Goering maintained the old airman point of view.' Taken ironically, the words constituted a just and fundamental criticism of Goering's air leadership.

The final prosecution speeches in condemnation of Goering followed at the end of July. Sir Hartley Shawcross said, 'Behind his spurious air of *bonhomie,* he was as great an architect as any in this satanic system.' On 31 August, Goering was back in the witness-box to make a final plea : 'I never decreed the murder of a single individual . . . I did not want war, nor did I bring it about.'

In September, Goering's wife Emmy was allowed to visit him in the Nuremberg gaol. They were not allowed to touch or kiss. Goering was cheerful and determined during these visits, but broke down after them. He knew they would be his last talks with Emmy.

On 1 October 1946, the President of the Court, Lord Justice Lawrence, read the judgement. Goering was sentenced to death by hanging. On the night of 15 October, some two hours before the time of his execution, and after having refused the last rites

of the Lutheran Church, Hermann Goering swallowed a phia‍l
of cyanide. Within five minutes he was dead after a number o‍f
shuddering, twisting convulsions. Goering's body was burne‍d
and his ashes scattered.

CHAPTER ELEVEN

Summing Up

IN JULY 1945, Goering told Major Evans, one of his American interrogators at the Mondorf gaol, that there would be statues erected in his memory all over Germany in the next fifty years. In this odd prophecy might be found two of the main characteristics of Goering's air leadership. He was a bad predictor of the future and his vanity was monumental. But there was a wide range of other elements in his personality which militated against his success as an air leader—bad temper, bad judgement, hastiness and lack of patience, unwillingness to listen or read at length, conceit and overconfidence boosted by his intake of drugs. He had, however, the external manner of a leader. It was the internal matter which was often defective. He certainly had courage and intelligence, but little humility or powers of strategic assessment. He was, in effect, a good ally of British, American and Soviet air power and a bad ally of Italian and German air power.

In his career as an air leader, in the First World War, he flattered to deceive. His aviation experience was limited. His spell as a reconnaissance crew member and as a commander of fighter squadrons covered only a negligible part of the modern military aviation spectrum.

From 1933 to 1945, when he needed to know all he could about the rapid succession of current technical air developments, he was constantly sidetracked by other commitments to the Third Reich, economic, police, political and diplomatic. He also spent too much time on his private art collection for a man with so many aviation things to do, and on entertaining at his hunting lodges, where he mixed business and pleasure.

But in his day, he and his air force added something to the equipment and methodology of modern air power. He was the first to translate the conception of mobility through air transport squadrons into large-scale reality in the period 1935-1941. His scheme of tactical close air support of ground forces, worked out with his air staff in the late 1930's, was far more advanced and efficient than in any other air force of that time. In the later stages of the Second World War, he lost the methodological lead in this sphere. The Junkers 87 dive-bomber was a specialist close-support plane which made a really effective Goering-cum-Udet contribution to the blitzkreig victories of 1939-40. Senior British army officers began to ask urgently for a Royal Air Force equivalent machine after the Ju 87 successes of May and June 1940 in France and the Low Countries. But in the later stages of the war the Luftwaffe lost its technological lead in air-ground support operations.

Perhaps his greatest weakness was a failure to foresee the key role of strategic air power, both in long-term air defence and long-range air attack. A leader who thinks that all air battles can be won in a matter of weeks or months is bound to be astray in any long-range aviation business. His belated realisation of the inadequacies of German aircraft production and of the need to create a bigger basic training organisation to deal with a long-term five-year war, which he himself had predicted more than once, was a cardinal cause of Luftwaffe disaster.

Goering also had a blind spot or two in the realm of naval aviation. In aerial mine-laying he and his air staff had a respectable World War Two record. But he was slow to develop aerial torpedo dropping—a technique in which the Luftwaffe relied too heavily on Italian help in 1940-41. He also failed to make adequate provision to support the German Navy in the Battle of the Atlantic. His decision to re-equip the naval air float-plane and flying boat squadrons of the German Air Force with land-based planes was much delayed. His serious attempts to verify Luftwaffe pilot claims of enemy ships sunk or damaged ranged from nil to negligible.

It is easy to criticise his choice of air commanders. Goering picked good and bad air leaders. Milch, Galland and Wever were good choices; Loerzer and Loehr less good. But Goering's real failure was to stifle much of the initiative of his senior air staff officers by his loud, brusque, dictatorial manner. He would hector them and subdue their views rather than quizz them gently, as one heard Air Chief Marshal Sir Charles Portal and General Carl Spaatz do at their air staff meetings. Goering was quick to blame and, sometimes, to apologise for his lapses.

It is hard to offer a definitive, general statement on Goering's patronage of technical air developments in the Luftwaffe. During his stewardship of German air affairs, the German Air Force was ahead of the rest of the world in developing jet planes, guided weapons and novelties such as V1 buzz-bombs. V2 rockets, of course, were the German Army's affair. Goering's air force was also first in the field with navigational beams for bombing aids. But on radar he was crucially late. German electronic scientists were ahead of the Reichsmarschall in this respect in the period 1935-40.

Perhaps the main criticism of Hermann Goering in the field of modern aero-space technical innovation is that he let his Fuehrer, Adolf Hitler, have too much say in the decisions to develop or not to develop war weapons. It is hard to know how far one should push this criticism. Mussolini cramped the style and technical development of the Italian Air Force in the Second World War, and Stalin did the same in the case of the Soviet Air Force long-range bombers in the 1930s. Dictators are not the best judges of long-term aviation policies, or so it would seem. But they do formulate them firmly at times.

Hitler's interference at all levels of air policy—in night fighter employment, in the use of the Messerschmitt 262 jet, the switching of air squadrons from one front to another, the day-light fighter defence of Germany, in aircraft production and in the bombing of Britain—was bad enough. But what was much worse for Goering's air leadership was the over-optimistic military strategy of the Fuehrer. The campaign decisions of Adolf Hitler made in the autumn of 1940—to attack in the Mediterranean and against the USSR—both made within a period of a few months, represented the height of strategic folly. In September 1940, the Wehrmacht had been checked in an attempt to invade Britain or to bring us to our knees. In the next three months, Hitler committed his Wehrmacht to two new wars, against the USSR and the British forces in the Mediterranean, while the problem of coping with Britain as a war base still gnawed at the vitals of his strategic purposes.

The spread of Hitler's military folly in the autumn of 1940

had a most fundamental effect on Hermann Goering's a
leadership. Saddled suddenly with the fresh responsibility
providing for and steering German air power in two new maj
campaigns, Goering found his aviation resources at first stretche
to the limit and then overextended to the point of impotence.

Even if Goering had succeeded in persuading Hitler not
attack Russia in June 1941—and he did try to dissuade th
Fuehrer—even so, his late 1940 air planning was still basical
defective. The multiple cracks were there, by the end of 194
for Goering and his air staff to behold. This applied to both th
Western and Mediterranean air fronts.

One may wonder if Goering ever looked at the Luftwaff
battle order and aircraft production position seriously in th
period October to December 1940, in terms of his known futu
commitments plus possible further undertakings, for examp
against US air power.

Let us assume that, in December 1940, he thought there w
hope of cancelling Barbarossa, of persuading the Fuehrer n
to attack the Soviet Union. Even so, Goering's policymakir
was not cut to the cloth of his other air commitments. The coas
line of Norway was much too thinly spread with the fight
cover needed to protect German merchant ships carrying vit
iron-ore, or to patrol over naval capital ships routed via Norwa
and taking a key part in the Battle of the Atlantic.

Goering's Air Force was also weak in the vital area of th
Bay of Biscay long before the end of 1940. German U-boa
operating from Brest and Bordeaux had no long-range fight
or bomber support of any dimensions. Indeed, Goering had
press some of his Henschel 126 army reconnaissance planes in
temporary service in this area for air patrol duties. They we
slow and short-ranged and utterly ill-suited for the nav
co-operation job they had to do.

Goering and his Fuehrer turned south to the Mediterranea
in planning harmony. They both harboured the dream of
successful Middle East strategy which would strike at the hea
of the British Empire. But again, by the end of 1940, and eve
more so in 1941, the gap between German air planning and a
reality was apparent in the Mediterranean. Goering's air leade
ship exchanged the strategic substance for the shadow wi
buccaneering insouciance. It had been a key part of his hopes

persuade Franco to provide air bases in Spain. From them, Goering confidently expected that the Luftwaffe would be able to stop the entry of British ships into the Mediterranean and help to eliminate Gibraltar, to be captured eventually by German airborne troops. In the Central Mediterranean, Malta was to have similar treatment as a result of the use of new Luftwaffe bases in Sicily. Meantime, Rommel was to gather his forces in North Africa and drive for Egypt. This was the essence of the Hitler-Goering plan at the turn of 1940-41.

There were already great cracks in the reality of Goering's air leadership in terms of his forward planning for the Mediterranean. His hopes were high and wild. There was no one to curb his aeronautical myopia. He also had some back luck.

In the light of all the German air aid given to General Franco in the Spanish Civil War, it was a reasonable German expectation that the Spanish leader would reciprocate and offer air bases in Spain to the Luftwaffe. But Franco, in this instance, though not later in the war against Russia, struck the pose of firm neutrality.

The fundamental failure in air terms of Goering's leadership in the air campaigns in the Mediterranean was his total inability to assess the forces required, even before the entry of the Soviet and American Air Forces against the Luftwaffe made his forward planning almost unreal. He was, by December 1940, committed to reduce Malta as an air and naval base and to provide tactical and air transport for Rommel's ground forces in North Africa and also to share the problems of the air escort and air protection of Italian ships supplying the Italo-German forces in Libya and Tripolitania.

What could Goering hope to achieve in 1941 in the Mediterranean theatre and elsewhere? Would the blitz on Britain go on or increase? What was to be the German air commitment against the Soviet Union? These and other Luftwaffe questions absorbed many minds outside Germany, including those of the British Chiefs of Staff, at the end of 1940. They simply could not believe that Goering really believed the nonsense of his own statements, when, for example, he gave orders for maximum air support blitzkrieg with maximum available forces.

That is why, towards the end of 1940, a puzzled Churchill and some of his senior advisers called for a special investigation into the expansion of German air power in 1941. The resulting Justice Singleton enquiry, dealt with rather briefly in Winston Churchill's war memoirs, produced no firm official British view. But RAF air intelligence stuck to its belief in a modest air expansion of ten per cent or so in front-line Luftwaffe strength in 1941, despite the vast new Goering air commitments. The basis of this prediction was mainly Goering's fatal inability to plan ahead in a realistic way. At the turn of 1940-41, his future as an air leader seemed assured in political terms but already very difficult indeed in operational terms. Thus, there were at least three separate operational areas to cater for in the Mediterranean theatre—Sicily-Malta, Rhodes-Egypt, and Libya-Tripolitania.

In the first half of 1941, that is before the German attack on the Soviet Union, it was already crystal clear that Goering's air resources in the Mediterranean were very limited. German air operations in the Eastern Mediterranean were confined to small-scale mine-laying and some reconnaissance of Egyptian target areas. There was no follow-up Luftwaffe bombing of British bases in Egypt. The attack on Malta was not pursued to its logical end because of the severe limitation of Luftwaffe air units in Sicily. And in the spring of 1941 there was dilution of even these German squadrons to meet the air support needs of Rommel's forces in North Africa.

Goering issued a series of hectic hectoring signals when he had complaints about the poverty of German air support for Hitler's ground forces in North Africa. Both Rommel and Froehlich, the latter the German air commander in this theatre, were urgent and trenchant in their requests for more air squadrons. The summer of 1941 came and went virtually without reinforcement. Goering's reaction amounted to no more than a mixture of empty promises and heated exasperation. Reinforcement came at the end of 1941; but it was at the expense of the Russian Front where the Luftwaffe was already dangerously thin on the ground.

It was, of course, the June 1941 attack on the Soviet Union which accelerated the slide of Goering's inability to plan ahead. In the summer of 1941 he was still, hopefully, a potential leader of blitzkrieg air success. But by the end of 1941 the unexpected resistance of the Soviet Army and Air Force had thrown all his air planning for the future out of focus. Like the British, American, Italian and Japanese strategists, he had grossly underestimated the fighting value of Stalin's armed forces.

Goering's vistas of early and spectacular victories in a matter of weeks or months on the Eastern Front and in the Mediterranean were now fading. But he still did not understand the planning currencies of either the next year or the year after. He simply was no long-term warrior.

The next year came and went. In 1942, the United States Army Air Force arrived in Europe, the war against the Soviet Union turned sour for the Wehrmacht, the air blitz on Britain receded, the British night blitz on Germany mounted, the Battle of the Atlantic was still in the forefront of German strategy. But German air support for German submarines and surface vessels was still a thing of puny dimensions. The four-engined Focke Wulf 200 was splendid, at times, in attacks on British shipping, but there were simply not enough of them to make a major impact. Output was only about half a dozen planes a month.

Once it was clear, at the end of 1942, that the Luftwaffe had to face the fury of three major air forces, British, American and Soviet, there was really little hope. The demise of Goering's Air leadership was almost inevitable. When Albert Speer took over the job of Minister of War Production in the Third Reich at the beginning of 1942, he had, initially, only a limited control over the policy of German aircraft production. Had he been switched from Nazi architecture to the manufacture of Luftwaffe planes back in 1940, and given major control of the German aero-space industry, he might, together with Milch, have achieved many new things. But once the accidental coalition of Britain, USA and the Soviet Union emerged from the vagaries of the Second World War, Goering's air leadership was probably doomed to a nadir of groping impotence, Speer or no Speer.

As long as these three major air forces could develop their aircraft industries and pilot training schemes, without major interference from German air power, the air defeat of Germany was virtually inevitable.

There are many excuses for the failure of Goering's leadership. Thus, he had little or no control over the Fuehrer's manic plans for quick and easy conquest. And so he could not easily foresee in time the future trend of the war and of the air forces needed. In some respects, the kind of criticism one makes of Goering could reasonably be made about other major air leaders. It is doubtful in December 1941, when the attack on Pearl Harbour was successfully executed, if any Japanese air leader foresaw the possibility of the holocaust of the American bombing of Japan in the last year of the war. To underestimate American air power was much in fashion among the Axis powers.

Then there are the pros and cons of military naval and air intelligence. It is true that Goering made many mistakes in judging enemy air potential, virtually throughout the Second World War, and also in the pre-war period. He paid little attention to the difficult problems of economic intelligence, to the technical development of enemy aircraft, enemy aircraft production, enemy damage and casualties sustained in air battles or to the characteristics of enemy air leaders. But which of the air powers of the world can claim an intelligence record free from major and repeated blemish in some of these fields? Certainly not Britain or the United States. As for Soviet intelligence, the gaps in their knowledge were extensive in the 1941-45 period, as we who worked with them quickly realised. Economic intelligence is a difficult subject. I doubt if modern computers, the study of cybernetics or the use of reconnaissance satellites have yet reduced the problems to manageable proportions. I know of no intelligence service in any country that gets hard reliable information on the enemy or potential enemy situation covering even half of the detailed economic ground that needs to be covered. To know the enemy is a military consummation devoutly to be wished; but, in the stern and expensive reality of military intelligence, one gropes and grasps at a mixture of conflicting straws blown to and fro by a varying quantity of hard information.

Goering was, as a man, ill-equipped to study the enemy seriously. His direct on-the-spot experience of the United States and the USSR was nil and of Britain very slight. His undoubted patriotism, his pre-occupation with many other things and his underestimate of the ranking requirements of senior intelligence officers—his top man was never more than a colonel, compared with an air vice-marshal in the Royal Air Force—his fatal instinct for brushing awkward problems aside, all resulted in crucial blind spots and in an unawareness of what he was up against.

Now and then he paid cursory lip service to British fighting ability. And he certainly reacted to the threat of the British bombing of Germany in the summer of 1940 in rapid fashion. But in the aggregate, he was usually blissfully unaware of enemy air potential except perhaps in the last year of the war. By then it was patently obvious and Goering had become an air leader only in notional terms.

The well-known story of Lord Dowding's difference with Winston Churchill in the fateful summer of 1940 showed how even one of the greatest leaders of a modern democratic country can unwittingly seek to waste the key substance of his country's air power. Had Dowding not protested to the point of resignation, a vital residue of British fighter squadrons might have been poured down the sink of a futile Allied air campaign in France. And what of British strategy in Greece later in 1940 which led to a handful of RAF squadrons being thrown into a hopeless battle against the might of the Luftwaffe? And the air defence of Singapore? All air leaders may suffer from the strategy of ruling politicians, though perhaps not as much as Goering suffered from the strategy of Hitler.

I know of no Goering official obituary, but I suspect that someone, somewhere, has paid an aviation tribute to him since his death which I have missed. But here are a few hundred words which attempt to sum him up as a man and as an air leader.

He was brave and loyal to his country, as he understood loyalty, both in victory and in defeat. His undoubted gifts of intelligence and forcefulness were marred by defects of temperament and character. He was a bluffer, worse still, a successful bluffer who then believed his bluff. He tended to boast easily and to believe the optimism of his vanity. As an air leader he had the right personality for quick victories and blitzkrieg successes, but his persistent lack of realism made him a bad air leader for the long haul of air power, for long-term planning, and for difficult armament, training or other problems that have to be thrashed out in detail in committee.

He was faithful to his leader, Adolf Hitler, to the point almost of stupidity. German Air Force pilots, air crews and air commanders held a wide range of views about Goering's air leadership of the Luftwaffe, but their affection for their Commander-in-Chief was fairly general and most marked in the period 1935-1940. However, some colleagues, such as Koller and von Greim, apparently felt that Goering should have been dismissed. Others, like Galland, felt that he merely needed to listen much more to good advice, for example about the importance of strengthening the Luftwaffe fighter arm.

What surprised me most about Goering's post-war reputation among some sections of the German Luftwaffe was the high regard in which he was still held even then. Yet murder and racial persecution are but two of the crimes against humanity of which Goering was justly accused at the Nuremberg Trials. If the Nuremberg Trial had been conducted by aviation judges and the indictments had been based on assessments of Goering's air leadership, he would surely have been found guilty on many more counts—failure to allow for sufficient wastage in battle, to build up adequate air reserves, either of pilots and air crews, in flying training schools, failure to study his foe except in small flippant doses, failure to consult knowledgeable and able colleagues to a sufficient extent, failure to push harder for key jet fighters, failure to oppose Hitler's strategic whims, lack of hard realism which is after all the real stuff of bombs, planes, radar, fuel, pilots and all the rest of the military aviation impedimenta, failure to think through his long-range problems, failure to keep in touch with the German Chiefs of Staff, failure to see, early in the war, that he had taken on much too much, failure to seek regular and proper treatment for his drug habits, and so on The list of personal and leadership inadequacies is long. The German Air Force deserved better leadership than it had.

The first flood tide of his political and military air successes, from 1935 to 1940, in Spain, Austria, the Rhineland, Czechoslovakia, Poland, Denmark, Norway, Holland, Belgium and France was a formidable flush of victories. It needed a cool long-sighted head to absorb them and not to treat them as guidelines for the future. But Goering was hot-headed, vain, optimistic and patriotic to excess. The run of victories would have been a heady mixture for any leader, especially one as rich and powerful as Goering. Then came the change. In the last half of 1940 from July to December, Goering was dealing in aviation currencies he did not understand. He himself once said to his second wife Emmy, 'I do not understand economics'. The economics of air power certainly eluded him. The costs in manpower and raw materials, the wastage of crews and planes, the organisation of factories and many other related things flitted briefly through his mind without making the impact needed. Instead of studying current affairs at Munich University in the early 1920's, he should perhaps have studied aeronautical engineering and electronics. But the woman he loved, and to whom Karinhall was in part a monument, encouraged him to play politics. The relationship between politics and the serious application of air power is, at best dubious, and at worst, disastrous.

Goering loved both his wives well; but he failed utterly to see the potential of women in the realms of air intelligence and air planning. His women's Air Force personnel, the so-called *Blitzmaedeln,* were used mainly for cypher work or on secretarial and clerical chores and for cooking; but not for contributing to air staff appreciations or for important aircraft reconnaissance photo interpretation as happened in the Royal Air Force.

In the final analysis, Hermann Goering's chief blind spot was himself. He was a great extravert. Such leaders, be they Generals Patton, McArthur or Reichsmarschall Goering, often fail to subject themselves to sufficient self-criticism.

The careers of most leaders, Napoleon, Churchill, Nelson, Marlborough and others, have had their peaks and troughs. Goering's peaks were mainly pre-war and in the first ten months of easy going between September 1939 and June 1940. The troughs then deepened and multiplied. Instead of turning more and more to his senior air colleagues for counsel he turned less and less. The military air forces ranged against the Luftwaffe grew apace and so did Goering's inability to co-operate and to take advice. But, to be fair, the powerful interfering hand of his Fuehrer continually cramped his air leadership. Could any aviation leader of the Second World War have coped successfully with the neurotic, frenzied, dictatorial outbursts of Adolf Hitler and still made military aviation logic from the consequences of his strategy? One has doubts about this. But in the 1930s, Goering might have done something to educate his master in the realities of air power—except that the Commander-in-Chief of the German Air Force was himself often unrealistic and seemed to enjoy disdaining reality. He preferred paintings to papers, high-quality Riesling to high-quality reportage, and the life of sybaritic man to the boredom of staff work.

Bibliography

BARTZ, KARL: *Swastika in the Air*. London, William Kimber 1956.

BAUMBACH, WERNER: *The Life and Death of the Luftwaffe*. New York, Coward-McCann 1960.

CHURCHILL, WINSTON S.: *The Second World War*. London, Cassell; I. *The Gathering Storm* (1948); II. *Their Finest Hour* (1949); III. *The Grand Alliance* (1950); IV. *The Hinge of Fate* (1951); V. *Closing the Ring* (1952); VI. *Triumph and Tragedy* (1954).

COLLIER, BASIL: *The Battle of Britain*. London, Batsford 1962.

COLLIER, RICHARD: *Eagle Day*. London, Hodder & Stoughton 1966.

DEMPSTER, DEREK and WOOD, DEREK: *The Narrow Margin*. London, Hutchinson 1961.

FRISCHAUER, WILLI: *The Rise and Fall of Hermann Goering*. London, Odhams 1960.

GALLAND, ADOLF: *The First and the Last*. London, Methuen 1953.

GRITZBACH, ERICH: *Hermann Goering, Werk und Mensch*. Berlin, Zentral Verlader N.S.D.A.P. 1938.

HEINKEL, ERNST: *Stormy Life*. New York, Dutton 1956.

ISMAY, LORD: *Memoirs*. London, Heinemann 1960.

KESSELRING, ALBERT: *Memoirs*. London, William Kimber 1953.

LEE, ASHER: *The German Air Force*. London, Duckworth 1947.

MACMILLAN, NORMAN: *The Royal Air Force in the World War*. George Harrap 1944.

MANVELL ROGER and FRANKEL, HEINRICH: *Goering*. London, Heinemann 1962.

OSTERKAMP, THEO : *Durch Hoehen und Tiefen Jagt ein Herz.* Heidelberg, Vowinckel 1950.

RICHARDS, DENIS and SAUNDERS, HILARY ST. GEORGE : *Royal Air Force* 1939-1945. London, Her Majesty's Stationery Office. I. *The Fight at Odds* (1953); II. *The Fight* (1954); III. *The Fight is Won* (1954).

SLESSOR, SIR JOHN : *The Central Blue.* London, Cassell 1956.

SPEER, AIBERT : *Inside the Third Reich.* London, Weidenfeld and Nicolson 1971.

WEBSTER, SIR CHARLES and FRANKLAND, NOBLE : *The Strategic Air Offensive against Germany.* London, Her Majesty's Stationery Office. I. *Preparation;* II. *Endeavour;* III. *Victory;* IV. *Annexes and Appendices.*

WILMOT, CHESTER : *The Struggle for Europe.* London, Collins 1952.

Index

References in italic indicate an illustration